CyberSociety

CyberSociety

COMPUTER-MEDIATED COMMUNICATION AND COMMUNITY

Steven G. Jones

SAGE PUBLICATIONS
International Educational and Professional Publisher
Thousand Oaks London New Delhi

For information address:

SAGE Publications, Inc.,
2455 Teller Road
Thousand Oaks, California 91320

SAGE Publications Ltd.
6 Bonhill Street
London EC2A 4PU
United Kingdom

SAGE Publications India Pvt. Ltd.
M-32 Market
Greater Kailash I
New Delhi 110 048 India

Printed in the United States of America

Library of Congress Cataloging-in-Publication Data

Main entry under title:

CyberSociety: Computer-mediated communication and community / edited by Steven G. Jones.
p. cm.
Includes bibliographical references and index.
ISBN 0-8039-5676-2. — ISBN 0-8039-5677-0 (pbk.)
1. Computer networks—Social aspects. 2. Communication.
3. Computers and civilization. I. Jones, Steve, 1961-
Tk5105.5.C92 1994
302.23—dc 20 94-29194

95 96 97 98 99 10 9 8 7 6 5 4 3 2 1

Sage Production Editor: Astrid Virding

Contents

PREFACE

Although communication via computers is not a new subject, such activity itself is exponentially increasing to the point where electronic mail is about as common as a phone call, or, as one of my undergraduate students put it, virtual reality is "just around the corner from commonplace" (Laird, 1993). It is not so ubiquitous that we all know what it is and how to use it, due, in part, to the fact that the technology is not really yet ready nor embraced by all. *CyberSociety,* though, is rooted in criticism and analysis of technologies that do presently exist and form the foundation for the media-ready pronouncements by everyone from MIT's Media Lab to Nintendo® about the wonders we are about to witness.

CyberSociety will not assist its readers to become more proficient at using any of a variety of tools for computer-mediated communication (CMC). Such assistance can be found in a variety of sources, of which the most useful are Brendan Kehoe's *Zen and the Art of the Internet* and a host of software-based guides to using computer networks. Nor will it more than briefly rehash the history of virtual reality (except where that history proves instructive), of the Internet, Usenet, and other forums wherein CMC can be found. We are, to borrow a title, entering Cyberspace: The Next Generation, and other sources exist for an understanding of the evolution of these technologies.

CyberSociety will, however, assist its readers to become aware and critical of the hopes we have pinned on computer-mediated communication and of the cultures that are emerging among network users. The prefix "cyber" derives from Greek and means "to pilot." Computer-mediated communication is one means (and, so far, the only means) with which we can fly in and out of societies, in this case ones formed by and in discussion groups, mailing lists, newsgroups, and other network "hangouts." Unlike face-to-face interaction, computer-mediated interaction can turn on a dime as we instantaneously move from one conversation to the next. An apt metaphor is the cocktail party. Its electronic version is in full swing on computer networks, and there are many rooms, many people. In some rooms, there is the *maskenbal,* where identities are unknown and change often. In other rooms, there are serious discussions, games, pickup lines galore, and long-term relationships. The doors to these rooms are most often unlocked, and *CyberSociety*'s authors peek in, mill about, engage in conversation, probe, analyze, and critique.

I am indebted to those authors. Their enthusiasm about the project and about computer-mediated communication not only constitutes this book but gives it life. They have patience, perserverance, faith, integrity, and diligence, and I will be forever grateful to them.

I am also indebted to Larry Grossberg at the University of Illinois, a colleague and friend since I was an Illinois undergraduate student. His guidance and assistance with this book have been invaluable. Likewise Sophy Craze, my editor at Sage, was thoughtful and caring and shepherded the work at every turn. Frank Christel, general manager of KWGS-FM at the University of Tulsa is a good friend and fellow cyberspace explorer without whom I would never have known about the furthest reaches (and then some) of the Internet. Lisa Freeman gave encouragement and advice in the early stages of the project, and I appreciate it greatly. The Computing and Information Resources staff at the University of Tulsa, in particular Reed Davis, Gary Szabo, Bob Chappelle, Tristia Watson, Cherie Stovall, and Rick Kruse, have always been helpful and ready to assist. I owe my colleague in the Faculty of Communication at the University of Tulsa, Joli Jensen, far more than words can convey. Her critiques of my work and the insights I gain from conversation with her are a high point of my academic life. Kerry Strayer and Jim Query helped me understand relevant areas of organizational communication. The students in my Media History courses at the University of Tulsa were very helpful, too, as they criticized my ideas alongside those of others and their own.

Support of the staff in the Faculty of Communication was invaluable. I particularly wish to thank Jan Reynolds, my research assistants Rachel Reynolds and Amanda Smith, and Frank Mulhern and Julie Schmidt for assisting with library research and interlibrary loan services. I also must thank Linda Strong and the staff at McFarlin Library at the University of Tulsa who were most helpful. Leila Khaled and many net.friends were very supportive, too. Special thanks are also due Richard Dover, George Gilpin, Kermit Hall, Tom Horne, Mike Hunt, George Jones, Sofia Jones, John Pauly, Al Soltow, and my colleagues at the University of Tulsa

Last, I want to thank Jodi White, whose company I missed on many evenings and weekends while I worked on this book and whom I will no doubt miss as I pursue other projects. Despite being physically apart she was always with me in my heart and thoughts. Her understanding and support are an everlasting gift.

Reference

Laird, A. (1993). *Computerscape with letters.* Unpublished manuscript prepared for Media History, Faculty of Communication, University of Tulsa.

INTRODUCTION: FROM WHERE TO WHO KNOWS?

Steven G. Jones

Follow the typical signs,
the hand-painted lines,
Down prairie roads.
Pass the lone church spire,
pass the talking wire,
From where
to who knows.
—"Gold Rush Brides,"
by 10,000 Maniacs
(written by Rob Buck and Natalie Merchant,

Our concept of cyberspace, cyberculture, and cyber-everything is, more than we care to realize, a European idea, rooted in Deuteronomy, Socrates, Galileo, Jefferson, Edison, Jobs, Wozniak, glasnost, perestroika, and the United Federation of Planets.
—Neal Stephenson, "In the Kingdom of Mao Bell,"
Wired, February 1994, p. 100

The ubiquitous nature of electronic communication has firmly manifested itself in computer-mediated communication (CMC). Through communication services like America Online, MCIMail, the Internet, Usenet, and numerous other mail, messaging, and bulletin board services (BBSs) electronically distributed, almost instantaneous written communication has for many people supplanted the postal service, telephone, and even the fax machine. There are more than 2 million Internet host computers, and it is estimated that some 3 million people use the Usenet news service accessible via Internet. Other computer communication networks spring to life seemingly every week, and even cable companies now venture into the networks to provide cable subscribers CMC connections.

Accompanying this manifestation is a resurgence in prophecy related to computers and computing. A large portion of that prophecy relates to virtual reality (VR) technology, which promises all flavors of reality on demand. Some of it is associated with the combination of audio and video in the computer that is to lead us to the long-promised connection between the radio, television, and computer. But increasingly, fewer comments are made about the wonders of technology and more about the new forms of community brought about by CMC, about the new social formations I have termed "cybersociety." This notion of community depends on CMC and on the ability to share thoughts and information instantaneously across vast distances.

Carey (1989) has eloquently argued that prophecy has accompanied the arrival of most every new communication (not to mention other) technology. What Carey and collaborator John Quirk argue is that "electrical techniques [are hailed] as the motive force of desired social change, the key to the recreation of a humane community, the means for returning to a cherished naturalistic bliss" (p. 115). Perhaps technology's numerous unfulfilled promises have led us to expect less naturalistic bliss, but expectations for social change and community remain. Evidence of the expectations for social change can be found in the sublimity with which electronic mail was said to have been important in the 1992 U.S. presidential election and in the speed with which the Clinton White House implemented an electronic mail system. As a press release touting the White House's e-mail connection claimed,

> Today, we are pleased to announce that for the first time in history, the White House will be connected to you via electronic mail. Electronic mail will bring the Presidency and this Administration closer and make it more accessible to the people. (letter from the president and vice president in announcement of White House electronic mail access, June 1, 1993)

Our hopes and expectations for community are evident in the everyday discourse on thousands of BBSs, on Usenet, in mail messages, and in interactive media like Internet Relay Chat (IRC). More important, these hopes lurk between the lines of that discourse in the assumptions that CMC users make about the connections they have to other users.

To examine those assumptions is to understand fundamentally human needs for contact, control, knowledge, the social and sociological elements of communication, and community. Each essay in this volume adds another facet to that examination by providing another glimpse of how the promises of technology and the reality of its use mesh, collapse, and reorganize and of the forms of cybersociety that are conjoined with that promise.

The "Net"

Cybersociety relies, of course, on the forms of CMC allowed by current computer network structures, and some discussion of those is in order. Excellent introductions to electronic mail, the Internet, and a host of other computer networks and software are readily available and I will not cover the ground they do.[1] Each can readily assist with connection to the variety of computer links described in *CyberSociety*'s chapters, and I suggest that the reader use this technology (if you have not already) to experience electronic mail, to examine the bulletin boards, lists, and newsgroups about which the contributors write. Unlike many other analyses and studies of contemporary society, one may enter the communities and discourse described in these chapters with relative ease. The issues with which sociologists and anthropologists, among others, have traditionally engaged when conducting their research are part of that discourse, for it becomes necessary to cover ground concerning participant observation, privacy, and biography. The best way to come in contact with those issues is to experience CMC.

As background to the following chapters, though, some introduction to the history of computer-mediated communication is useful. The connections in place for the most widely discussed computer network, the Internet, were formed in the 1960s and early 1970s when the U.S. Department of Defense and several research universities, via DARPA (Defense Advanced Research Program Agency), linked computers. The resulting network, Arpanet, allowed for access to each site's computers not only for communication but for research. The latter role, though, took a back seat to the use of Arpanet as a means for researchers to share information by way of electronic mail. Initially, such mailing was in the form we are accustomed to from using the post office: Individual messages are sent from one person to another.

However, it quickly became clear that messages often contained information to be shared by many users, and thus mailing lists were created. These lists allowed one person to mail one message to a central point from which that message was "bounced" or "reflected" to others who subscribed to the list. Eventually, lists became specialized to particular topics, and the terms "bulletin board" and "mailing list" came to have some interchangeability. Bulletin boards, though, generally referred to computers one could reach by dialing through standard phone lines with a computer modem and linking with another computer. The effect of each, board and list, was similar in many ways, as both provided news and information to users and came to be subsumed under the cateogry of "newsgroup." Newsgroups gather the messages posted by users in a centralized fashion and permit interaction with posted messages by way of simple means of reply. Lengthy threads are created by individual messages that generate dozens, even hundreds, of replies. The largest manifestation of newsgroups is known as the Usenet, a massive repository of thousands of newsgroups accessible from most any computer with a connection to the Internet.

Other computer networks grew during the 1970s, and various software and hardware protocols were developed that enabled them to connect to Arpanet, and it, in turn, morphed into the Internet thanks to the National Science Foundation's appropriation of advanced computing.

The Internet essentially serves as the main connecting point for many other networks. It has, in a sense, come to be a "backbone" by which networks link up with each other. A common estimate is that there are over 30,000 computer networks with over 1.5 million computers connected through the Internet, and the Internet's number of users grows by 10% monthly.

The Internet is a decentralized network, and its management occurs via the NSF. However, no one group manages it. Instead, a variety of groups, such as the Internet Society and InterNIC, circulate information and resolutions and do research on the network's needs.

There are several purposes the Internet can serve, but the two its users most frequently engage with are electronic mail and newsgroups. Not coincidentally, these two purposes form the basis for CMC and are the ones most discussed in *CyberSociety,* and it is those I address in the opening chapter.

However, they are not necessarily the place to begin to understand all of the connections between CMC and community, especially as technologies continue to converge. Virtual reality (VR) technology and even computer games like Nintendo®'s and Sega™'s, for example, provide still more arenas for communication and interaction. As Cheris Kramarae points out in the second chapter, VR "affects even those of us who have no intention of putting on VR glove and headset."

Kramarae finds compelling connections between the "information revolution," VR, entertainment, and sensation, strongly evoking critiques of the direction we seem to be pushing new technologies. For her, VR may portend "an interest in moving to a more sanitized world without the messes we've made," or, to put it another way, in distancing ourselves from the physical world we have just as equally created as the virtual worlds we may create.

Indeed, the creation of new worlds is at the heart of what all new communication technologies seem to be destined for. Part of that creative process involves narrative, part involves technology, and part involves social interaction. As Mary Fuller and Henry Jenkins note, the impulse to create new worlds is deeply rooted in the human psyche. Their insightful connections between exploration of space, new world narratives, and graphic interfaces like Nintendo® point out that our efforts at electronic discovery through technologies like VR or other CMC forms have strong historical roots. They identify "the appetite for encountering a succession of new spaces," and such an appetite also motivates the development of new communication technology. They borrow from De Certeau to claim that "spatial relations [are a] central organizing principle of all narratives" (p. 64, this volume). As CMC is rooted in narrative, it is clearly important to understand the travel stories that users tell, implicit ones as well as explicit ones, and Fuller and Jenkins provide a basis for that understanding.

Narrative is an important focus of study for anyone seeking to comprehend the variety of CMC available, as it is important to ask questions about power in relation to it. Who will secure the "master" narrative (if there will be one) concerning CMC? Some say software will enable all users to contribute to, or create, an unlimited amount of narratives and texts. The development of Mosaic software by the National Center for Supercomputing Applications (NCSA) at the University of Illinois, for instance, links still images, video, and audio to text-based documents and is not much more difficult to use than a fancy word processor. It is, though, only in its formative stages. Most other software used for CMC relies exclusively on text, and consequently we must examine the forms of textual interaction provided via the computer screen. As Ted Friedman writes in Chapter 4, perhaps some type of "software theory" is needed, a kind of intersection of literary criticism and computer-mediated text, to engage questions of self and identity via the cognitive mapping that takes place while one "plays" computer games. Friedman finds that computer games "mark a fundamental challenge to familiar conceptions of individual autonomy," at least in part due to the constraints placed on one's conception of self within a game created by others (software designers).

The notion of self and its relation to community is one that must be taken up critically, and the other contributors to *CyberSociety* do so. Given, for instance, the mutability of identity in Usenet, where it is possible to post messages anonymously and pseudonomously, how are we to negotiate social relations that, at least in the realm of face-to-face communication, were fixed by recognition of identity? One answer to that question comes in the form of the previously mentioned constraints on CMC users. The developers of Eudora, an electronic mail software package, for instance, in early versions made it possible to send messages adopting anyone else's name by using their e-mail address. Later versions of Eudora circumvented this software loophole by appending the word "unverified" in parentheses next to the e-mail address of the sender if the message originated without a password.

Still other means of fixing identity and conduct have developed over time, and in Chapter 5 Margaret McLaughlin, Kerry Osborne, and Christine Smith examine the evolution of standards of conduct on Usenet. Their work, like others in *CyberSociety,* begins to ask questions about power in the social relations being formed via CMC. Such work speaks directly to the creation of community via CMC, as the development of standards of conduct is in a sense the development of a moral code, a system of values, akin to the ones that arise and are revised in most social formations. For McLaughlin and her coauthors, the patterns of conduct that accrete on Usenet point to "evidence of community" similar to "the discursive working-out of community standards of behavior." Such evidence does not, however, make Usenet communities any less amorphous and ephemeral, and consequently the question that needs to be asked is this: In a near entirely ephemeral world, how does an individual, much less a community, maintain existence?

Pointing toward one direction that may answer that question, Richard MacKinnon in Chapter 6 examines the notion that individuals exist as "persona" on Usenet, and "at this level . . . the fear of vanishing from existence is ever present and near." MacKinnon uses Hobbes's Leviathan to examine the relationship between online and offline identity and power. Although Hobbes's 17th-century political theory may lack immediacy in relation to 20th-century CMC, the connection between Hobbes's proposal for monarchy as the ideal for social organization and MacKinnon's use of Gene Spafford as a Usenet "monarch" and newsgroup moderators as themselves monarchs makes for a compelling argument that Leviathan may be among Usenet's personae. An earlier version of MacKinnon's work has sparked a great deal of discussion on Usenet and is available electronically at numerous sites on the Internet. In this version, he focuses some arguments and furthers his search for Leviathan.

MacKinnon's efforts point to one of the most compelling questions concerning CMC: Who are we when we are online? The question becomes even more important as new technologies are developed for creating "agents" or "alters" that roam the network for us when we are away from our terminals. Each of *CyberSociety*'s last three chapters seeks to address this question. As Nancy Baym notes in Chapter 7, members of a newsgroup dedicated to discussion of soap operas "creatively exploit the system's features in order to play with new forms of expressive communication, to explore possible public identities." Interestingly, Baym finds that rather than fearing a loss of identity, newsgroup users value anonymity "because it creates opportunities to invent alternative versions of one's self and to engage in untried forms of interaction."

The preeminent arena for realtime interaction on the Internet is the MUD, or Multi-User Dimension. In a MUD, many users can interact using a text-based communication system and collaboratively created spaces. Elizabeth Reid's examination of MUDs in Chapter 8 points to an active process of community building in what is essentially a virtual reality environment constructed through texts. The latter may not be particularly surprising; after all, we have, in a sense, created virtual worlds since the invention of writing. The former, though, is startling, because rarely have those worlds been created simultaneously among people at such great physical distance from each other. Importantly, Reid notes that MUDs "rarely resemble scripts or books." In other words, though text-based, MUD discourse combines elements of the written and spoken, which itself points to the "naturalness" of the environments that MUD users create. The spontaneity with which discourse and dialogue can occur affects the text itself, and MUDs are an arena within which users communicate in real time and with little time to construct carefully written texts.

On another front, newsgroups do allow users time to consider messages and responses, and in Chapter 9, Alan Aycock and Norman Buchignani examine a Usenet incident involving the posting of messages and responses to them that calls into question whether we will alter our notions about the conventional categories of authority, genealogy, and madness. Aycock and Buchignani find strong conservative impulses in all three realms rather than a willingness among Usenet users to question those categories. As we seek to know whether the social formations we encounter online are indeed new ones, their work is critical.

And, indeed, *CyberSociety* is at heart an attempt to understand and probe into these formations. One reason why such an attempt is needed is to understand the framing of reality that CMC brings about. As Chayko (1993) claims,

> In modern everyday life, it is difficult (and becoming impossible) to definitively classify experience as "real" or "not real"; it is more helpful to determine the degree or "accent" of reality in an event. The frames we once used, conceptually, to set the real apart from the unreal are not as useful as they once were; they are not as sturdy; they betray us. As they become ever more fragile, we require new concepts and understandings. (p. 178)

The purpose of this book is to provide a few such concepts and understandings. It also emphasizes that new social formations may require new forms of inquiry, too. How will sociologists, ethnographers, communication scholars and anthropologists, for instance, grapple with issues related to studying electronic communities? The essays in *CyberSociety* are evidence of some answers to that question. They are descriptive, but not prescriptive. The interest is to understand the everyday life of the network and its citizens, to, as Carey (1993) puts it, engage in "a sociology of border crossing, of migration across the semipermeable membranes of social life that constituted . . . disorderly fronts" (p. 179). In this case, the fronts are on our computer screens, beckoning us to go from the "where" of our own boundaries to a "who knows?" that, like any new frontier, is colonized first by our imagination and thought.

Note

1. Among the best of these introductory texts are the following:

Badgett, T., and Sandler, C. *Welcome to . . . Internet: From Mystery to Mastery.* New York: MIS Press, 1993. 324 pp. ISBN 1-55828-308-0.

Braun, E. *The Internet Directory.* New York: Fawcett Columbine, 1994. 704 pp. ISBN 0-449-90898-4.

Dern, D. P. *The Internet Guide for New Users.* New York: McGraw-Hill, 1994. 570 pp. ISBN 0-07-016511-4.

Engst, A. C. *Internet Starter Kit for Macintosh.* Indianapolis, IN: Hayden, 1993. 641 pp. ISBN 1-56830-064-6.

Estrada, S. *Connecting to the Internet: A Buyer's Guide.* Sebastopol, CA: O'Reilly & Associates, Inc. 1993. 170 pp. ISBN 1-56592-061-9.

Falk, B. *The Internet Roadmap.* San Francisco: Sybex, 1994. 263 pp. ISBN 0-7821-1365-6.

Fraase, M. *The Mac Internet Tour Guide: Cruising the Internet the Easy Way.* Chapel Hill, NC: Ventana Press, 1994. 288 pp. ISBN: 1-56604-062-0. Ventana has published a similar book by Fraase for the DOS-based computer.

Gilster, P. *The Internet Navigator.* New York: John Wiley, 1993. 470 pp. ISBN 0-471-59782-1.

Kehoe, B. P. *Zen and the Art of the Internet.* Englewood Cliffs, NJ: PTR Prentice Hall, 1993. 112 pp. ISBN 0-13-010778-6. An early version of Kehoe's book is available in electronic form at a variety of Internet sites.

Krol, E. *The Whole Internet Catalog & User's Guide.* Sebastopol, CA: O'Reilly & Associates, 1992. 376 pp. ISBN 1-56592-025-2.

Quarterman, J. S. and Smoot, C. *The Internet Connection: System Connectivity and Configuration.* New York: Addison-Wesley, 1994. 271 pp. ISBN 0-201-54237-4.

Smith, R., and Gibbs, M. *Navigating the Internet.* Carmel, IN: Sams Publishing, Inc., 1993. 500 pp. ISBN 0-672-30362-0.

Some, such as Engst's book, come with a floppy disk containing essentially all of the software required to get any computer with a modem hookup connected to the Internet or commercial networks like CompuServe, Delphi, and GEnie, which themselves provide Internet access.

References

Carey, J. (1989). *Communication as culture.* Boston, MA: Unwin-Hyman.

Carey, J. (1993). Everything that rises must diverge: Notes on communications, technology and the symbolic construction of the social. In P. Gaunt (Ed.), *Beyond agendas* (pp. 171-184). Westport, CT: Greenwood.

Chayko, M. (1993). What is real in the age of virtual reality? "Reframing" frame analysis for a technological world. *Symbolic Interaction, 16*(2), 171-181.

1

UNDERSTANDING COMMUNITY IN THE INFORMATION AGE

Steven G. Jones

Whether by choice or accident, by design or politics (or some complex combination of each), the United States (followed closely by many other countries) is embarking on a building project the likes of which have not been seen since the Eisenhower era. Indeed, there are startling parallels between the current project, the "information highway," and the one spurred on by both world wars, the interstate highway system—not the least of which is the reliance on the word "highway" and the romantic connotations of the open road (and that Vice President Al Gore, Jr.'s father was instrumental in the development of the federal highway system). Another parallel is the initially military motivation for highway building (established by Thomas Jefferson, among others) and the military origins of the most prominent information highway, the Internet, in defense department computer networks linked to university research centers.

Patton (1986), in his history of the U.S. interstate system, says that it was

> the most expensive and elaborate public works program of all time, offer[ing] a vision of social and economic engineering. It was planned to be at once a Keynesian economic driver and a geographic equalizer, an instrument for present prosperity and the armature of a vision of the future. It was at once the last program of the New Deal and the first space program. (p. 17)

The information highway being vociferously championed by the Clinton administration and by Vice President Al Gore also combines ideas about the economic and social direction of the United States. It is in a sense the first program of the new New Deal and, some say, the last space program. Patton's comments about the effects that interstates have had on cities and communities bear especially close scrutiny, as they evoke images of what the information highway may as well do to social formations. Highways, Patton says,

> have had monstrous side effects. They have often rolled, like some gigantic version of the machines that build them, through cities, splitting communities off into ghettos, displacing people, and crushing the intimacies of old cities. . . .
> While promising to bring us closer, highways in fact cater to our sense of separateness. (p. 20)

Critical to the rhetoric surrounding the information highway is the promise of a renewed sense of community and, in many instances, new types and formations of community. Computer-mediated communication, it seems, will do by way of electronic pathways what cement roads were unable to do, namely, connect us rather than atomize us, put us at the controls of a "vehicle" and yet not detach us from the rest of the world.

If that is to be so, it is not premature to ask questions about these new formations. What might electronic communities be like? Most forecasters, like Howard Rheingold (1993), envision them as a kind of ultimate flowering of community, a place (and there is no mistaking in these visions that it is place that is at stake) where individuals shape their own community by choosing which other communities to belong to. Thus a paradox long haunting America is solved in a particularly American way; we will be able to forge our own places from among the many that exist, not by creating new places but by simply choosing from the menu of those available. Another of the many questions we must ask about electronic communities is: What is the nature of individual members' commitments to them? In the physical world, community members must live together. When community membership is in no small way a simple matter of subscribing or unsubscribing to a bulletin board or electronic newsgroup, is the nature of interaction different simply because one may disengage with little or no consequence?

Perhaps the most important question for the purposes of this book is: How do we study computer-mediated community? Like other social groups, these are palpable, yet evanescent to CMC users. Although we can "freeze" electronic discourse by capturing the text and information it may contain, how do we ascertain the interpretive moment in electronic discourse, particularly as it engages both reading and writing? The authors of the following chapters attempt to answer that question in a variety of ways. All of them are aware of and alert to the possibilities and pitfalls of embracing traditional methods of social research to study nontraditional social formations, and all cultivate what Chayko (1993) calls a "special sensitivity" to distinctions between the virtual and the real. As she writes, that sensitivity is required for us to study the

> new ways in which we "carve out" reality by framing experience, and to the nature of such newly constituted "realities." It is one of the tasks of sociologists to problematize "what is real." Rather than assume that the real world is "out there" to be learned about and internalized, we recognize that there is no reality apart from what social actors make of it. (p. 172)

This is particularly important ground as it relates, in Berger and Luckmann's (1967) terms, to the "social construction of reality." That reality is not constituted *by* the networks CMC users use; it is constituted *in* the networks. It would be far easier to understand the physical, or hardwired, connections than to understand the symbolic connections that emerge from interaction. To again borrow from Carey (1989), much of our energy has been directed toward understanding the speed and volume with which computers can be used as communication tools. Conspicuously absent is an understanding of how computers are used as tools for connection and community. Carey makes the distinction between transmission and ritual views clear: "Communication under a transmission view is the extension of messages across geography for the purposes of control, the . . . case under a ritual view is the sacred ceremony that draws persons together in fellowship and commonality" (p. 18).
The distinctions between the two views of communication Carey draws are critical to understanding the full range and scope of CMC. It would seem we now have our global village or community, not just via CMC but by way of the many media of communication ever present. Everywhere we go we can "tap into" that community with a cellular telephone, a personal digital assistant, a modem, or a satellite dish. But connection does not inherently make for community, nor does it lead to any necessary exchanges of information, meaning, and sense making at all. Barnes and Duncan (1992) borrow from James Clifford: "When we write we do so from a necessarily local setting" (p. 3). The primary act involved in CMC is that of writing. Like Ong's (1982) description of authorship, that act is *intensely* local, for, although we may be certain of an audience, we are unable to verify its existence just as we are unable to verify its interpretation of our writing.

That uncertainty is central to the act of writing, as Ong sees it. It may also be central to the desire for control and feedback that Beniger (1986) believes caused the "control revolution." Beniger's thoughts are focused on the rapid technological innovation at the end of the late 19th century that heralded the introduction of basic communication technologies and, he says, restored the economic and political control lost during the Industrial Revolution:

> Before this time, control of government and markets had depended on personal relationships and face-to-face interactions; now control came to be reestablished

> by means of bureaucratic organization, the new infrastructure of transportation and telecommunications, and system-wide communication via the new mass media. (p. 14)

The need for control is obvious when viewed as a problem of geography, at once created and solved by transportation and communication. But when viewed as outside the frame of transportation and from the perspective of ritual, the predicament is one that we continue to face: How do we attend to the social connections impinging on us, the connections we at once desire (e-mail, telephone, fax, etc.) and despise (for they take up more and more of our time and energy)? Again, control is sought after, but it is not sought for the purposes of power but for the purposes of its inverse, restraint. As Carey (1993) put it, "Human intelligence has lodged itself, extrasomatically, in the very atmosphere that surrounds and supports us. Yet, back at home, we have a surplus of disorder and disarray" (p. 172). The very surfeit of knowledge and information leads toward chaos, and ever greater efforts are made at controlling the disorder with information-navigating devices like HyperCard®, Gopher, Veronica, and Mosaic.

Such disorder and the attempts to control it underscore the mythic investment we have in computer technology. The chaos and confusion generated by the opening of new frontiers led us to devise means of communication and transportation as if those means were one, part and parcel of the same process. Rail and road followed river and stream, to be supplanted by telegraph wire, telephone wire, and fiber-optic cable. (One ought to wonder what wireless communication as it develops in all its manifestations will truly bring, as the link between communication and transporation, forged by history, dissolves.) Jenkins and Fuller's chapter in this volume on new world narratives and Nintendo is precisely the analysis needed to make explicit the links between our new media and our history.

It is important, too, for us to not only understand the parallels between new world narratives and CMC narratives but to understand their differences. In a modern world, there is a need for control related to structure and homogenization, to the reversal of entropy. Such reversal comes to us in the guise of connections and associations that overcome geography and physical space. Computer-mediated communication will, it is said, lead us toward a new community: global, local, and everything in between. But the presence of chaos inexorably draws us away from that ideal as the need for control becomes greater and greater. It is most accurate to claim, as Carey (1993) does, that when it comes to proselytizing CMC, "these are ideas that people want or need to be true merely because it would be bewildering to be without them" (p. 172).

It may as well be "bewildering" for us to create and learn the norms of on-line worlds, for to learn them is a complex process. It may bring people together insofar as such learning is often collaborative, but it is equally as often frustrating and off-putting. Nevertheless, there is a sense that we are embarking on an adventure in creating new communities and new forms of community, and that sense is fueled by two motives: first, that we *need* new communities and, second, that we *can* create them technologically. Such motives, in turn, arise from what Soja (1989) has called "postmodern geographies," the tensions caused by differentiation and homogenization in the (re)production of space. In the case of CMC, what allows for the reproduction of space is the malleability with which identity can be created and negotiated, an issue several of the authors in *CyberSociety* take up. Consequently, one must question the potential of CMC for production of social space. Could it perhaps *re*produce "real" social relations in a "virtual" medium?

It is more likely that social relations emerging from CMC are between the two poles of production and reproduction. Pushing too close to either pole puts at risk whatever new social construction of reality may arise. And yet any new social formations are at risk of being mythologized and incorporated into the "rhetoric of the electrical sublime" that Carey (1989) identifies. All media, for instance, have been touted for their potential for education. Radio and television, in particular, were early on promoted as tools for education, and CMC is no different. In an article on computer technology in schools, one author wrote, "At a time when American schools are receiving less and less money to cope with growing social upheaval, telecomputing seems to offer a glimmer of hope, enlivening both teachers and students even as it compels a striking realignment of relationships within the classroom" (Leslie, 1993, p. 90).

There is no doubt that CMC is linked inextricably to education. Even the Corporation for Public Broadcasting (CPB) now seeks

> to develop community-wide education and information services. These publicly accessible interactive services will take full advantage of widely available communications and information technologies, particularly inexpensive computers linked by telephone lines.
>
> Who will mobilize the development of high-quality, non-commercial, educational and public services that will provide all Americans with the opportunities for learning, staying healthy, and participating in cultural and civic affairs —services crucial to the well-being of society as a whole? (from 1993 solicitation guidelines)

The CPB's comments parallel those made when radio and TV were introduced (the emphasis then was on broadcasting in the public interest, convenience, and necessity). Even Jaron Lanier, a pioneering virtual reality programmer and engineer, has said, "Television wasn't planned well enough and I think it's been a real disaster in this country" ("Virtual Reality," 1992, p. 6). Similarly, Quarterman (1993) has said, "Radio and television produced a different society. Computer networks will, too. Perhaps this time we can avoid a few mistakes" (p. 49). Such comments obfuscate the power behind decisions that go into planning and organizing media. Who will plan, how will we plan, and how will we account in our planning for unanticipated consequences? Media regulation in the U.S. has hardly been the most successful enterprise. Why should we believe regulating CMC will be different?

At the heart of comments like Lanier's and Quarterman's is a pervasive sense that we can learn from the "mistakes" we believe we've made using older media. Computer-mediated communication (and computers generally) gives us a sense that we can start over and learn from the past. Their comments point out that we have a fundamental need, or at least hope, for something better to come from future media.

But what exactly are we hoping *for*? The answer to that question is necessarily linked to questions about who we are hoping to be as a society, and that, in turn, is tied to issues of identity and discourse. Who are we when we are on-line? The question becomes even more important as new technologies are developed for creating "agents" or "alters" that roam the network for us when we are away from our terminals.

The possibility of new social formations is certainly alluring and is one of those ideas we seem to "want or need to be true." Another related idea we seem to need is, of course, the concept of virtual reality. What is most interesting, though, is that virtual reality is hardly less "bewildering" than non-virtual reality. The systems of cultural significance and methods of social control that *CyberSociety*'s contributors describe in on-line worlds in some instances parallel ones we are already accustomed to and in some instances do not. In all instances, though, they do form a new matrix of social relations. What impulses those formations are propelled by is an important matter that should not be overlooked. Cybersocieties are not organized simply for the transmission of information, nor do they "have to do something nontrivial with the information they send and receive" (Licklider & Taylor, 1968, p. 21). In fact, much of what is done with CMC is trivial. As Chesebro and Bonsall (1989) note, CMC may "promote efficiency at the expense of social contact" (p. 221). However, it is unlikely that many in contemporary society find the values explicit in Chesebro and Bonsall's statement antagonistic. CMC brings us a form of efficient social contact.

I believe that is an important point, for it speaks to the issue of community formation in a postmodern world. CMC allows us to customize our social contacts from fragmented communities. Few have studied this phenomenon comprehensively, although a step in the right direction was taken by Linda Harasim, editor of the anthology *Global Networks*. Harasim (1993) finds that social communication is a primary component of computer-mediated communication and is well able to organize thoughts about the use of CMC around social rather than solely work functions. However, none of those contributing to the anthology she edited probe satisfactorily into the nature of CMC's social use, preferring to claim, in the final analysis, that we simply seek community by whatever means it is available.

This is probably true, particularly insofar as we seek community other places as it dissolves in the spaces we physically inhabit. But we then must ask, as Benedikt (1991, p. 125) does, "What is space?" Forceful arguments about the ways technology shapes social relations have been made by numerous social scientists and philosophers, including Lewis Mumford and Marshall McLuhan. But space is not social relations, and vice versa. Mumford (1934) in particular notes a shift in society's interests, away from the abstraction of time and space and toward a desire to *use* space and time. CMC gives us a tool with which to use space for communication.

CMC, of course, is not just a tool; it is at once technology, medium, and engine of social relations. It not only structures social relations, it is the space within which the relations occur and the tool that individuals use to enter that space. It is more than the context within which social relations occur (although it is that, too) for it is commented on and imaginatively constructed by symbolic processes initiated and maintained by individuals and groups. The difficulty in defining space is clear in the zeal with which many have latched onto other derivative terms. For instance, yet more evidence of the prophetic nature of rhetoric about CMC is the pervasive use of the word "cyberspace," coined by William Gibson, a writer of fiction, to put a finger on a space at once real in its effects and illusory in its lack of physical presence. The "space race" of the 1950s and 1960s is indeed over. We no longer look to the stars and the thermodynamic engines that will transport us to them but to sites unknown and unseen (perhaps unseeable) and the ever smaller electronic engines that seem to effortlessly and without danger bring this space to us.

But is it even possible to pin down space to any particular definition? As Benedikt (1991) correctly observes, "Space, for most of us, hovers between ordinary, physical existence and something other" (p. 125). Where we find it hovering is, as Soja (1989) notes, in "socially produced space, [where] spatiality can be distinguished from the physical space of material nature and the mental space of cognition and representation, each of which is used and incorporated into the construction of spatiality but cannot be conceptualized as its equivalent" (p. 120).

Computer-mediated communication is, in essence, socially produced space, and it is these spaces that the chapters in *CyberSociety* examine. And such examination comes with self-reflection, for the authors of these chapters are likewise engaged in the construction of narratives concerning socially produced space. Having learned from and engaged with disciplines like anthropology, sociology, psychology, communication, and many others, these authors probe and question the interpretive acts and narratives they construct along with the ones they study.

The importance of CMC and its attendant social structures lies not only in interpretation and narrative, acts that can fix and structure, but in the sense of mobility with which one can move (narratively and otherwise) through the social space. Mobility has two meanings in this case. First, it is clearly an ability to "move" from place to place without having physically traveled. But, second, it is also a mobility of status, class, social role, and character. Like the boulevardiers or the denizens of Nevsky Prospect described by Berman (1982), the citizens of cyberspace (or the "net," as it is commonly called by its evanescent residents) "come here to see and be seen, and to communicate their visions to one another, not for any ulterior purpose, without greed or competition, but as an end in itself" (p. 196). The difference between those on the net and those on the street is encompassed in a distinction made by Soja (1989): "Just as space, time, and matter delineate and encompass the essential qualities of the physical world, spatiality, temporality, and social being can be seen as the abstract dimensions which together comprise all facets of human existence" (p. 25).

In cyberspace, spatiality is largely illusory (at least until Gibson's accounts of its visualization are realized), and temporality is problematized by the instantaneity of CMC and the ability to roam the net with "agents," software constructs that are automated representatives able to retrieve information and/or interact on the net. What is left is social being, and that too is problematic. Is the social actor in cyberspace mass-mediated, a mass-mediator, a public figure, or a private individual engaged in close, special interrelation? As Soja sees it in a summary of the dialectic between space and social life,

> The spatio-temporal structuring of social life defines how social action and relationship (including class relations) are materially constituted, made concrete. The constitution/ concretization process is problematic, filled with contradiction

> and struggle (amidst much that is recursive and routinized). Contradictions arise primarily from the duality of produced space as both outcome/embodiment/ product and medium/presupposition/producer of social activity. (p. 129)

No matter how ill-defined the space of cyberspace, the space we occupy as social beings is as affected by CMC. As Gillespie and Robins (1989) note, "New communications technologies do not just impact upon places; places and the social processes and social relationships they embody also affect how such technological systems are designed, implemented and used" (p. 7).

Soja's comments and the questions that arise from them speak to the heart of the many contradictions and problems embodied in CMC. On the one hand, it appears to foster community, or at least the sense of community, among its users. On the other hand, it embodies the impersonal communication of the computer and of the written word, the "kind of imitation talking" Ong (1982, p. 102) aptly describes. In that fashion, CMC wears on its sleeve the most important dichotomy that Jensen (1990) identifies in her book *Redeeming Modernity.* Jensen writes that traditional life, supposedly, "was marked by face-to-face, intimate relationships among friends, while modern life is characterized by distant, impersonal contact among strangers. Communities are defined as shared, close, and intimate, while societies are defined as separate, distanced, and anonymous" (p. 71).

Can CMC be understood to build communities and form a part of the conduct of public life, as other forms of communication seem to, or does CMC problematize our very notions of community and public life? CMC may yet be the clearest evidence of Beniger's (1987) "pseudo-community," part of the "reversal of a centuries-old trend from organic community—based on interpersonal relationships—to impersonal association integrated by mass means" (p. 369). Even if it is, the most important question is: How is it that a mass medium can be so closely related to (in some cases, equated with) a community?

A danger in the current assessments of cyberspace and cyberspatial social relations is the implacability of Carey and Quirk's "mythos of the electronic revolution" previously mentioned. For instance, Benedikt (1991) has claimed that in cyberspace, "to which every computer is a window, seen or heard objects are neither physical nor, necessarily, representations of physical objects but are, rather, in form, character and action, made up of data, of pure information" (pp. 122-123). Now, one most imminent danger (arising in part from the commodification of information) is that information is itself understood as a physical entity. It is important to remind one's self that computer data is essentially binary information based on the manipulation of strings of ones and zeros, themselves no more "physical" than our imagination allows them to be. In the operation of an audio compact disc player, the compact disc's bits of information are decoded by the player and converted to sound waves representative of (although nevertheless analogous to) the sound waves encoded during recording. The sound certainly retains "high fidelity," thanks largely to the enormous quantities of information encoded by the disc. In the operation of cyberspatial social relations, bits of information are decoded by users and converted to analogues of mediated and interpersonal social relations. The danger lies in the sense that cyberspatial social relations maintain "high fidelity" to those analogues. First, there is no prerequisite for such a homology. Second, any presupposition of a homology also assumes and fixes the rebirth of prior social relations, engineered along with the machines that make them palpable.

The importance of the disapointment that engineered communities have brought cannot be understated. We can no more "build" communities than we can "make" friends or, at least, as David Harvey (1989) points out, "the potential connection between projects to shape space and encourage spatial practices . . . and political projects . . . can be at best conserving and at worst downright reactionary in their implications" (p. 277). Harvey follows Heidegger through to his connections to fascism, a condition the nets have generally avoided, but his points, particularly as they concern political life, ought to be heeded by CMC users. Definitions of community have largely centered around the unproblematized notion of place, a "where" that social scientists can observe, visit, stay, and go. Their observations had largely been formed by examination of events, artifacts, and social relations within distinct geographic boundaries. The manifestation of political struggle as boundaries shift, break apart, and re-form has largely been overlooked, and the perspectives presented in *CyberSociety* are a first step toward redirecting observation and interrogation.

Communities formed by CMC have been called "virtual communities" and defined as "incontrovertibly social spaces in which people still meet face-to-face, but under new definitions of both 'meet' and 'face'. . . . [V]irtual communities [are] passage points for collections of common beliefs and practices that united people who were physically separated" (Stone, 1991, p. 85). In that sense, cyberspace hasn't a "where" (although there are "sites" or "nodes" at which users gather). Rather, the space of cyberspace is predicated on knowledge and information, on the common beliefs and practices of a society abstracted from physical space. Part of that knowledge and information, though, lies in simply knowing how to navigate cyberspace. But the important element in cyberspatial social relations is the sharing of information. It is not sharing in the sense of the *transmission* of information that binds communities in cyberspace. It is the ritual sharing of information

(Carey, 1989) that pulls it together. That sharing creates the second kind of community that Carey (1993) identifies as arising from the growth of cities during the late 19th and early 20th century, the one

> formed by imaginative diaspora—cosmopolitans and the new professionals who lived in the imaginative worlds of politics, art, fashion, medicine, law and so forth. These diasporic groups were twisted and knotted into one another within urban life. They were given form by the symbolic interactions of the city and the ecology of media, who reported on and defined these groups to one another, fostered and intensified antagonisms among them, and sought forms of mutual accommodation. (p. 178)

Such a formation is reoccuring in the discourse within CMC and without it, in the conversations its participants have on-line and off, and in the media coverage of electronic communication, electronic communities, and virtual reality.

The Community Along the Highway

In *The Postmodern Condition,* geographer and theorist David Harvey (1989) refers frequently to "time-space compression": "processes that so revolutionize the objective qualities of space and time that we are forced to alter, sometimes in quite radical ways, how we represent the world to ourselves" (p. 240). Harvey finds such compression central to understanding the now commonplace (and perhaps dated) concepts of the world as a "global village" or "spaceship earth." As part of his analysis of shifts in the history of capitalism, he identifies a change in spatial organization from feudal to Renaissance Europe. As regards the former, he writes,

> In the relatively isolated worlds . . . of European feudalism, place assumed a definite legal, political, and social meaning indicative of a relative autonomy of social relations and of community inside roughly given territorial boundaries. . . . External space was weakly grasped and generally conceptualized as a mysterious cosmology populated by some external authority, heavenly hosts, or more sinister figures of myth and imagination. (pp. 240-241)

Morris (1992) has criticized Harvey's reduction of complex problems to simple dualities. In particular, Morris writes, "Global problems are posed with a sense of urgency verging on moral panic, but then existing practical experiments in dealing with these on a plausible scale are dismissed for the usual vices ("relativisim," "defeatism"), reclassified as what they contest ("postmodernism"), or altogether ignored" (pp. 271-272). Still, at least two points that Harvey makes are important for the study of CMC and community. First, external space is in some sense no more firmly grasped today, although it is conceptualized in a variety of ways linked to objective representation via maps, photographs, and other visual media. Second, the relative autonomy of which Harvey speaks has given way since the Renaissance "to the direct influence of [the] wider world through trade, intra-territorial competition, military action, the inflow of new commodities, of bullion and the like" (Morris, 1992, p. 244). Social isolation becomes a difficult proposition for any contemporary community. Computer-mediated communities are in a sense "practical experiments" dealing with "global problems," and Morris's critique is all the more sharp as she points out Harvey's fallacy that "geographically 'global' space requires a philosophically *transcendent* space of analysis" (Morris, 1992, p. 273). Which of these spaces, if any (or all), is to be addressed in studies of CMC?

It is clear that studies of community have embedded a similar fallacy. The study of community followed a course similar to that which Harvey describes and Morris critiques as it evolved from attempts to describe and "write" communities in an isolated (almost antispatial) fashion to attempts to grapple with the complexities of overlapping and interlinked communities.

In assessing the history of community studies one finds that space was understood less as socially produced and more as that which produced social relations. So, for instance, Stacey (1974) identified the threads running through definitions of community in the sociological study of community. These include territory, social system, and sense of belonging. The first element, territory, however, is meant as a boundary within which a community maintains the other two elements. Similarly, Bell and Newby (1974) identified a variety of elements present in most definitions of community: social interaction based on geographic area, self-sufficiency, common life, consciousness of a kind, and possession of common ends, norms, and means. Bell and Newby also included ideas about social systems, individuality, totality of attitudes, and process as commonalities in approaches to community studies.

The most useful deconstruction of conceptions of community comes from Effrat (1974), who categorizes three main ones:

1. Community as solidarity institutions
2. Community as primary interaction
3. Community as institutionally distinct groups

Effrat's categories betray not only a Western sociological bias (which she admits) but a root in structured social action particularly well-defined in the

Chicago school of sociology. It is an "instrumentalist" perspective based on involvement and interaction, concepts somewhat easier to measure, at least, than community but nonetheless difficult to describe qualitatively. Such a perspective stems also from one of the earliest community studies, Warner's (1963) *Yankee City,* which Warner claimed would cross-sectionally represent American communities. The desire driving these studies is that of the social scientist who seeks to generalize from conditions of study as close to the "laboratory" as possible.

It is difficult to import definitions that use these elements and ideas to computer-mediated communication. Of Effrat's categories, the third, community as institutionally distinct groups, makes the most sense in the context of computer use. CMC is rarely a solidarity institution in Effrat's terms; that is, it rarely functions to produce solidarity. It may be a primary interaction, in a particularly narrow sense, insofar as relationships that CMC engenders may be close ones, and the content of communication may also make computer mediation the primary source of interaction. Yet viewed that way, primary interaction is virtually a function of a community defined as an institutionally distinct group, that is, a function of belonging to some social group or category.

It is most critical to attend to Etzioni's (1991) "I and We" paradigm:

> the idea that both individual and community have a basic moral standing; neither is secondary or derivative. To stress the interlocking, mutually dependent relationship of individual and community, and to acknowledge my mentor, Martin Buber, I refer to this synthetic position . . . (the We signifies social, cultural and political, hence historical and institutional forces, which shape the collective factor—the community). (p. 137)

The contributors to this book attend precisely to that paradigm and to the three criteria that Etzioni uses to focus community: scope, substance, and dominance (pp. 144-149). Each criterion focuses too, in its way, on the argument Calhoun (1980) makes that "we need to develop a conceptualization of community which allows us to penetrate beneath simple categories . . . to see a variable of social relations. The relationship between community as a complex of social relationships and community as a complex of ideas and sentiments has been little explored" (p. 107). The former has been an element of CMC study from the start. Some of the earliest ideas about CMC recognize that computer-mediated community will affect our considerations of space. As Licklider and Taylor saw it in 1968,

> What will on-line interactive communities be like? In most fields they will consist of geographically separated members, sometimes grouped in small clusters and

> sometimes working individually. They will be communities not of common location, but of *common interest*. In each geographical sector, the total number of users . . . will be large enough to support extensive general- purpose information processing and storage facilities . . . life will be happier for the on-line individual because the people with whom one interacts most strongly will be selected more by commonality of interests and goals than by accidents of proximity. (pp. 30-31)

The relation between "fields" and "interests" is not questioned in that article, nor is the connection between "common interest" and Calhoun's concept of "community as a complex of ideas and sentiments" followed up, but of greater importance is the belief that "accidents of proximity" lead one to be unhappy. Serendipity in its usual sense plays no part in either world that Licklider and Taylor (1968) describe; only a kind of will to interact among others with (undefined) "common interests" is operational. Yet geography does play a role, for it, at the very least, serves as the site and center of the machine that they state will serve us as we escape the social constraints that location has placed on us.

Walls (1993), in a chapter on global networks, attempts to subdivide community into those that are "relationship focused" and those that are "task focused," but the subdivision only provides insight into the functions of particular user groups rather than into the connections between users and hardly accounts for Calhoun's conception of community. Frederick (1993) borrows from Harasim's (1993) concept of "networlds" and Rheingold's (1993) notion of "virtual communities" to identify "nonplace" communities. None of these all too brief forays into CMC and community hit the mark. What is missing is the concomitant conceptualization of space and the social, the inquiry into connections between social relations, spatial practice, values, and beliefs. The ability to create, maintain, and control space (whatever we call it—virtual, nonplace, networld) links us to notions of power and necessarily to issues of authority, dominance, submission, rebellion, and cooptation, notions that Etzioni (1991) establishes as primary criteria of community. Just because the spaces with which we are now concerned are electronic it is not the case that they are democratic, egalitarian, or accessible, and it is not the case that we can forego asking in particular about substance and dominance.

Concerns about these issues have not only been underrepresented in the study of CMC, they have also been lost in community studies. In his classic study of communities and social change in America, Bender (1978) critiques community sociology as the study of "locality-based action" that emphasizes territory at the expense of culture:

> The identification of community with locality and communal experiences with rather casual associations has quietly redefined community in a way that puts it at odds with its historical and popular meaning . . . drain[ing] the concept of the very qualities that give the notion of community cultural, as opposed to merely organizational, significance. (p. 10)

For Bender, communities are defined not as places but as social networks, a definition useful for the study of community in cyberspace for two reasons. First, it focuses on the interactions that create communities. Second, it focuses away from place. In media that shift not only the sense of space but the sense of place, decentering (although not removing) the consideration of territory is necessary to permit entry of notions of power and its analysis.

Pseudocommunity and the Decentering of Place

Several authors, most notably Beniger (1987) and Peck (1987), have written about pseudocommunity: "the great societal transformations of the 19th century . . . a sharp drop in interpersonal control of individual behavior: from traditional communal relationships (*Gemeinschaft*) to impersonal, highly restricted association or *Gesellschaft* . . . from face-to-face to indirect or symbolic group relations" (Beniger, 1987, p. 353). Beniger borrows from Tonnies's (1967) work to bring the distinctions between Gemeinschaft and Gesellschaft into a discussion of mass-mediated discourse. For Beniger, a pseudocommunity is one in which impersonal associations constitute simulated personalized communication, what he calls "a hybrid of interpersonal and mass communication" (p. 369). His and Peck's criticisms of pseudocommunity center on the insincerity (or inauthenticity) of communication that it represents and the goals toward which that communication may be directed. It is natural that such criticisms ought to be part of an awareness of CMC, for it is, to say the least, difficult to judge sincerity in electronic text. Rheingold (1993) asks the appropriate questions:

> Is telecommunication culture capable of becoming something more than what Scott Peck calls a "pseudo-community," where people lack the genuine personal commitments to one another that form the bedrock of genuine community? Or is our notion of "genuine" changing in an age where more people every day live their lives in increasingly artificial environments? New technologies tend to change old ways of doing things. Is the human need for community going to be the next technology commodity? (pp. 60-61)

The most important of these questions is the one that asks whether or not our notions of the "genuine" are changing. One of the measures of genuine community ought to be its relationship to action (political or otherwise). As Taylor (1992) notes in *The Ethics of Authenticity,* political powerlessness feeds alienation from community. Does participation in on-line communities increase or decrease individuals' feelings of power? Is it a technology that embodies Taylor's ethic as its users spin off identities, or is it one that technologizes and reduces that ethic by problematizing identity and, with it, authenticity? As others in *CyberSociety* have noted, perhaps it does, but it probably does not. Part of the reason for such an assessment is that it is difficult to determine just what would constitute on-line political and personal action. The connections between computer-mediated community and the social and political worlds that users are part of offline are unclear, much like the connections between advertising and consumer behavior or between television and direct effects. Moreover, it is important to not slide by questions of access to computer-mediated communities, as they are related to power. Quarterman (1993) claims that "although power may come from the barrel of a gun, as Chairman Mao said, it is often preserved by secrecy. In networking, secrecy is not power and may not even be possible. Therefore, networking is subversive" (pp. 48-49). Yet Quarterman does not explain why secrecy may be impossible, nor does he seem sensitive to the powerful role that information and its absence may play in society. As Robert Doolittle (1972) has noted, the rhetorical and political elements that most often con- stitute communities include common understandings that action and effort will lead to the realization of achievements for the common good. The situ- ation in which we find computer-mediated communities at present is that their very definition as communities is perceived as a "good thing," creating a solipsistic and self- fulfilling community that pays little attention to political action outside of that which secures its own maintenance. Community and power do not necessarily intersect, but such solipsism is a form of power itself, wielded by those who occupy the community. Branscomb (1993) has pointed out, "More important than the substance of the legal rules that are likely to arise governing electronic communications is the question of what group will determine which laws or operating rules shall apply" (p. 99).

Part of what is already occurring, as explained by several of this anthology's contributors, is the creation of multitechno/cultural groups that determine operating rules for their own domain. But what is occurring additionally as the Internet and other computer networks sprout commercial nodes is the agglomeration of capital and its concomitant pressures on groups that already have some power. The arguments those groups (and others) often marshal to persuade government, industry, and citizens that computer networks must remain "free" are based on the very idea that it is only for lack of constraint that community could exist via CMC. However, community itself is a structuring concept—and a strong one given the almost primordial pull of symbolic force the word "community" continues to have.

Community as Culturally Constructed Category

Creating and maintaining community has traditionally been valued as a commendable goal. Bell and Newby (1974) wrote of the theoretical inheritance brought to definitions of community that " 'community' was thought to be a good thing, its passing was to be deplored, feared and regretted" (p. 21). That inheritance was left by modernism, and in some ways is part of postmodernism too, at least insofar as the tensions between modernity and postmodernism are sometimes still implicated in its theoretical discourse. The importance of that inheritance is the rhetorical use of community in social planning and the strength of persuasion the term "community" contains. In her book, *Redeeming Modernity,* Jensen (1990), borrowing from Robert Nisbet, identifies "the community/society dichotomy [that] references social relations," and claims that "what is at stake in this dichotomy, in American social thought, is the issue of connection—how we are to link up to each other in America" (p. 71). Jensen's questions about the ties that bind us ought to be asked in light of CMC. How is computer-mediated communication to link us up?

We have some answers insofar as links have already been made and others are envisioned. The scholarly literature examining computer-mediated communication has been expanding, as scholars in various fields probe and examine the nature of this form of communication. What can be learned from these forays that seek to assess not only the present state of CMC but its future?

Several threads, or categories, emerge from a close reading of the literature, predicated on the notion of CMC's effects on social relations. CMC, it is claimed, will

1. Create opportunities for education and learning
2. Create new opportunities for participatory democracy
3. Establish countercultures on an unprecedented scale
4. Ensnarl already difficult legal matters concerning privacy, copyright, and ethics
5. Restructure man/machine interaction

It is instructive and interesting to examine each claim in its own right. However, the contributors to this anthology will traverse this ground. Interestingly, the unifying principle among these claims is that orgnizational change will precipitate their occurrence. As Marvin (1988) notes in her brilliant study of the earliest electrical communication devices, *When Old Technologies Were New,* assumptions about technological change tell us what we believe the technology is supposed to do, which in turn reveals much about what we believe *we* are supposed to do. It would seem, then, that rather than reinvent or re-create social relations, or even reexamine culturally constructed definitions of community we already have, we believe we are supposed to reorganize social relations around a new technology.

The most important reorganization is the force with which the ideal of face-to-face communication is brought to the center of arguments about the structure of communication technology. Some evidence of this is found in the use of terms like "interactivity" to describe (and promote) new technology that allows for user feedback. As Rafaeli (1988) sees it,

> Interactivity is generally assumed to be a natural attribute of face-to-face conversation, but it has been proposed to occur in mediated communication settings as well.
>
> [I]nteractivity is an expression of the extent that in a given series of communication exchanges, any third (or later) transmission (or message) is related to the degree to which previous exchanges referred to even earlier transmissions. . . . This complex and ambitious definition misrepresents the intuitive nature of interactivity. In fact, the power of the concept and its attraction are in the matter-of-factness of its nature. The common feeling is that interactivity, like news, is something you know when you see it. (pp. 110-111)

Rafaeli goes on to criticize the use of interactivity as a "buzzword" but does not overlook a fundamental question: Why should face-to-face communication serve as an ideal? The most likely answer is that it is a form of communication that we identify and associate with community, with Gemeinschaft, and face-to-interface communication we associate with the impersonal communication that Beniger decries has led to "pseudocommunity."

Yet Michael Schudson (1978) has noted that

> when we criticize the reality of the mass media, we do so by opposing it to an ideal of conversation which we are not inclined to examine. We are not really interested in what face-to-face communication is like; rather, we have developed a notion that all communication *should* be like a certain model of conversation, whether that model really exists or not. (p. 323)

Computer-mediated communication permits us the "feeling" that Rafaeli emphasizes, but we are too media-savvy to be misled to believe that CMC has achieved the face-to-face ideal. We thus totter between the belief that CMC will, to borrow from Marshall McLuhan, "retribalize" us by engaging us in an ideal form of communication we have abandoned, and the belief that our interaction will become mechanized and lack the "richness" of face-to-face conversation. The development of CMC fits Schudson's (1978) idea that the face-to-face ideal is "in part a consequence of mass media": "First, the mass media have contributed to making the 'egalitarian' criterion of ideal communication more prominent and more possible to realize. . . . The mass media have had a second effect in making the conversational ideal more frequently realizable" (p. 326).

Creating software (and hardware) for CMC has become a race to provide the most "lifelike" interaction possible, a race characterized by extreme attentiveness to information richness and simulation. Each checkpoint in this race asks whether or not we have taken a step toward realizing the "conversational ideal" about which Schudson writes. Yet, even in face-to-face interaction, much of what is most valuable is the absence of information, the silence and pauses between words and phrases. Cohen (1985) critiques the idyllic (and often romantic) view of face-to-face interaction, too:

> The idea that, in small-scale society, people interact with each other as "whole persons" is a simplification. They may well encounter each other more frequently, more intensively and over a wider range of activities than is the case in more anonymous large-scale milieux. But this is not to say that people's knowledge of "the person" overrides their perception of the distinctive activities (or "roles") in which the person is engaged. (p. 29)

Nevertheless, we are reassured by the belief that the reality our eyes perceive in face-to-face communication is more real (or less manipulable) than other media by which we perceive reality. That belief reasserts itself in the understanding we have that what mediated reality lacks is sufficient "richness" to convey nonmediated reality. Each belief fuels the bias toward filling cyberspace with information and gives rise to two distinct ideas: first, that unused space is wasteful and, second, that more information is desirable and better. The trend in CMC, as in other areas of computing, has been to provide greater speed and more levels of organization to cope with that bias, and computer-mediated communication has been viewed from the perspective of organizational communication scholarship for quite some time. That perspective brings a bias, and I will examine it in a moment. Regarding community most directly, though, the bias most readily discernible is toward the removal of boundaries. Yet, as Cohen (1985) notes, it is "boundary [that] encapsulates the identity of the community" (p. 12). Face-to-face interaction does not necessarily break down boundaries, and to adopt it as an ideal will likewise not necessarily facilitate communication, community building, or understanding among people.

CMC and Organization

Although the study of organizational communication has only recently begun to intersect with community studies, particularly in the field of health communication, much of the literature examining CMC is from an organizational perspective and stems from studies of the introduction of computers in the workplace. The work of Rice (1984, 1987, 1989; Rice & Love, 1987; Rice & McDaniel, 1987) as well as that of Sproull and Kiesler (1991) is exemplary and develops ideas about the changes that electronic mail brings to organizations. The main body of their scholarship examines patterns of interaction and communication through telecommuting, teleconferencing, e-mail, and the like and asks questions about management, work, and the future of traditional organizational structures unbound from "the conventional patterns of who talks to whom and who knows what" (Sproull & Kiesler, 1991, p. 116).

There are two key elements to this form of analysis of CMC. First, it assumes that distance and space are to be centrally overcome and controlled, not in the sense that an individual is to control them but in the sense that a technology centrally and universally used will permit "almost unlimited access to data and to other people" (Sproull & Kiesler, 1991, p. 116). Almost in the same breath, however, Sproull and Kiesler argue for centralized oversight and control of access, claiming that

> it is up to management to make and shape connections. The organization of the future will depend significantly not just on how the technology of networking evolves but also on how managers seize the opportunity it presents for transforming the structure of work. (p. 123)

The issue, however, is less changes to "the structure of work" and more the control of access to information and people. That access is based on two principal assumptions about the use of computers found in many analyses of CMC: Computers cut across/break down boundaries, and computers break down hierarchies. Both of these assumptions are based on the idea that modifications to present social systems and reactions to social concerns can best be achieved by using a new technology on old problems. It is not unusual to find such assumptions when any new technology is put to use, as Marvin (1988) notes. Similarly, Hiltz and Turoff (1978) note, in relation to electronic mail, that there is a tendency to view new technology as simply a more efficient method or tool for confronting or improving an existing technology or situation.

Yet, as the contributors to *CyberSociety* point out, computers just as easily create boundaries and hierarchies. As Ross (1990) points out in a terrific essay, itself available on-line, there is a "tendency to use technology to form information elites," and evidence of such formations can be found in the romanticizing of the hacker as a countercultural hero (p. 15), in the elevation of privacy as a critical issue for computer users, and in the fervor with which PGP and other data encryption devices are being adopted.

The speed with which we may form new hierarchies and reorganize existing ones, particularly such as those on Usenet, does little to mitigate the fact that they are indeed present. They may rise and fall more quickly, but they are just as ubiquitous. Rheingold (1993) goes so far as to determine that computer-mediated communities will "grow into much larger networks over the next twenty years" (p. 58) but does not question or examine how that growth will be accompanied by structuring and hierarchies within networks.

Indeed, it is difficult to understand just how hierarchy and community can coexist via CMC, in part because of the seemingly anarchic (or at least unstructured) nature of many computer networks. A common denominator linking hierarchy and community is identity, not only in terms of one's sense of self but also in terms of one's sense of others. CMC provides ample room for identity but not for its fixing and structuring. Ross (1990) notes that "access to digital systems still requires only the authentication of a signature or pseudonym, not the identification of a real surveillable person, so there exists a crucial operative gap between authentication and identification" (p. 24). As some of the authors in *CyberSociety* point out, one can have multiple identities in cyberspace; moreover, one can shift identities rather easily, taking on characteristics of others' identities. It even is possible, as MacKinnon shows, to functionally locate personae via CMC.

The Illusion of Community

Issues of identity ought to be front and center with those of community as CMC develops. As Cheney (1991) correctly claims, "One's identity is somehow related to the larger social order. However [there is] disagree[ment] . . . on what kind of relationship this entails" (p. 10). What is most important is that identity is related directly to the increase in size of social organizations. The necessity to "keep track" of individuals by way of Social Security numbers and other bureaucratic devices that connect an individual to a larger entity make identification a matter of organization too, rather than a matter of self-definition. Cheney's (1991) comment that "there has been a transformation of the term 'identity' from its 'sameness' meaning to its 'essence' meaning" (p. 13) is significant precisely because identity as mediated in cyberspace carries no essential meanings. Alliances based on "sameness" may form and dissolve. Yet the ideas that Cheney borrows from Burke that assist him in developing a definition of identity "associated with the individual that must draw upon social and collective resources for its meaning" (p. 20) do not apply equally in CMC. CMC users may use similar resources to develop and structure meaning but without the affective alliances that Cheney implies are necessary.

Rheingold (1993) attempts to define how identity will be constructed via CMC:

> We reduce and encode our identities as words on a screen, decode and unpack the identities of others. The way we use these words, the stories (true and false) we tell about ourselves (or about the identity we want people to believe us to be) is what determines our identities in cyberspace. The aggregation of personae, interacting with each other, determines the nature of the collective culture. (p. 61)

One might suppose the same is true as to the aggregation of particular traits that determine the nature of the individual. However, the symbolic processes that Rheingold elides through use of such words as "encode" and "unpack" (themselves taken from the language of computer software) are fraught with unproblematized assumptions about the work that humans perform in search of their own identities and those of others. Interaction ought not be substituted for community, or, for that matter, for communication, and to uncritically accept connections between personae, individuals, and community inadvisable.

It will be unfortunate, too, if we uncritically accept that CMC will usher in the great new era that other media of communication have failed to bring us. It is not, as virtual reality pioneer Jaron Lanier says, that television has failed us because it "wasn't planned well enough" ("Virtual Reality," 1992, p. 6); it is that organization and planning are not necessarily appropriate processes for constructing or recapturing the sense of community for which we are nostalgic. Bender (1978) sharply criticizes those who seek "to recapture community by imputing it to large-scale organizations and to locality-based social activity regardless of the quality of human relationships that characterize these contexts" (p. 143). Instead, Bender finds community in the midst of a transformation and asks us to heed his call that we not, by way of our nostalgia, limit definitions of community to that which "seventeenth-century New Englanders knew" (p. 146), although with electronic town hall meetings and the like we seem to be doing precisely that. One example can be found in Rheingold's work. Although often critical in much of his writing, it is clear from the comparisons that Rheingold (1993) makes to other forms of community that what he calls "virtual communities" are predicated on nostalgic (and romantic) ideals:

> It's a bit like a neighborhood pub or coffee shop. It's a little like a salon, where I can participate in a hundred ongoing conversations with people who don't care what I look like or sound like, but who do care how I think and communicate. There are seminars and word fights in different corners. (p. 66)

> Virtual communities might be real communities, they might be pseudocommunities, or they might be something entirely new in the realm of social contracts, but I believe they are in part a response to the hunger for community that has followed the disintegration of traditional communities around the world. (p. 62).

Of course, it is difficult to imagine what new on-line communities may be like, and it is far easier to use our memories and myths as we construct them. What is more important than simply understanding the construction we are undertaking is to notice that it is peculiar and particular to the computer. Because these machines are seen as "linking" machines (they link information, data, communication, sound, and image through the common language of digital encoding), to borrow from Jensen (1990), they inherently affect the ways we think of linking up to each other, and thus they fit squarely into our concerns about community. Media technologies that have largely been tied to the "transportation" view of communication mentioned earlier were developed to overcome space and time. The computer, in particular, is an "efficiency" machine, purporting to ever increase its speed. But unlike those technologies, the computer used for communication is a technology to be understood from the "ritual" view of communication, for once time and space have been overcome (or at least rendered surmountable) the spur for development is connection, linkage. Once we can surmount time and space and "be" anywhere, we must choose a "where" at which to be, and the computer's functionality lies in its power to make us organize our desires about the spaces we visit and stay in.

The question remains, though, whether or not the communities we may form by way of CMC will, or even ought to, be part of our public culture. If so, then perhaps it would be best to not understand them as communities. As

Bender (1978) writes, "Our public lives do not provide an experience of community. The mutuality and sentiment characteristic of community cannot and need not be achieved in public. We must be careful to distinguish between these two contexts of social experience" (p. 148). The manner in which we seek to find community, empowerment, and political action all embedded in our ability to use CMC is thereby troubling. No one medium, no one technology, has been able to provide those elements in combination, and often we have been unable to find them in any media. CMC has potential for a variety of consequences, some anticipated, some not. A critical awareness of the social transformations that have occurred and continue to occur with or without technology will be our best ally as we incorporate CMC into contemporary social life.

References

Barnes, T. J., & Duncan, J. S. (1992). *Writing worlds.* London: Routledge.

Bell, C., & Newby, H. (1974). *The sociology of community.* London: Frank Cass & Company, Ltd.

Bender, T. (1978). *Community and social change in America.* New Brunswick, NJ: Rutgers University Press.

Benedikt, M. (1991). Cyberspace: Some proposals. In M. Benedikt (Ed.), *Cyberspace* (pp. 119-224). Cambridge: MIT Press.

Beniger, J. (1986). *The control revolution.* Cambridge, MA: Harvard University Press.

Beniger, J. (1987). Personalization of mass media and the growth of pseudo-community. *Communication Research, 14*(3), 352-371.

Berger, P. L., & Luckmann, T. (1967). *The social construction of reality.* New York: Anchor Books.

Berman, M. (1982). *All that is solid melts into air.* New York: Simon & Schuster.

Branscomb, A. W. (1993). Jurisdictional quandaries for global networks. In L. M. Harasim (Ed.), *Global networks* (pp. 57-80). Cambridge: MIT Press.

Calhoun, C. J. (1980). Community: Toward a variable conceptualization for comparative research. *Social History, 5,* 105-129.

Carey, J. (1989). *Communication as culture.* Boston, MA: Unwin-Hyman.

Carey, J. (1993). Everything that rises must diverge: Notes on communications, technology and the symbolic construction of the social. In P. Gaunt (Ed.), *Beyond agendas* (pp. 171-184). Westport, CT: Greenwood.

Chayko, M. (1993). What is real in the age of virtual reality? "Reframing" frame analysis for a technological world. *Symbolic Interaction, 16*(2), 171-181.

Cheney, G. (1991). *Rhetoric in an organizational society: Managing multiple identities.* Columbia: University of South Carolina Press.

Chesebro, J. W., & Bonsall, D. G. (1989). *Computer-mediated communication.* Tuscaloosa: University of Alabama Press.

Cohen, A. (1985). *The symbolic construction of community.* London: Tavistock.

Doolittle, R. J. (1972). *Speech communication as an instrument in engendering and sustaining a sense of community in urban and poor neighborhoods: A study of rhetorical potentialities.* Unpublished doctoral dissertation, Pennsylvania State University.

Effrat, M. P. (1974). *The community: Approaches and applications.* New York: Free Press.
Etzioni, A. (1991). *The responsive society.* San Francisco: Jossey-Bass.
Frederick, H. (1993). Computer networks and the emergence of global civil society. In L. M. Harasim (Ed.), *Global networks* (pp. 283-296). Cambridge: MIT Press.
Gillespie, A., & Robins, K. (1989). Geographical inequalities: The spatial bias of the new communications technologies. *Journal of Communication, 39*(3), 7-18.
Harasim, L. M. (Ed.). (1993). *Global networks.* Cambridge: MIT Press.
Harvey, D. (1989). *The condition of postmodernity.* Oxford: Blackwell.
Hiltz, S. R., & Turoff, M. (1978). *The network nation: Human comunication via computer.* Reading, MA: Addison-Wesley.
Jensen, J. (1990). *Redeeming modernity.* Newbury Park, CA: Sage.
Laird, A. (1993). *Computerscape with letters.* Unpublished manuscript prepared for Media History, Faculty of Communication, University of Tulsa.
Leslie, J. (1993, November). Kids connecting. *Wired, 1*(5), 90-93.
Licklider, J.C.R., & Taylor, R. W. (1968). The computer as a communication device. *Science & Technology, 76,* 21-31.
Marvin, C. (1988). *When old technologies were new.* Oxford: Oxford University Press.
Morris, M. (1992). The man in the mirror: David Harvey's "condition" of postmodernity. *Theory, Culture & Society, 9,* 253-279.
Mumford, L. (1934). *Technics and civilization.* New York: Harcourt, Brace & World.
Ong, W. (1982). *Orality and literacy.* London: Methuen.
Patton, P. (1986). *Open road.* New York: Simon & Schuster.
Peck, M. S. (1987). *The different drum: Community-making and peace.* New York: Simon & Schuster.
Quarterman, J. S. (1993). The global matrix of minds. In L. M. Harasim (Ed.), *Global networks* (pp. 35-56). Cambridge: MIT Press.
Rafaeli, S. (1988). Interactivity: From new media to communication. In R. P. Hawkins, J. M. Wiesmann, & S. Pingree (Eds.), *Advancing communication science: Merging mass and interpersonal processes* (Sage Annual Reviews of Communication Research, Vol. 16, pp. 110-134). Newbury Park, CA: Sage.
Rheingold, H. (1993). A slice of life in my virtual community. In L. M. Harasim (Ed.), *Global networks* (pp. 57-80). Cambridge: MIT Press.
Rice, R. E. (1984). *The new media: Communication, research, and technology.* Beverly Hills, CA: Sage.
Rice, R. E. (1987). Computer-mediated communication and organizational innovation. *Journal of Communication, 37*(4), 65-94.
Rice, R. E. (1989). Issues and concepts in research on computer-mediated communication systems. In J. A. Anderson (Ed.), *Communication yearbook* (Vol. 12, pp. 436-476). Newbury Park, CA: Sage.
Rice, R. E., & Love, G. (1987). Electronic emotion: Socioemotional content in a computer-mediated communication network. *Communication Research, 14,* 85-108.
Rice, R. E., & McDaniel, B. (1987). *Managing organizational innovation: The evolution from word processing to office information systems.* New York: Columbia University Press.
Ross, A. (1990). Hacking away at the counterculture. *Postmodern Culture, 1*(1), 1-43.
Schudson, M. (1978). The ideal of conversation in the study of mass media. *Communication Research, 12*(5), 320-329.
Soja, E. (1989). *Postmodern geographies: The reassertion of space in critical social theory.* London: Verso.

Sproull, L., & Kiesler, S. (1991, September). Computers, networks and work. *Scientific American,* pp. 116-123.
Stacey, M. (1974). The myth of community studies. In C. Bell & H. Newby (Eds.), *The sociology of community* (pp. 13-26). London: Frank Cass & Company, Ltd.
Stone, A. R. (1991). Will the real body please stand up? Boundary stories about virtual cultures. In M. Benedikt (Ed.), *Cyberspace* (pp. 81-118). Cambridge: MIT Press.
Taylor, C. (1992). *The ethics of authenticity.* Cambridge, MA: Harvard University Press.
Tonnies, F. (1967). *Community and society.* Lansing: Michigan State University Press.
Virtual reality: A new medium and a new culture. (1992, November). *Communique,* p. 6.
Walls, J. (1993). Global networking for local development: Task focus and relationship focus in cross-cultural communication. In L. M. Harasim (Ed.), *Global networks* (pp. 153-166). Cambridge: MIT Press.
Warner, L. (1963). *Yankee city.* New Haven, CT: Yale University Press.

2
A BACKSTAGE CRITIQUE OF VIRTUAL REALITY

Cheris Kramarae

They are called "tools to amplify the mind" ("Virtual Reality," 1992). They are computer-generated viewing devices, acoustical chips, and sensors that provide individual users with multiple sensory information—sound, sight, touch—to simulate real or fantastic environments. The makers of the virtual reality programs promise us that we can immerse ourselves in new environments, as if we were really on the battlefields or driving a tractor through the fields or playing in a personal bordello. The existing cyberspace simulations are not refined, and it will be years, if ever, before the computer illusions will be confused with our non-computer-assisted experiences. However, virtual reality programs and promises are attracting a great deal of attention and funding, and they say a lot about visions of the future. In many ways, these visions differ in very real and important ways from the visions of feminists who are also interested in changing our relationships to each other and our environments.

In this chapter, I use feminist speculative fiction to critique virtual reality literature. Both concern the vision, sound, feel, and taste of possible worlds. Feminist speculative fiction as a genre has been accused by some critics of presenting a nostalgia for a never-never time with an emphasis on matriarchal relationships, a oneness with the earth, and a resistance to technology. Such criticism is simplistic and inaccurate as feminist speculative fiction deals with many issues in a rich variety of methods. Yet even the feminist "cyberpunk" novels have received relatively little popular, commercial, and academic interest (see, e.g., Smith, 1993, for a discussion of Olivia Butler's *Xenogenesis*). This is, in part, because the feminist speculative fiction authors do challenge, through utopias and dystopias, the prevailing conceptions of bodies, genders, relationships (including to the earth), and sexual violence.

The issues mentioned here have implications for everyone, including those who are not girls or women[1] and those who do not use computers. I'm going to write about virtual reality as it affects even those of us who have no intention of putting on VR gloves and headset.

Throughout the 1980s, when computers were discussed there was a lot said about the information revolution, about the ways that computers can spread information across class and national boundaries. The stress on information has been unfortunate, as if there were shared ideas about what constitutes information, and as if this information or knowledge (the two words were often used as synonyms) could be transferred via computers or any other way in a manner and form beneficial to everyone. The *Encyclopedia Britannica* was often given as an example of information or knowledge that can be digitized and made more accessible to many. Feminists' critiques of the contents of editions of that encyclopedia run to more pages than the object itself. The encyclopedia is, of course, a very limited work containing not the knowledge of people around the world but, rather, some of the beliefs and interests of a relatively small number of people. Yet the encyclopedias are heavily used in education settings and are taught as knowledge—containing the kinds of things one has to know if one is to be considered educated. In the first wave of justification of selling and investing in computers, encyclopedias were there, ready to be converted into a new form to help distribute the Information Revolution everywhere—for a price.

Now, increasingly, the focus in the professional, popular, and scholarly publications is on virtual reality (VR). When VR is discussed, we notice that the focus on information has disappeared and what is mentioned repetitively is sensation. What is coming is entertainment and interaction. The computer was an extension of the book and thus had educational functions—many thought of it as the book with a TV screen. VR, however, is discussed as an extension of the computer and movies, with a focus on entertainment—the computer with feelies. Even the electronic networks are changing, with increasing numbers of interactive computer games like the MUDs (Multi-User Dungeons).[2] Some things are changing, but in many respects it's back to the future. It is not a revolution as much as a little shifting around in the play plot.

Here, I want to discuss where boys and girls, and men and women, in the United States are in what is being described, by those who say they are in the know, as another revolution in the ways we will interact and know ourselves (e.g., "We are contemplating the arising shape of a new world," writes Michael Benedikt, 1991, p. 23). In many respects, the changes aren't as dramatic as the rhetoric is. First, then, a few comments on the terminology being used for many of the activities, designs, processes, dreams and nightmares of what is called "information" technologies, or, increasingly, "the technology" or, once again without much regard for the natives, "the new frontier."

Cyberspace

This word comes from William Gibson's book *Neuromancer.* Gibson describes it as "a consensual hallucination. . . . [People are] creating a world. It's not really a place, it's not really space. It's notional space." Gibson and John Barlow state, "Cyberspace is where you are when you're talking on the telephone" (quoted in *Mondo 2000,* 1992, p. 78). Another definition by Randy Walser in "Autodesk Cyberspace Project": "Cyberspace is the medium that gives people the feeling they have been transported, bodily, from the ordinary physical world to worlds purely of imagination." (cited in *Mondo 2000,* 1992, p. 264). If this sounds like the effects of several drugs you know, you are thinking along the same lines as many involved in creating cyberspace. Timothy Leary is dramatically involved in discussions of cyberspace, as men (and it is mostly men) talk about ways of extending life and senses.[3] Some people use the term "cyberspace" interchangeably with "virtual reality." In general, "cyberspace" is used to refer to the worldwide computer-mediated communication (CMC) network where words and graphics are shared, and friendships and power relations are manifested.

Virtual Reality (VR)

Timothy Leary says we have been living in virtual reality since the proliferation of television sets. VR differs primarily from TV in that VR makes the experience interactive rather than passive (cited in *Mondo 2000*, 1992, p. 262). Howard Rheingold (1991) asks us to

> imagine a wraparound television with three-dimensional programs, including three-dimensional sounds and solid objects that you can pick up and manipulate, even feel with your fingers and hands. . . . Imagine that you are the creator as well as the consumer of your artificial experience, with the power to use a gesture or word to remold the world you see and hear and feel. (p. 16)

Brenda Laurel (1991) writes that, for her, VR brings the experience of acting, a way of exploring existence from the perspectives of varied characters, situations, and worlds not otherwise encountered in our everyday lives. Laurel worked on "Wild Palms," which was promoted as TV's first attempt at showing virtual reality; however, she doesn't think that even interactive television represents the future: "It's a dead end" (quoted in McCarthy, 1993)[4] with a lot of scary and hopeful possible successors to it "depending on who owns the interactive media of the future" (Antonopulos & Barnett, 1992, p. 12). Unlike most of the programmers interested in virtual reality, she is working with electronic storytelling, "a very female-dominated" activity, with the technology as an audience (Antonopulos & Barnett, 1992, p. 12). Laurel's approach is a good illustration of the importance of paying close attention to the interests of many rather than just to the statements of those who have the loudest and best financed statements about what computers can and should be programmed to do.

VR exists in various fairly rudimentary (in terms of what is talked about as coming) forms. A couple of examples: The first BattleTech Center opened in 1990 at Chicago's North Pier. The game is based on networked military tank simulators. Players pay and sign in at the front desk and are matched up with others to make teams. The teams play in a room decorated as the war room of a starship, with TV monitors filling up a wall. Each player gets a BattleTech console, which is steered like a battle tank, with floor pedals and throttle. Speakers around the players supply the sounds of machinery and battle. The joystick has triggers and buttons for controlling weapons systems. The idea is not to beat the machine but to beat the enemy either individually or in teams. As one report states, "What gives realism and challenge to the Battletech experience is the fact that you play against living opponents rather than the algorithms of a computer's program" (Hsu, 1993, p. 102). Scott Crandall, the VR entrepreneur who plans to open BattleTech franchises in other cities, says, "There is an exciting kind of bonding with virtual reality that goes on even with members of the opposing team. You admire quick moves and get excited by a competitor who challenges you, who gives you a good experience" (description and quote from Pimentel & Teixerira, 1993, pp. 211-212). The company that created the game reports that BattleTech is a huge success in Japan also (Newquist, 1993).

Most VR "entertainment" work is taking place in the United States, in part because the U.S. defense industry has invested so many (tax) dollars in VR projects and now wants to find other uses for their work (Newquist, 1993). However, in Great Britain there are also commercial applications using the technology. For example, in Nottingham, England, in a storefront in one of the city's nightclub areas, Andy and Paul Smith and Justin Webster have built one of the world's first LBE (location-based entertainment) centers. You can watch players through a large window before you walk into the office and wait for your turn. The playroom has four virtuality units. The largest depicts a medieval village and forest. The play: a new version of *Dungeons and Dragons*®, a game played, in the past often intensively, most often by boys and men. This new game, Legend Quest, is played in virtual reality. Each player chooses from 18 possible characters (elf, human, dwarf characters; the gender can also be chosen). The virtuality system is equipped to customize your character—the person others in the game will see and hear. After all, if you say you are an elf you need to be seen as short and to be heard as speaking in a higher voice. The goal of the game is to live rather than die from foul play or other dangers, succeed in 10 challenges, and defeat the evil master of the dungeon. If this sounds familiar it's because all-too-familiar knowledges, stories, adventures, and stereotypes operate in virtual reality. The creativity doesn't come in the form of new legends. We can expect many more medieval imaginations, cops-and-robbers, sex, and other mayhem from other creators of VR.

Legend Quest has been hugely successful. More than 1,500 players signed up for lifetime memberships in the first eight weeks (at £5 each). Outside of the commercial play, some of the characters meet to plan strategies and pig roasts (Delaney, 1993).

It seems to me that the potential major change here is some erosion of the classic body/mind split. VR, like all other imaginative situations, has the potential for changes in gender stereotypes, but while, as in other kinds of play-acting, women and men can temporarily change their gender, there is little to suggest major overhauls of those so-called sex roles in VR programming.[5] As Brenda Laurel says, the guys who are designing the programs are the guys whose business it is to sell sexual stereotypes, and so the new programs become "another means of enforcing the gender landscape rather than a means of liberation" (Antonopulos & Barnett, 1993, p. 12).

Desktop VR

For some, desktop virtual reality is a more comfortable, accessible VR system than immersion virtual reality. Some users of current immersion VR suffer from "simulator sickness" because of the sensor lag—you turn your head but the sensors cause a delay that might disorient. Desktop VR systems can be used to show potential customers products that are in the design or production stage; the effects, on the product and its environment, of altering the shape, size, and color can be seen from all angles. For teachers, there are promises of desktop VR programs that will allow them and their students to go places they can't or shouldn't go. For example, a project funded by the Department of Employment and a number of companies in Great Britain allows students at West Denton High School in Newcastle upon Tyne to move around a factory floor with interactive machines that, if real, could be dangerous to the novice operator of lathes. The real and the VR machines are operated by push-button controls, so the student can learn the safe procedures, such as correct rotation maneuvers, before venturing into the real factory where mistakes could result in problems for the machines and operators. Learning Spanish? Might be more fun to wander around a VR home, interacting with objects that display their names in Spanish (Tait, 1993).

Many of the people writing about VR say that its potential is limited only by the imagination of those working on the programs. That's my worry. I'm concerned about the limited imagination of those working on and using the programs. And I think we all need to be concerned.

Women and Cyberspace

Looking at the programs and the discussions of the programs, we see that women *are* in this cyberspace but in the same basic ways they have been in the rest of men's technology creations, not as primary decision makers but primarily as tools or concepts to be used in the creations of men. I'm not discussing here whether women will have their own Virtual Vernon programs to correspond to the sensationally successful (in terms of copies sold) *Virtual Valerie.* Just as there was *Playgirl* after *Playboy* and the video game *PacWoman*™ after *PacMan*™, there will be a Virtual Vernon after *Virtual Valerie.*

What I'm concerned about is the place of girls and women in the designing and analyzing of our futures. Given the supposed concern of educational administrators about the past gender, race, and class inequities in our school systems, and given the stated goals of providing meaningful education to students from a variety of backgrounds, we would think that those administrators might be encouraging all manner of studies and providing support to those who are studying the genderizing of the computer studies and programs inside and outside the classrooms. They are not.

We can define the problems of access to common electronic programs as occurring at two levels. First, the hardware and software. As anyone who looks with even semi-keen eyes can see, girls and women do not have the access that boys and men have. Studies that indicate that many little boys quickly learn that they can and may push girls off classroom computers should be of great concern to all of us, as should be the assumptions on campuses about the people who most need the new equipment. The distribution of hardware and software seems to have a direct correlation to the distribution of women and men teachers across the campus. Will we see that biology professors are assumed to need computers but that those teaching nursing classes do not?

Second, there is a problem of access to relevant databases, bulletin boards, and newsgroups. While there are thousands of on-line discussion groups to be found via electronic searches, very few of the electronic forums are germane to the feminist student and scholar (Ebben & Kramarae, 1993).[6]

Our own research and our experience in organizing a working colloquium —Women, Information Technology, and Scholarship (WITS)—at the University of Illinois at Urbana-Champaign makes clear to us that girls and women will have to work, often under difficult circumstances, to alter the trends and to find or create funding for computer equipment and programs and other relevant and useful resources. Judging from what is going on, and not going on, in cyberspace these days, it is vital to all of us that women do this finding and creating. The social critic and speculative fiction writer Marge Piercy gives us some insight as to what might happen to us if we don't. I suggest that, instead of renting films such as *The Lawnmower Man* or *Terminator 2* from the video shop, you borrow Piercy's (1991) *He, She, and It* from the library and read, the old-fashioned way, about the 21st century as she thinks it can be predicted by present events and conditions. In the future that she sees, the environment is, of course, a mess, and the world has been divided into 23 great corporate enclaves. Most people, the day workers and gang niños and unemployed, live outside the enclaves in the dangerous environment and air of the Glop.

Some people live within a wrap in one of the free towns, the choice of those with a minority religion, a sexual orientation not condoned by the multis, or an archaic desire for freedom. The techies of 2061 are, as today, "making those elaborate worlds people play at living in instead of worrying about the one we're all stuck with" (p. 7). Food as we know it is very scarce, with most people living on "vat food," organisms grown in large vats. Spikes, the interactant programs in which the players are projected into the drama, are very intense (more intense than the stimmies in which users just experience what an actor sees, feels, and touches); people tell "of kids found dead who had replayed favorite adventure or porn scenes until they starved to death" (p. 32). Few people read.

The Jewish women in one of the free towns talk about how they have always considered that access to books and various information is part of what they consider human. One woman says, "Most folks press the diodes of stimmies against their temples and experience some twit's tears and orgasms, while the few plug in and access information on a scale never before available. The many know less and less and the few more and more" (p. 194). The problem is not with the existence of various technologies—long ago people became cyborgs in various stages, with artificial knees and hips, kidney and heart transplants, contact lenses, and second skins needed for protec- tion from the sun; we're all cyborgs, writes Piercy, who has read Donna Haraway's article "A Manifesto for Cyborgs" (pp. 50, 431). The problem is partly too much time spent on manufactured fantasies and too little dealing directly with people in their nonprogrammed environments. Piercy is very concerned with past history as well as future, and thus she deals with the ways that minorities, and those majorities who are considered minorities, survive. The women build real-life relationships that give them protection, love, and mental stimulation. Shira, the "shero" of the novel, is also able to experience love with a cyborg man but only because he has been programmed primarily by women.

In her acknowledgments, Piercy points out that, given the present realities, her fictional world is not fantasy:

> Be aware that even now companies are working on sensor nets that permit a person to "walk into" data and experience it as real objects in imaginary space [VR]. As for the destruction of the ozone layer and the results of global warming, your local library surely has this information, as mine did. (p. 432)

Cyberspace, like earthspace, is not developing as a viable place for women. A *Time* article on "cybertech" states that "what once seemed like a passing fad for preteen boys has grown into a global money making machine that is gobbling up some of the most creative talents in Hollywood and tapping the coffers of media and communications conglomerates eager to get in on the action" (Elmer-Dewitt, 1993, p. 68; reprinted by permission). U.S. manufacturers of video games take in $5.3 billion a year, more than people spend in going to the movies. The several versions of *Mortal Kombat* are a brutal sensation (introduced with a $10 million media blitz), with lots of digitized blood and gore. Now we have the "almost full-immersion" video "games" with titles such as *Comanche Maximum Overkill* and *Doom.* It's not only what the simulations contain that is of concern (e.g., girls and women being threatened or lots of men being killed) but all the missing characters and topics. Although many people become very concerned about any talk of censorship, I see very little public concern about the general problem of what is called "entertainment" in this country.

The WITS women are very interested in the new technologies and talk about potentials for increasing communication among women, of making child care easier and better for all, and of making their professional lives better rather than more difficult and dangerous. We talk about the importance of being active participants in the learning process and the value of multiple learning modes (rather than assuming that everyone enjoys learning by waiting for the program to crash). We talk about easy access to a broad array of information (including such basics as telephone numbers and household information) and information retrieval customized to one's personal history (see Banich & Wilson, 1993, p. 67). We are writing and reading essays that deal with the working conditions of women working at cheap rates in other countries to produce the computer parts that have allowed the rapid increased buying of personal computers in the United States. We are asking questions about the impact of technological change for rural women in the United States and elsewhere and questions about social and health issues that come with the new technologies. We are discussing the masculinity of science and what that means for all our work in all disciplines.

In general, these are not the issues one sees and hears in "malestream" publications and other forums. Below I mention just a few of the issues I do see discussed in those forums. Men's talk about VR is at the moment mostly speculative fiction; I critique that talk via feminist speculative fiction.

Ecology

Frank Biocca points out that virtual reality "will allow all kinds of protean forms of visual and physical expression without transforming physical reality. . . . [I]t is suggested that virtual reality is a green technology." Jaron Lanier agrees that "media technology is a minor contributor to the ecological malaise of our planet. . . . To the degree that it might encourage telecommuting that is probably more important than anything else" (Lanier & Biocca, 1992, p. 169).

We'll leave aside the mention of telecommuting, a very promising and problematic concept these days especially for the women who try to work two jobs—working for a company while watching the children, without benefit of union support or day care. What about the argument that VR takes little fossil energy and avoids trampling on the grass? Some of my friends say that if they had just an hour a week to roam around in their favorite place—say, the west coast of Oregon, or the Isle of Skye—that gives them pleasure and stimulation they could then be happier and more productive in the cornfields of Illinois. And some VR advocates point out the values of being able to place people *in,* for example, the rainforests of the world, to encourage understanding and conservation.

Agreed. I'm waiting for the Oregon coast VR program with inexpensively created waves and smells. However, these programs do use lots of electricity. And we can guess that, as with computers, VR equipment will quickly become antiquated and junked when newer models become available. In addition, I worry about programs that encourage us to leave for extended periods the dirt and water of the actual places we live in. In many real lives, the man sits at the breakfast table or in his evening chair reading the newspaper while the woman dresses the children, fixes meals, and answers the phone. I can imagine the man of the house putting on his gloves and headset and visiting Costa Rica while the woman of the house stays in the real house, changing the diapers and fixing the meals. I'd like more discussion of this as we talk about the ecological benefits of VR. Does the interest in moving away from the earth and the environment we've created come from an interest in moving to a more sanitized world without the messes we've made?

Sally Gearhart (1991), author of the feminist speculative fiction *Wanderground: Stories of the Hill Women,* has called for "an end to technology," writing that we are growing more and more dependent on Western science and technology, with the result being that we are virtually helpless when it fails, as in the nuclear meltdown at Three Mile Island and in the many failures of computers that leave consumers stranded in airports and library patrons without a catalogue. More important, in our dependency on technology we stand in an adversarial relationship to our environment. To study and control our environment we alienate ourselves from it, she writes. Technology as it is being used leads to power, domination, and control—in a failed relationship to our planet. Gearhart (1991) writes, "An extraterrestrial observing our polluted and diseased planet would have to conclude that homo sapiens, the inventor of technology, was an evolutionary blunder and should now silently . . . steal away" (pp. 83-85).

She suggests that if we knew we were to have no more of us we might change our character pretty quickly and quit poisoning, killing, and beating up on each other (actions that haven't shown much interest in species preservation anyway) and become more appreciative of our environment. If we can't or don't want a voluntary cessation of reproduction, we have another option offered by her *Wanderground*—the training of our senses so that, for example, we hear and see with more sensitivity and we learn to live much more cooperatively with other animals so as to bring some harmony to all. I'm watching to see what other animals will appear in VR programs. In the VR literature, I see references to some creatures called "interstellar pukoids" and "nasty phlegm throwers," but except for a few discussions about rainforest plants and animals, there seems to be little interest in rethinking our relationship with our environment. In fact, the interest seems to be in distancing humans from it, away from the dirt and also away from the pollution we have caused.

Intimacy/Communication Enhancement

Rheingold (1991) writes,

> The secondary social effects of technosex are potentially revolutionary. If technology enables you to experience erotic frissons or deep physical, social, emotional communication with another person with no possibility of pregnancy or sexually transmitted disease, what then of conventional morality, and what of the social rituals and cultural codes that exist solely to enforce that morality? Is disembodiment the ultimate sexual revolution and/or the first step toward abandoning our bodies? . . . perhaps cyberspace is a better place to keep most of the population relatively happy, most of the time. . . .
>
> Privacy and identity and intimacy will become tightly coupled into something we don't have a name for yet. (pp. 352-353)

This focus on intimacy as technosex is pervasive in VR discussions. For example, during a half-hour program about VR presented on PBS May 1, 1992, a speaker on the virtues of VR asked listeners to image the following: You are traveling. You get to the hotel and you miss your wife. You ring up your wife and then you can have sex over the glove/phone link.

For many men in particular, heterosexual intimacy means primarily sex, whereas women more often talk about intimacy in terms of general closeness, including sharing thoughts and discussing problems. This conflict of interests is clearly going to be played out once again in the New Media. The alt.sex.news groups on the Internet have very high traffic, with mostly men exchanging messages. We see unrequested body parts "visuals" (e.g., "breasts" composed of computer keyboard letters and punctuation marks) e-mailed to women, and digital printouts posted in computer labs as university nets are used to transmit pornography (Kramarae & Taylor, 1993). In France, the national fiber-optic Minitel system is largely funded by phone sex (Stefanac, 1993).

Cybersex

Now, cyberbabes. We can't be surprised, given the current culture and given the real-life creators and manufacturers of the new games, that the New Media develops so clearly and with so little new creativity from the Old. For example, using Interotica's program *NightWatch,* the user/voyeur is provided with a VR female guide who points out a number of fantasy possibilities. The guide takes on the behaviors suggested by the player, eventually becoming his personal ideal for this situation. Linda Jacobson, editor of *CyberArts,* writes:

> Smut on paper or video is much more benign than interactive stroke books. These products show men that they can have control over women. You can force them to do your bidding and they do it willingly. I am absolutely opposed to censorship, but I think men have to be made aware that this kind of thing can make women feel very uncomfortable. (quoted in Stefanac, 1993, p. 41)

Sex will (has?) become another sport, like hunting and shooting tanks and hostile aliens. *Collaborative* interaction will likely mean it can be a men's team sport. It will again be removed from intimacy as many women know or wish it. Brenda Laurel says, "The computer game genre has grown . . . with programmers utterly devoted to an adolescent male demographic and a very white, First World Western view of what's interesting to kids . . . shooting and killing and blowing things up. . ." (quoted in Bright, 1992, p. 66).

With VR you can also reach out and grab someone. In a passage that's been reprinted in a number of publications, Rheingold (1991) writes,

> Picture yourself a couple of decades hence, dressing for a hot night in the virtual village. Before you climb into a suitable padded chamber and put on your 3D glasses, you slip into a lightweight (eventually, one would hope, diaphanous) bodysuit, something like a body stocking, but with the kind of intimate snugness of a condom. Embedded in the inner surface of the suit, using a technology that does not yet exist, is an array of intelligent sensor-effectors—a mesh of tiny tactile detectors coupled to vibrators of varying degrees of hardness, hundreds of them per square inch. . . .
>
> Now, imagine plugging your whole sound-sight-touch telepresence system into the telephone network. You see a lifelike but totally artificial visual representation of your own body and of your partner's. . . . Your partner(s) can move independently in the cyberspace and your representations are able to touch each other, even though your physical bodies might be continents apart. (p. 346)

But no need to wait the decades. *Virtual Valerie* exists. It's not called information but, rather, a game or pornography, depending on whether you think of the CD-ROM *Virtual Valerie* as openness and freedom or as sexist and exploitive.[7] Because she has sold so well, she is one of the best known but still only one of a number of cyberbabes. Earlier, *Valerie*'s creator, Mike Saenz, created *MacPlaymate* for the Mac. He writes that he wanted to create something new:

> Most games are performance tests—violent performance tests. Most look as if they've been programmed by sadistic nerds—this is largely because they were.
>
> I wanted to create a nonviolent interactive simulation that a user could enjoy simply for the experience. . . . Virtual Valerie . . . she's your cybernetic fantasy! . . .

> This is our chance to create a whole new form of erotic art. . . . When I explain virtual reality to the uninitiated, they just don't get it. But they warm immediately to the idea of virtual sex. . . . I have a silly idea for a product called Strip Teacher. She goes, "Tell me the name of the thirteenth president of the United States and I'll show you my tits." (quoted in *Mondo 2000,* 1992, pp. 272, 274)

I'll venture that he's not thinking of this product as primarily an educational experience.

Saenz continues, "I think lust motivates technology. The first personal robots, let's face it, are not going to be bought to bring people drinks" (quoted in *Mondo 2000,* 1992, p. 275).

One multimedia consultant and author writes,

> Once you start thinking about sex at a distance, it's amazing how many other questions about future possibilities present themselves, questions about big changes that might be in store for us. Given the rate of development of VR technologies, we don't have a great deal of time to tackle questions of morality, privacy, personal identity, and even the prospect of a fundamental change in human nature. When the VR revolution really gets rolling, we are likely to be too busy turning into whatever we are turning into to analyze or debate the consequences. (Rheingold, 1991, p. 350)

No time to discuss these questions? Who determines how fast this process goes or whether it goes at all? Human nature? What might that be? That's a very strange term these days when we are starting to acknowledge and respect many natures, many knowledges, many perspectives.

The journal *NewMedia* states the problem on one cover as "Digital Sex, Technology, Law & Censorship" with a photo of a nude woman covered only by the words. (If we want to begin to understand the problem, we can wonder why not a photo of a nude man with genitalia hanging out? Would that sell as many copies or mean the same?) The argument is basically the same as those we've heard so many times: The First Amendment guarantees each of us free speech. Why, then, isn't there concern about those who don't have access to free speech and those whose free speech is impeded by the *Virtual Valerie* programs? If I made a program that portrayed men in the ways women are portrayed in these programs, I'd likely be dead very shortly. Freedom of expression is only for a relatively few adults, almost none of whom are women who counter the "malestream" voices. Neither our boys nor our girls are hearing or seeing many choices.

And as important, these forms of intimacy come without any necessity or even desirability of giving to another. Piercy (1991) writes of the simulations of the 21th century: "You watch or rent a stimmie and you enter that actor or actress. You feel what they feel. They're yours. But you don't belong to them. You are freed from the demands of reciprocity" (p. 382). Another writer comments on this freedom from worries of responsibilities for others:

> Imagine a cyberspace mate whom you see only when you want to—one designed to your specifications, who doesn't argue, doesn't require medical care, never goes away. For some, such a virtual world might be addictive and debilitating. For others, it might be kind. (Mort, 1992, p. 191)[8]

Another writer calls virtual reality "the emotional condom of the 21st century" (Ulrich, 1992). We can talk about the differing ways of expressing closeness.

You've heard the feminist critiques of men's ways of expressing intimacy. Men disclose less and mostly about current events, sports, and money; they think sex is primarily *doing* rather than being; they have more but less intimate same-sex friends, and their friendships are based more on activities rather than talking things over.

Recently, some communication researchers have pointed out that the research on men's and women's friendships has been female biased.[9] In focusing on differences we have often overlooked that girls and boys, women and men, all want relationships that are validating and satisfying. Men, the argument continues, have taken a different rather than less meaningful path to closeness. They do things for those about whom they care. Also, they show friendship by sharing activities rather than expressing feelings through talk. Sharing joint activities (rather than the sharing of information, feelings, and secrets) is also an active way of cultivating closeness, these critics point out. Through the sharing of activities men have reported that they create feelings of interdependence and affinity and experience personal development (Swain, 1989). Other critics have suggested that men's relative unwillingness or disinterest in talking about personal matters means that in intimate interactions with women it becomes very difficult to have discussions about problems. (Maybe one of the reasons why women are, in general, better at reading nonverbal cues is that they have to learn that when the best man in a woman's life washes the car he is really saying things like "I understand that you are feeling bad about the death of your cat and the fact that you have an unexplained lump on your elbow and I'm doing my best to tell you that I am also concerned, that I think that the lump might be caused by the stress that you and I have been under at work. I really care about you and your mental and physical health and I'm showing it the only way I know how. I'm saying all this and the car is clean. What more would you want?") We should talk more about this, however difficult it might be for some. Electronic sex and intimacy, as illustrated and planned in VR, is very limited and limiting.

Community/Shared Dreams and Possibilities

Of course, VR can make possible ways of sharing and building an environment together. Not all will be games such as *Roger Wilco,* which was introduced with questions such as "Who's the well-oiled androidess pictured on the cover of this issue [*InterAction,* June 1993], and why is she out to splatter a genetically jumbled Roger?"[10] We can develop new ways of sharing.

Jaron Lanier says, "If virtual reality is used in a way where people using it improvise the content of worlds together, collaboratively, then virtual reality would seem to come closest to providing [a] kind of shared dream space." Later, he adds, "Some voomies [virtual movies] will actually be experiences where people can come in and play dimensional versions of baseball" (quoted in Lanier & Biocca. 1992, pp. 156, 159). Well, that's one kind of collaboration—again not highly imaginative.

Alternatively, we can imagine that neighbors and city planners could use a VR context to consider what kind of towns we want to create or rebuild. One architect writes about possibilities:

> Imagine a neighborhood in which transit was within three blocks and ran conveniently every ten minutes. . . . Imagine that the streets were tree-lined and free of speeding cars—a neighborhood in which some trips could be made conveniently on foot, transit, or bike. . . .
>
> The neighborhood would be near a village green with daycare, recreation and a town hall surrounded by homes and fronted on one side by a retail center . . . accessible from the neighborhood and an arterial roadway. This area would contain a library, a post office, professional offices and a transit station. (Calthorpe, 1993, pp. 11-13)

I'd like to walk around that neighborhood, with my neighbors, trying it out. What about people who are in wheelchairs? Is there any lighting or other devices that would make it safe for women and gay men to walk home at night from the transit station? What is needed to make it easy to carry or wheel groceries from that retail center? Theoretically, people of varying ages with varying needs and interests would be able to work out a desirable neighborhood together—and then work to have some of the features installed in their real neighborhood. Sounds pretty good.

Collective, decentralized administration is a feature in many feminist speculative fiction novels. However, as Margarit Eichler (1981) points out, while the speculative societies in many feminist novels place a greater value on beautifying and equipping public rather than private space, this is the opposite of the real situation we have today.

Unless the creators and marketers of VR programs make some radical changes in what they think important and can convince others to try something new, we won't have a lot of neighborly walks. Further, democratic decisions imply equality of human worth and absence of stratification systems (although individuals might achieve recognized expertise in some areas). Gender, race, and age equality is hardly thinkable today. Any simulated neighborhood and any neighborly walk program would have to have educational programs built in to enable us to learn how to walk with an egalitarian gait and talk as if the needs of all members are important, which would necessitate a reevaluation of the social contributions of all peoples. They would be impressive programs. I'd like to see some initial tries. Given that this society is in the business of more and more traffic congestion, a rapidly deteriorating environment, and more formal and informal segregation, we need some new scenarios badly. I think we have to do a lot of thinking and talking about these issues before VR is going to bring us more community and sharing.

Limiting Danger and Hostilities

Sex and war are mentioned under this category. The military can test out equipment and operators through VR; in fact, the military has been a heavy promoter of VR.[11] But VR can serve in other ways. Jaron Lanier, former chair of the board and chief scientist at VPL, a major manufacturer of virtual reality technology, coined the term virtual reality and has obviously done a lot of thinking about the uses of VR and the U.S. culture of the future. He writes, "There's no doubt that all of us—and let's say adolescent boys in particular —go through a period where they are interested in killing things and aggression. . . . [I]f they do it in a playground, it's part of a fluid process which continues to grow and change" (quoted in Lanier & Biocca, 1992, p. 164).[12]

Mike Saenz predicts that "sophisticated sex simulation will be ubiquitous and accepted as legitimate entertainment education and therapy." He suggests that "just as a flight simulator is used to train pilots before they climb into a real plane, I think sex simulation could be used to prevent unwanted pregnancies and warn about sexually transmitted diseases" (quoted in Stefanac, 1993, p. 40). Is this man suggesting that *Virtual Valerie* be used in the junior high sex ed classes? Would many educators agree? If not, why not, if sex simulation is to be used as an educational device?

In Marge Piercy's novel, one of the good features of cyberspace is that people are able to project themselves in the Net the way they think of themselves. The women, for example, can appear as active and strong.[13] However, when we listen to most creators of current programs and to those who will set up the rules and boundaries of what we imagine, we can see that cybersex in general is not going to be about strong and active women.

We can imagine dangers and hostilities increasing with the VR programs.

Words and Writing in These New, Better Worlds

The communication, information, and sensation revolutions and industries have not been designed for, or opened to, women. While many teachers may wonder what will happen to the printed word as words and people become electronic, many of us also wonder just what the exclusion will look like with the new changes. Dale Spender (in press) points out that the era of books was not one that included women as writers:

> Looking back now we can see that *women were worse off after the introduction of print* than they had been before it. And this wasn't a case of women deciding that they didn't like the medium, that it was anti-female, or that they didn't want to have anything to do with it. It was a straightforward instance of exclusion. Women were locked out of the powerful information medium for 500 years. It was not until the 1970s, and the establishment of women's presses in the western world, that women were able to exercise any influence within the medium. It was not until women were the owners of presses, not until they were independent publishers, editors, sales people and booksellers, that women were able to speak in their own voice, and to break through the "sound barrier" in significant numbers.

It's been men and their technologies, with women as their tools. Remember the typewriter? Initially, the typists were men. Then, as it became a common machine in offices used mainly to print the words of men, the typewriter, as the operator was called, became a woman. The telephone was designed and made for men and their businesses (in some places, "social calls" initially cost more than "business calls"), but women were employed to do the switching until new technology took care of most of that. Eventually, computers will be constructed to print the words spoken to them, but for now, many women work in many computer centers tapping away, typing businessmen's words. In general, women are employed to do what the men don't want to do and the machines can't do yet.

Teaching writing with the uses of computers breaks the tradition somewhat because both men and women are learning to type their compositions. However, if we track the students through universities and into their workplaces, we find that women and men have very different dealings with computers and other machinery. And if we look at the activities of the middle-class girls and boys who will eventually come into the composition classes, we see very different dealing with computers. We all know this, of course. We know that it's primarily the middle-class boys who are spending long hours playing "games" on computers. I think that if we are concerned about our students and what they are learning from us and the rest of the culture, we need to look closely at these differences. We need to consider the changing definitions of sex, gender, intimacy, privacy, and identity and also the remaining gender hierarchy that continues to construct the basis of sex, gender, intimacy, privacy, and identity.

The viewers and voyeurs of the New Media perhaps are not fundamentally different in interests and tastes from the viewers and voyeurs of the past and current media. A survey of the BattleTech players found that the players still read newspapers as well as books and magazines (Pimentel & Teixerira, 1993, p. 214). There is an explosion of writing going on the Internet—"the biggest boom in letter writing since the 18th century: . . . Words have been decoupled from paper" (Saffo, 1993, p. 48). It's not a matter of whether we'll use the new technologies; of course we will as we have access to them. Perhaps VR will not live up to the expectations of its current advocates; perhaps other entertainment, thought to be closer to "the ultimate experience," will come along, leaving VR as mostly hype rather than reality. But whatever happens, I think analysis of the gendered work and play of these technologies makes clear that nontraditional forms of expression contain much of the same old ideas about gender roles.

Assuming that we think the gender splits and hierarchies of the past, current, and (unless there are major changes) the future are destructive, what can we do? First, we need to pay mind to what's going on with the activities of millions of young boys and girls. Many working-class children have little access to computers in or outside the classroom; for many children here and in other countries, life is about just trying to live. Many middle-class boys are becoming electronic demons on the nets and play all the computer games they can get their hands on; the girls are not. The reasons for the very different experiences that girls and boys have with the new technologies are many, but all involve the very present gender, race, and class divisions that remain in our culture because those who have the most power to do something basic to alter this situation don't want to or really don't know how to. We need to continue to watch, listen, analyze, and make interventions when we can, particularly in times of change. The fake spaces of VR, like the fake spaces of all our imagination and writing, can provide freedoms of various sorts, but they are designed and constrained by powerful structured forces of assumptions and goals; they are not equally friendly environments or opportunities for everyone.

If we want to establish community of any sort, we will continue to want to transcend our own experiences, our own realities. Current VR programming, with its roots in male science fiction, television and movie scripting, is one way to go. The feminist speculative fiction writers show us other ways. Marge Piercy's work gives us a critique of sci-fi plotting. Joanna Russ, Octavia Butler, Doris Lessing, Suzette Haden Elgin, and Anne McCaffrey are also playing serious games with history and gender assumptions. Ursula Le Guin, in *Always Coming Home* (1984), illustrates a way in which literary genres, music and drawing can combine in culturally rich ways to present alternative ways of thinking, of imagining.[14]

In sum, how much flexibility everyone has in imagining our selves and our collective future is the real fantastic question.

Notes

1. Gender is usually mentioned when girls and women are present, as if boys and men have no gender. Gender is thought to be female related, just as, in the United States, race is thought to be Black, Hispanic, or Indian related. Because of the importance of gender in our society—functioning as a fundamental division and hierarchy— gender is always present in our interactions, whether single sex or mixed sex. The feminist and Queer Nation movements are bringing some changes to this binary opposition, but many people still write and talk about two sexes.

2. One user reports, "I was on a MUD a few weeks ago and somebody was like, 'Oh, I heard you were real easy. I heard you spread like peanut butter' " (Margie, 1993, p. 80).

3. Jaron Lanier points out that it's still possible to determine whether you are in VR or on drugs: "Put your hand on your eyes and see if you're wearing Eyephones or not. That simple" (quoted in *Mondo 2000,* 1992, p. 264).

4. Laurel is designing interactive media for diverse populations. "We're trying to look at a lot of things—culture, age, gender—to understand what we need to do a better job of designing for people with really, really different characteristics" (quoted in McCarthy, 1993, p. 42). She is building *Placeholder,* a virtual environment for two people, based on Native American stories. Her approach is so different from that of most people working in the computer industry that she says, "I do feel like an alien among more established business-as-usual communities" (quoted in McCarthy, 1993, p. 42).

5. The programming thus far seems to be relying heavily on traditional ideas of masculinity and sex drives. Sally Gearhart and Peggy Cleveland (1975) write about the invention of *The Sex Drive*: "the moment when man knew himself to need his physical body but sought it outside himself in the other rather than repossess his own" (p. 55).

6. Margie (1993), researching a story on "cyberspace" for *Sassy,* checked out the Women On-Line forum, where the posts were overwhelmingly from males (85% or more while she was looking). Margie reports that "Someone guessed that 'less than one percent of the people on line

are actual females, and only one-tenth of those I would actually describe as women. The rest are feminazis and bored obese trashbag-wearing housewives. . . .' Very nice" (p. 80).

7. Some people argue that *Virtual Valerie* does have some educational content; she is anatomically correct, supposedly, and her various orifices and organs can be explored.

8. Does this sound something like many johns' attitudes toward prostitutes?

9. See the critical review offered by Julia Wood and Christopher Inman (1993).

10. This "well-oiled androidess" belongs to a long line of science fiction female aliens with immense, engorged breasts, which, Robin Roberts (1993) suggests, evoke the image of frightening mother. The nearly naked women of the covers and stories of science fiction novels "emphasize the biological differences between male and female," differences that have led some critics to point out that in science fiction male and female are different species (p. 41).

11. The U.S. Air Force led the way in the development of virtual reality. In the late 1960s, the Air Force developed training simulators for pilots. With its Virtual Environment Workstation Project, NASA has done a lot of the recent work in adding depth and movement vertices to the programs (see Newquist, 1992, pp. 93-95).

12. Called by others (and perhaps himself) the visionary high priest of VR, Lanier, 32, was fired from his own company in December 1992 by a French electronics conglomerate that called in its overdue loans (see Snider, 1993, pp. 76-80).

13. Donna Haraway also conceives of the cyborg as a potentially liberating figure (see the discussion by Claudia Springer, 1993).

14. Now, if the fakespace companies signed Ursula (who is conversant with many friends using many vocabularies—visual, verbal, music, textural, graphics, and animation), we would have a mix for many.

References

Antonopulos, Spiros, & Barnett, Andrea. (1992). [Interview with] Brenda Laurel. *boing boing, 10,* 12.

Banich, Marie, & Wilson, Betsy. (1993). Imagining the ideal information technology. In H. Jeanie Taylor, Cheris Kramarae, & Maureen Ebben (Eds.), *Women, information technology, and scholarship* (p. 67). Urbana: University of Illinois Center for Advanced Study.

Benedikt, Michael. (1991). *Introduction to cyberspace: First steps.* Cambridge: MIT Press.

Bright, Susie. (1992). *Susie Bright's sexual reality: A virtual sex world reader.* Pittsburgh, PA: Cleis Press.

Calthorpe, Peter. (1993, Spring). Redesigning the American dream. *Co-op American Quarterly,* pp. 11-13.

Delaney, Ben. (1993). Where virtual rubber meets the road. *Virtual Reality 93: Special Report,* pp. 15-18.

Ebben, Maureen, & Kramarae, Cheris. (1993). Women and information technologies: Creating a cyberspace of our own. In H. Jeanie Taylor, Cheris Kramarae, & Maureen Ebben (Eds.), *Women, information technology, and scholarship* (pp. 15-27). Urbana: University of Illinois Center for Advanced Study.

Eichler, Margarit. (1981). Science fiction as desirable feminist scenarios. *Women's Studies International Quarterly, 4*(1), 51-64.

Elmer-Dewitt, Philip. (1993, September 27). The amazing video game boom. *Time,* pp. 66-72.

Gearhart, Sally. (1991). An end to technology. In John Zerzan & Alice Carnes (Eds.), *Questioning technology: Tool, toy or tyrant?* (pp. 83-85). Philadelphia: New Society.

Gearhart, Sally, & Cleveland, Peggy. (1975). On the prevalence of stilps. *Quest, 1,* 53-64.
Gibson, William. (1984). *Neuromancer.* New York: Ace Books.
Gibson, William, & Barlow, John. (1992). Cyberspace. In *Mondo 2000.* New York: HarperCollins.
Hsu, Jeffrey. (1993). Virtual reality. *Compute, 15,* 100-102.
Kramarae, Cheris, & Taylor, H. Jeanie. (1993). Women and men on electronic networks: A conversation or a monologue. In H. Jeanie Taylor, Cheris Kramarae, & Maureen Ebben (Eds.), *Women, information technology, and scholarship* (pp. 52-61). Urbana: University of Illinois Center for Advanced Study.
Lanier, Jaron, & Biocca, Frank. (1992). An insider's view of the future of virtual reality. *Journal of Communication, 42,* 150-172.
Laurel, Brenda. (1991). Virtual reality design: A personal view. In Sandra Helsel & Judith Paris Roth (Eds.), *Virtual reality: Theory, practice, and promise* (pp. 95-99). London: Meckler.
Le Guin, Ursula, with Barton, Todd (composer) & Chodos, Margaret (artist). (1984). *Always coming home.* New York: Harper & Row.
Margie. (1993, May). Hi girlz, see you in cyberspace! *Sassy,* pp. 72, 73, 80.
McCarthy, Susan. (1993, June). Techno-soaps and virtual theater. *Wired,* pp. 40, 42.
Mondo 2000. (1992). New York: HarperCollins.
Mort, John. (1992, September 22). Electronic concept, still in its infancy, both a promise and a threat. *Kansas City (Missouri) Star,* p. 19.
Newquist, Harvey P., III. (1992). Virtual reality's commercial reality. *Computerworld, 26*(13), 93-95.
Newquist, Harvey P., III. (1993). The fruits of war for fun and profit. *Virtual Reality 93, Fall Special Report,* pp. 11-14.
Piercy, Marge. (1991). *He, she and it.* New York: Fawcett Crest.
Pimentel, Ken, and Teixerira, Kevin. (1993). *Virtual reality: Through the new looking glass.* New York: Intel/Windcrest/McGraw-Hill.
Rheingold, Howard. (1991). *Virtual reality.* New York: Summit Books.
Roberts, Robin. (1993). *A new species: Gender and science in science fiction.* Urbana: University of Illinois Press.
Saffo, Paul. (1993, May/June). Hot new medium: Text. *Wired,* p. 48.
Smith, Stephanie A. (1993). Morphing, materialism, and the marketing of Xenogenesis. *Genders, 18,* 67-86.
Snider, Burr. (1993, May/June). Jaron. *Wired,* pp. 76-80.
Spender, Dale. (in press). *Nattering on the nets.* Melbourne, Australia: Spinfex.
Springer, Claudia. (1993, Winter). Muscular circuitry: The invincible armored cyborg in cinema. *Genders, 18,* 87-101.
Stefanac, Suzanne. (1993, April). Sex and the new media. *NewMedia,* pp. 38-45.
Swain, Cott. (1989). Covert intimacy in men's friendships: Closeness in men's friendships. In Barbara J. Risman & Pepper Schwartz (Eds.), *Gender in intimate relationships: A microstructural approach* (pp. 71-86). Belmont, CA: Wadsworth.
Tait, Andy. (1993). Authoring virtual worlds on the desktop. *Virtual Reality 93: Special Report,* pp. 11-13.
Ulrich, Allen. (1992, March 7). Here's reality: "Mower" is less. *San Francisco Examiner.*
Virtual reality [cover story]. (1992, October 5). *Business Week,* pp. 96-100, 102, 104-105.
Walser, Randy. (1992). Autodesk Cyberspace Project. In *Mondo 2000.* New York: HarperCollins.
Wood, Julia, & Inman, Christopher. (1993). In a different mode: Masculine styles of communicating closeness. *Journal of Applied Communication Research, 21,* 279-295.

3

NINTENDO® AND NEW WORLD TRAVEL WRITING: A DIALOGUE

Mary Fuller

Henry Jenkins

Mary Fuller: We want to start by telling you two stories.

Henry Jenkins: Here's the first. Princess Toadstool is kidnapped by the savage King Koopa. Two brave brothers, Mario and Luigi, depart on a series of adventures to rescue her. Mario and Luigi, simple men of humble beginnings (in fact, Italian American plumbers), cross a vast unexplored space, encountering strange creatures, struggling against an inhospitable landscape. Finally, they confront and best the monarch and his minions in a life and death struggle. In the process, the Super Mario Brothers not only restore the princess to her people but also exert control over this strange new world and its curious resources.

MF: My story is really a collection of stories, which I can probably evoke for you in some form just by mentioning a few key words: Walter Raleigh, Roanoke, the Lost Colony, Virginia Dare. Or Jamestown, John Smith, Pocahontas, John Rolfe. I want to draw for the moment not on the complexities and particularities of these stories but on what is simple and popular, what can be evoked as an indistinct impression: the saleable, inaccurate, recurrent myth of the captive princess and her rescuers (Virginia Dare, the first child born in what was to become the "Lost Colony"; Pocahontas, a genuine princess who became a candidate for rescue—or kidnapping —thanks to her own gesture of rescuing John Smith; Smith himself, both a hero of humble origins and a kind of princess in drag who represented his entire career as a repeated experience of captivity and rescue by women; or, for that matter, Virginia itself, personified by English apologists for colonization as a virgin to be rescued from savages). Nintendo®'s Princess Toadstool and Mario Brothers is a cognate version of this story.

What we want to get at is not these alluring narratives of Princess Toadstool, Pocahontas, and Virginia Dare (or of Mario, Luigi, and John Smith) but another shared concern in our material that seems to underlie these more memorable fictions in a constitutive way. Both terms of our title evoke explorations and colonizations of space: the physical space navigated, mapped, and mastered by European voyagers and travelers in the 16th and 17th centuries and the fictional, digitally projected space traversed, mapped, and mastered by players of Nintendo® video games. Simply put, we want to argue that the movement in space that the rescue plot seems to motivate is itself the point, the topic, and the goal and that this shift in emphasis from narrativity to geography produces features that make Nintendo® and New World narratives in some ways strikingly similar to each other and different from many other kinds of texts.

HJ: This chapter is the result of a series of conversations we've been having over the past four years. Our conversations began with hesitant efforts by each of us to understand the other's area of specialization but have grown in frequency and intensity as we began to locate points of contact between our work. We hope that what follows will reflect the process of that exchange, opening questions for future discussion rather than providing answers for immediate consumption.

MF: This work is a confessedly exploratory attempt at charting some possibilities of dialogue and communication between the disparate professional spaces we inhabit. Yet the association between computer software and the Renaissance "discovery" of America is not exactly new. A computer software firm in Boston claims in its advertisement, "Sir Francis Drake was knighted for what we do every day . . . The spirit of exploration is alive at **The Computer Merchant**" (*Boston Computer Currents*, September 1990, p. 34). More generally, discussions of virtual reality have widely adopted a language borrowed from this earlier era: One headline reads, "THE RUSH IS ON! COLONIZING CYBERSPACE" (*Mondo 2000,* Summer 1990, no. 2, cover).

HJ: The description and analysis of virtual reality technologies as the opening up of a new frontier, a movement from known to unknown space, responds to our contemporary sense of America as oversettled, overly familiar, and overpopulated. Howard Rheingold's (1991) *Virtual Reality* un-self-consciously mimics the rhetoric of earlier promoters and settlers when he promises to share with his readers the account of "my own odyssey to the outposts of a new scientific frontier . . . and an advanced glimpse of a possible new world in which reality itself might become a manufactured and metered commodity" (p. 17). Or consider Timothy Leary's proclamation in that same book: "We live in a cyber-culture surrounded by limitless deposits of information which can be digitalized and tapped by the individual equipped with cybergear. . . . There are no limits on virtual reality" (Rheingold, 1991, p. 378). Virtual reality opens new spaces for exploration, colonization, and exploitation, returning to a mythic time when there were worlds without limits and resources beyond imagining. Technologists speak of the "navigational systems" necessary to guide us through this uncharted realm. The advent of this new technological sphere meets the needs of a national culture which, as Brenda Laurel suggests, finds contemporary reality "too small for the human imagination" (quoted in Rheingold, 1991, p. 391). Few of us have donned goggles and powergloves to become settlers of this new cyberspace, although both heroic and nightmarish accounts of virtual reality proliferate in popular culture. Many of us have, however, interacted with digitalized space through Nintendo® games. We felt it might be productive to take seriously for a moment these metaphors of "new worlds" and "colonization" as we look more closely at the spatial logic and "cognitive mapping" of video games.

MF: One has to wonder why these heroic metaphors of discovery have been adopted by popularizers of the new technologies just as these metaphors are undergoing sustained critique in other areas of the culture, a critique that hardly anyone can be unaware of in the year after the quincentary of Columbus's first American landfall. When John Barlow (1990) writes that "Columbus was probably the last person to behold so much usable and unclaimed real estate (or unreal estate) as these cybernauts have discovered" (p. 37), the comparison to cyberspace drains out the materiality of the place Columbus discovered, and the nonvirtual bodies of the pre-Columbian inhabitants who did, in fact, claim it, however unsuccessfully. I would speculate that part of the drive behind the rhetoric of virtual reality as a New World or new frontier is the desire to recreate the Renaissance encounter with America without guilt: This time, if there are others present, they really won't be human (in the case of Nintendo® characters), or if they are, they will be other players like ourselves, whose bodies are not jeopardized by the virtual weapons we wield. The prospect of seeing VR as a revisionary reenactment of earlier history raises issues that we address only in passing: One would be the ethics and consequences of such a historical revision; another would be to ask whether it *is* accurate to say that VR is unlike Renaissance discovery in having no victims, that at no point does it register harmfully on real bodies that are not the bodies of its users. These kinds of questions frame our discussion, which has a narrower focus on the specificities of Nintendo® games and voyage narratives as rhetorical and cultural artifacts. If the simple celebration of expansiveness borrowed from the age of discovery for virtual reality no longer seems adequate to the texts and experiences it once described, it seems no less important to map the narrative and rhetorical configurations of these texts themselves, which have provided model and metaphor for so much later experience, their authors', in Derek Walcott's (1986) words, "ancestral murderers and poets" (p. 79).

The kinds of New World documents I have in mind are ones like Columbus's *Diario* (1492-1493) or Walter Raleigh's *Discoverie of the large, rich and beautiful empire of Guiana* (1596) or John Smith's *True Relation of such occurrences and accidents of noate as hath hapned in Virginia* (1608)—that is, chronologically structured narratives of voyage and exploration, from ships' logs to more elaborate texts. At the outset, one might expect these narratives of travel to and return from what was at least conceptually another world to assume a different kind of structure than, in fact, they do: a romance or quest motif, the ironic contrasts of utopian fiction, or at least an overt "theme." Such expectations are largely disappointed. One literary critic complains that the travel journal underwent no sustained development as a literary form but conforms more or less consistently to a formulaic pattern: "The abstract reads, we sailed, did and saw this and this, suffered and were saved or lost, made such and such encounters with the savages, hungered, thirsted, and were storm worn, but some among us came home" (Page, 1973, p. 37). Part of the problem lies outside the texts, in that practical strategies embedded in the material diverge from the demands of narrative coherence: the same critic complains that the carefully prepared climax of Jacques Cartier's *Brief Récit* is spoiled when Cartier decides to sail for home instead of waiting for a long anticipated Indian attack. Reading the voyage narratives from the perspective of conventional narrative expectations is an experience of almost unremitting frustration. Yet these texts, if they are not conventional narratives, are equally clearly not transparent records of an experience that itself demands no commentary. On the contrary.

And so one wants first to find a way of characterizing their structure and its shaping imperatives on its own terms and second, to account for their reception, their uses and pleasures for audiences then and now. This is material that was produced and printed in extraordinary quantity. Richard Hakluyt, one of the founding members of the Virginia Company, made a lasting name for himself by collecting and publishing documents of voyages by his contemporaries, documents ranging the gamut of possibilities from ethnographic survey to narrative poem to navigational instructions. Hakluyt's first collection appeared in 1582 as a slim quarto volume. By 1601, the third and final collection, *The Principal Navigations . . . of the English Nation,* took up three large folio volumes totaling almost 900 pages (12 volumes in the modern edition). Hakluyt's work was continued by Samuel Purchas, whose *Hakluytus Posthumus*, appearing in 1625, had expanded to 4,262 pages. Simply on the basis of volume, these documents would impose themselves on our attention, whatever their narrative shape.

HJ: Nintendo®, similarly, plays an increasingly visible role with the American imagination. By the end of 1990, one of three homes in the United States owned a Nintendo® system. My household was one of them, and I wanted to know more about how we might discuss these phenomenally popular games as cultural artifacts, as popular narratives, and as a new media for mass communication. As I discovered when asked to review two recent books on Nintendo® (Kinder, 1991; Provenzo, 1991; see Jenkins, 1993), current accounts lack any serious discussion of the particularity of Nintendo® as a means of organizing cultural experience; the writers fail to address what it meant to be playing the games rather than watching or reading them. Both books seemed interested in talking about Nintendo® for other reasons: in one case in terms of issues of pedagogy, in the other in terms of issues of intertextuality, but both offered accounts that presuppose that traditional narrative theory (be it literary or film theory) can account for our experience of Nintendo® in terms of plots and characters.

This application of conventional models to an emergent form seemed unsatisfying because it ignores the way that game players discuss the experience of play and the ways that the games are marketed to their consumers. Plot is not a central feature of Nintendo®'s sales pitch. Ads talked about interactivity rather than characterization ("Nintendo® gives you power to choose") and about atmospheres rather than story lines ("awesome graphics"). Nintendo®, a 100-year-old playing card company little known outside Japan, revitalized the declining American video game market by moving from the simple, abstracted spaces of Pong or Pac-Man™ to create an ever changing and visually fascinating arena for play.

Nintendo®'s central feature is its constant presentation of spectacular spaces (or "worlds," to use the game parlance). Its landscapes dwarf characters who serve, in turn, primarily as vehicles for players to move through these remarkable places. Once immersed in playing, we don't really care whether we rescue Princess Toadstool or not; all that matters is staying alive long enough to move between levels, to see what spectacle awaits us on the next screen. Mario's journey may take him by raft across a river of red hot molten lava, may require him to jump from platform to platform across a suspended city, or may ask him to make his way through a subterranean cavern as its ceiling collapses around him. The protagonist of a sword and sorcery game may struggle against a stormy sea, battle a massive serpent, confront a pack of wolves who rule a frozen wasteland, or combat an army of the dead that erupt from the trembling earth, all in search of lost fortunes and buried gold. A game like *Lemmings* puts us in charge of an army of tiny creatures, willing slaves who live and die at our bidding and who dig tunnels or construct bridges to allow us to continue to venture deeper into the game space. For the most part, the technological limitations of the game systems mean that we move left to right through this space, but designers may simulate other kinds of movement, such as an elevator in the *Ninja Turtles®* game that allows us to battle our way higher and higher into Shredder's command center or racing games that allow us to skim forward along a winding racetrack getting closer and closer to the glistening city that looms on the horizon. The more sophisticated Super Nintendo® system allows for multiple levels of graphics that interact with each other in ever more complex fashions. The art of game design comes in constructing a multitude of different ways we can interact with these visually remarkable spaces.

Most of the criteria by which we might judge a classically constructed narrative fall by the wayside when we look at these games as storytelling systems. In Nintendo®'s narratives, characters play a minimal role, displaying traits that are largely capacities for action: fighting skills, modes of transportation, preestablished goals. The game's dependence on characters (Ninja Turtles, Bart Simpson, etc.) borrowed from other media allows them to simply evoke those characters rather than to fully develop them. The character is little more than a cursor that mediates the player's relationship to the story world. Activity drains away the characters' strength, as measured by an ever shifting graph at the top of the screen, but it cannot build character, since these figures lack even the most minimal interiority. Similarly, plot is transformed into a generic atmosphere—a haunted house, a subterranean cavern, a futuristic cityscape, an icy wilderness—that the player can explore. This process becomes most visible when we look at games adapted from existing films or television programs; here, moments in the narrative trajectory become places in the player's itinerary, laid out as a succession of worlds we must travel through in order to reach our goals. Playing time unfolds in a fixed and arbitrary fashion with no responsiveness to the psychological time of the characters, sometimes flowing too slow to facilitate player interest and blocking the advance of the plot action, other times moving so fast that we can't react quickly enough to new situations or the clock runs out before we complete our goals. Exposition occurs primarily at the introduction and closing of games: For instance, the opening of Super Mario World™ reminds us that the Princess has once again been kidnapped. The game's conclusion displays the reunion of Princess and champion and a kind of victory tour over the lands that Mario has conquered. But these sequences are "canned": Players cannot control or intervene in them. Often, a player simply flashes past this exposition to get into the heart of the action. These framing stories with their often arbitrary narrative goals play little role in the actual experience of the games, as plot gives way quickly to a more flexible period of spatial exploration. Although plot structures (kidnapping and rescue, pursuit and capture, street fighting, invasion and defense) are highly repetitive (repeated from game to game and over and over within the game, with little variety), what never loses its interest is the promise of moving into the next space, of mastering these worlds and making them your own playground. So although the child's play is framed by narrative logic, it remains largely uncontrolled by plot dictates.

The pleasure of spatial spectacle may be most visible in games that do not seem to require anything more than the most rudimentary spaces. *Street Fighter II*™, one of the most popular Nintendo® games in recent years, basically centers around a kickboxing tournament that could have been staged in any arena. The game, however, offers players a global array of possible spaces where the individual competitions can occur: a Brazilian dock, an Indian temple, a Chinese street market, a Soviet factory, a Las Vegas show palace. In the Indian sequence, elephants sway their trunks in the background. Water drips from the ceiling into a Japanese reflecting pool. In Spain, flamenco dancers strut and crowds cheer as the combatants struggle for dominance. All of these details constitute a form of visual excess ("eye candy," as computer enthusiasts call it), a conspicuous consumption of space. Such spectacular visions are difficult to program, unnecessary to the competition, yet seem central to the game's marketing success.

MF: It sounds to me as if not only space but culture is being consumed, used and also used up as local cultures from India to Las Vegas shrink into a procession of ornamental images. Each is "colorful," yet none is really alien. Certainly, the ability to register local differences varied among Renaissance travel narratives: The same image might begin its career as close observation at first hand and reappear in progressively more stylized and ornamental forms detached from its original reference, as John White's drawings of North Carolina Algonquians reappeared on the engraved frontispiece to Theodor de Bry's *America* and were, in turn, reproduced as illustrations for John Smith's adventures in Virginia. One might also think of the famous Rouen entry of Henri II, where an entire Tupi village was recreated, employed for a day or so as a place for the performance of Brazilian life, and then burned.

If Nintendo® feeds the appetite for encountering a succession of new spaces (as well as helping to create such an appetite), that same appetite was, of course, central to these New World narratives. In turn, there were pressures on texts to conform to a locodescriptive form, the equivalent in writing of Nintendo®'s scrolling succession of spaces. One precursor of the travel narrative would be the logbook, in which a grid divides the page into spaces for date, time, compass bearing, wind, speed, and, finally, notes. The logbook presents a succession of indexed spaces on the page that correspond to a succession of days and places. Implicitly, each of these spaces is of equal importance: The grid predisposes its user to make *some* notes in each space but not too many. Athough the logbook was a technical tool of long-distance navigation, its form strongly influenced land-based narratives that followed arrival.

As an instance of a locodescriptive project both in action and writing, John Smith's strategy of successively exploring and mapping all the rivers around Jamestown contrasted with the Virginia Company's desire to impose grander, more recognizable, and more goal-oriented trajectories on the travels of the colonists: to find a gold mine, a passage to China, or Raleigh's Lost Colony. These ultimate objectives, held as in suspension, enabled Smith's presence in Virginia and his day-by-day progress through the natural and human geography of the Chesapeake. This configuration, of "story" as pretext for narratives of space, is (as we suggested at the outset) a common one in this material. Voyages and narratives that set out in search of a significant, motivating goal had a strong tendency to defer it, replacing arrival at that goal (and the consequent shift to another kind of activity) with a particularized account of the travel itself and what was seen and done. Hernán Cortés (1986) walked into Tenochtitlan in 1534, becoming master of its gold and other resources; yet the bulk of his Second and Third Letters concerns not this period of achieved conquest and consumption but the survey of points on the way there and then a second survey of points passed through on the drive to reconquer the city through more conventional military means. Even goal-driven narratives like those of Raleigh or Columbus at best offered only dubious signs of proximity in place of arrival—at China, El Dorado, the town of the Amazons—phenomena that, interpreted, erroneously suggested it was just over the horizon, to be deferred to some later date.

Rhetorical as well as documentary goals bear on the narratives, which aim not only to describe but to persuade. That is, Walter Raleigh wanted to find El Dorado, and he also wanted to produce a narrative that would stimulate interest in Guiana and persuade Elizabeth to restore him to favor. The imperative that operates on his text in consequence is less that of coherence than of completeness, a (doubtless, loaded) inventory of what was done and seen, one that provided at once both an alternate, more diffuse kind of justification for the discovery and motives and informational resources for a repeat performance. Ralph Lane, one of the Roanoke Colony's governors, noted that the particularity of his account is "to the end it may appear to you . . . that there wanted no great good will . . . to have perfected this discovery"—of a rumored mine the company never set out towards (Lane, 1979, p. 309). Even in the *Discoverie of Guiana,* a text whose teleology is announced in the title, the actual search for Guiana, the narrative concomitants of searching for something, get lost in a welter of details, of events and places that have little to do with El Dorado but that occupied the days of the voyage. The sequenced inventories of places and events replace, defer, and attest to an authentic and exculpating desire for goals the voyages almost invariably failed to reach.

Given the inconclusiveness I've described, it was the ability to move in space (rather than to arrive) that generated and structured narrative; John Smith wrote primarily about the times he was in motion, not the times he was sitting in Jamestown. The resulting narratives were, in turn, organized by elapsed time (sequences of dates) but also determined by it. Henry mentioned that "characters" in Nintendo® can be described less in terms of learning and transformation than in terms of resources gradually expended in the course of the game. This sense of a trajectory dictated not by change or crisis but by expenditure, the gradual running out of a fixed quantity of time or resources, is an almost universal feature of the narratives I study because it was an equally frequent phenomenon in the voyages and colonial experiments they document. Many documents record the consequences of poorly managing resources —the season for sailing passing as one sits windbound in an English harbor, a crew mutinying at the idea of sailing beyond Ireland, food running out in the middle of the winter or the middle of the ocean (this one over and over), having to write home hypothetical accounts of the treasures you would discover if you had better boats or more food or it were not so late in the year. These documents end not because some resolution or conclusion has been achieved but because something has run out. To give another example, John Smith's ability to trade for corn to feed a starving colony was unarguably more critical than the story about the rescue of the Lost Colony that the Virginia Company tried to impose on him or the story about Pocahontas that he recounted 16 years after the event and 6 years after her death.

HJ: Although we've noted the experimental nature of this chapter's juxtapositions, there is, in fact, a precedent for them in Michel De Certeau's work in successive books on New World discourse (*Heterologies,* 1984a) and on the politics of consumption in contemporary popular culture (*The Practice of Everyday Life,* 1984b). While we are claiming space as the organizing principle for two kinds of narrative, as what makes them different from novels, for example, De Certeau (1984b) lays out a grand claim for spatial relations as the central organizing principle of all narratives: "Every story is a travel story—a spatial practice" (p. 115). Our cultural need for narrative can be linked to our search for believable, memorable, and primitive spaces, and stories are told to account for our current possession or desire for territory.

De Certeau's analysis of "spatial stories" provides tools for talking about classes of narratives that have proven difficult to discuss in terms of traditional notions of plot or character. Consider, for example, the emergence of science fiction in the late 19th and early 20th century as a means of creating imaginary spaces for our intellectual exploration. The adventure stories of Jules Verne drew upon centuries of travel writing as they recounted a variety of trips to the moon, under the sea, into the center of the earth, or around the globe. The technological utopian writers often created static plots (a man from our present goes to the future) that allowed them simply to describe the landscape of tomorrow; one can draw a direct line from the moment in Edward Bellamy's *Looking Backward,* where the book's protagonist stands on his balcony and surveys Boston's future, to the train cars that allowed visitors to the 1939 New York World's Fair to ride above and look down upon Futurama. Hugo Gernsback's *Amazing Stories* magazine was full of chronicles of "odysseys" across the uncharted wilderness of Mars or Venus and encounters along the way with strange flora and fauna. Writers often modeled these aliens' worlds after the American West so that they could cross-market their stories to both western and science fiction pulps. A focus on plot and characterization was slow to develop in this genre that seemed so obsessed with going "where no one has gone before."

A similar claim could be made for various forms of fantasy writing. Trips to Oz or Narnia or through the looking glass, adventures in Middle Earth, or quests for the Grail all seem to center as much on the movement of characters through space as on the larger plot goals that motivate and give shape to those movements. Maps appear in fantasy novels with the same frequency and function that genealogies appear in the great 19th-century novels, suggesting the relative stress the two forms give to spatial relations and character relations. It is not surprising that science fiction, fantasy, and sword-and-sorcery stories provide much of the iconography of the Nintendo® games.

Nintendo® may also be linked to another class of spatial stories, the amusement park rides that as early as turn-of-the-century Coney Island adopted popular fictions into spaces we can visit and explore. Walt Disney's *Peter Pan* becomes a ride by flying ship across the landscape of London and Never-Never-Land, *Snow White* turns into a runaway mine car tour, and *20,000 Leagues Under the Sea* is remade into a submarine ride. The introduction of virtual reality technology to the Orlando, Florida, amusement parks results in a succession of ever more intense "tours" of the stars, the oceans, the human body, the World of Hanna-Barbera, and the dawn of time. Nintendo®'s constant adaptation of plot-centered contemporary films into spatial narratives represents a miniaturization of this same process. The tamed frontier of the virtual new world has, from the first, been sold to us as a playground for our world-weary imagination, as a site of tourism and recreation rather than labor and production. Public interest in virtual reality is directly linked to the amusement park's long history of satisfying popular demand for spatial difference, spectacular attractions, affective stimulation, and sensual simulation. De Certeau's description of Jules Verne's stories as focused around the related images of the *Nautilus*'s porthole (a windowpane that "allows us to see") and the iron rail (that allows us to "move through" fantastic realms) has its obvious parallels in these amusement park attractions that invite us to look upon and travel through but not to touch these spectacular spaces (De Certeau, 1984b, p. 112). What is a spectacle at the amusement park ("Keep your hands in the car at all times") becomes a site of more immediate interaction in the Nintendo® game that asks us to act upon and transform the places it opens to our vision.

MF: Voyage narratives were almost never presented as recreative texts, whatever they might become for later readers. Two exceptions are Richard Willes's *Historie of travel* (London, 1577) and Andre Thevet's *Les singularitez de la France antarctique* (Paris, 1558). Although a narrative like Thomas Harriot's *Brief and True Report of the New Found Land of Virginia* (London, 1588) might offer a catalogue of America's abundant flora and fauna, the items of the catalogue were presented not as strange things to wonder at but as "marchantable commodities," goods for use and sale, the potential for industrious activity. Leisure in the New World was pejoratively characterized as idleness, associated with disease, mendacity, and social disorder. In most places the English settled, colonists had to do some work to feed and shelter themselves; when a company shipwrecked on the uninhabited Bermudas and found an Edenic land of temperate weather and dreamlike abundance, its leaders found means to take the company back to starvation in Jamestown. The project of colonizing itself was, in the English case, less a matter of acquiring a native workforce than of finding work for what contemporaries envisioned as the teeming masses of England's unemployed. Virginia's colonists were there (at least in theory) to labor, not to look, and labor was directed to activating the commercial potentials of the land.

HJ: For De Certeau (1984b), narrative involves the transformation of place into space (pp. 117-118). Places exist only in the abstract, as potential sites for narrative action, as locations that have not yet been colonized. Place may be understood here in terms of the potential contained as bytes in the Nintendo® game cartridge or the potential resources coveted but not yet possessed in the American New World. Places constitute a "stability" which must be disrupted in order for stories to unfold. Places are there but do not yet matter, much as the New World existed, was geographically present, and culturally functioning well before it became the center of European ambitions or the site of New World narratives. Places become meaningful only as they come into contact with narrative agents (and in the construction of the New World in Mary's Renaissance stories, only Europeans are understood as narrative agents). Spaces, on the other hand, are places that have been acted upon, explored, colonized. Spaces become the location of narrative events. As I play a Nintendo® game and master it level by level, I realize the potentials encoded in the software design and turn it into the landscape of my own saga.

The place-space distinction is closely linked to De Certeau's discussion of the differences between "maps" and "tours" as means of representing real-world geographies. Maps are abstracted accounts of spatial relations ("the girl's room is next to the kitchen"), whereas tours are told from the point of view of the traveler/narrator ("You turn right and come into the living room") (De Certeau, 1984b, pp. 118-122). Maps document places; tours describe movements through spaces. The rhetoric of the tour thus contains within it attention to the effects of the tour, its goals and potentials, its limitations and obligations. A door is a feature of a place, or it may be a potential threshold between two spaces. One of my favorite games, *A Boy and His Blob,* places the resources of its imaginary world fully at our disposal. The blob can be transformed into everything from a blowtorch to a stepladder depending on what flavored jellybean we feed him, and as a result, the mutating blob contains endless possibilities for acting upon and transforming the virtual playing space. The pleasure of the game lies in creating our own paths, tunneling down deeper and deeper into its cavernous world. The blob, the various levels, the jellybeans exist as potentials that only become narratively meaningful when we act upon them and bring them into our control.

De Certeau is thus interested in analyzing and documenting the process by which we "mark off boundaries" within the narrative world, by which characters map, act upon, and gain control over narrative spaces. Just as narratives involve movement from stability through instability and back again, narratives also involve a constant transformation of unfamiliar places into familiar spaces. Stories, he argues, are centrally concerned with "the relationship between the frontier and the bridge, that is, between a (legitimate) space and its (alien) exteriority" (De Certeau, 1984b, p. 126). He continues: "The story endlessly marks out frontiers. It multiplies them, but in terms of interactions among characters—things, animals, human beings" (De Certeau, 1984b, p. 126). Plot actions, he argues, involve the process of appropriation and displacement of space, a struggle for possession and control over the frontier or journeys across the bridges that link two spaces together. Such terms will, of course, be familiar to anyone who has thought about the discovery and colonization of America. Yet Nintendo® also enacts a constant struggle along the lines that separate known and unknown spaces—the line of the frontier—which is where the player encounters dangerous creatures and brutal savages, where we fight for possession and control over the story world. As De Certeau (1984b) notes, the central narrative question posed by a frontier is "to whom does it belong?" (p. 127). The frontier here is apt to be technological and urban rather than primitive and pastoral (or, as in the Mario Brothers games, a strange mix of the two) but then Mary's settlers were also mapping their adventures on spaces already occupied by someone else's culture. The frontier line is literalized through the breakdown of story space into a series of screens. The narrative space is not all visible at once. One must push toward the edge of the screen to bring more space into view.

The games also often create a series of goalposts that not only marks our progress through the game space but also determines our dominance over it. Once you've mastered a particular space, moved past its goalpost, you can reassume play at that point no matter the outcome of a particular round. These mechanisms help us to map our growing mastery over the game world, our conquest of its virtual real estate. Even in the absence of such a mechanism, increased understanding of the geography, biology, and physics of the different worlds makes it easy to return quickly to the same spot and move further into the frontier.

A related feature of the games are warp zones—secret passages that, like De Certeau's bridges, accelerate one's movement through the narrative geography and bring two or more worlds together. Knowledge about warp zones, passwords, and other game secrets are key items of social exchange between game players. More to the point, they have become important aspects of the economic exchange between game companies and players. Nintendo® engages in a playful yet lucrative form of "insider trading," selling secret tips about traversing the game space to consumers either through 1-900 hotlines or through subscriptions to *Nintendo® Power* magazine, which markets detailed maps of the many worlds and levels of popular games and tips for coping with the local flora and fauna or crossing difficult terrain.

The maps and charts that *Nintendo® Power* publishes are curious documents. Strictly speaking, they are not maps at all, not abstract representations of geographic places. The magazine simply unfolds the information contained on many different screens as a continuous image that shows us the narrative space from the player's point of view, more or less as it will be experienced in the game. (The closest analogy would be something like Japanese scroll painting.) Surrounding these successive representations of the screen space is a narration or "tour" that identifies features of the landscape and their potentials for narrative action, as in this text from a discussion of *Adventure Island 3*: "Lush jungle regions dominate Stage 2. However, a remote island to the southwest appears to be snowed under. How unusual! One of the largest waterfalls known to mankind will be encountered in Stage 2. Its cascading torrents may be too much for the loin-clothed island hero. To the south, Higgins will be lost in the mist". The text may also suggest possible ways of acting upon this space and point toward the forms of resources and knowledge needed to survive there: "The Spiders shouldn't give Higgins too much trouble. Some move up and down and some of them don't. There may be hidden Eggs in places such as this." At times, the text may also focus our attention back onto the larger narrative context, onto character disputes or goals that frame the game action: "The volcanos are erupting! Higgins had better act fast so he can rescue his girlfriend and get out of there. Because of the tremendous heat, the supply of fruit is shrinking. There won't be much time for decision making. The aliens, astonished that Higgins made it this far, will be waiting!" ("Adventure Island 3," *Nintendo® Power*, October 1992, no. 41, pp. 8-13)

Such representations of virtual space bear close resemblance to De Certeau's description of early maps that "included only the rectilinear marking out of itineraries (performative indications chiefly concerning pilgrimages), along with the stops one was to make (cities which one was to pass through, spend the night in, pray at, etc.) and distances calculated in hours or in days, that is, in terms of the time it would take to cover them on foot. Each of these maps is a memorandum prescribing actions" (De Certeau, 1984b, p. 120). Much like these earlier maps, the Nintendo® documentation focuses on the specific narrative actions to be performed upon these spaces, purposes to be pursued and sites to be visited, rather than a universalized account of the possible places that exist independent of the reader's goals and desires. In most cases, however, the game company withholds crucial information, and the final stage of the game remains unmapped and undocumented. Players must still venture into an unfamiliar and uncharted space to confront unknown perils if they wish to master the game.

MF: As Henry's citation from De Certeau suggests, we might locate Nintendo®'s treatment of space in relation to a history of cartography. The Renaissance was, in fact, the moment when mapmaking shifted from providing locally oriented maps of previous trajectories and observations by coastal navigators (rutters) to the universalized overview of the Mercator projection. Yet the "universalized overview" was still conceptual rather than actual; the information needed to map the globe was still being gathered in arenas of intense competition and secrecy.

I've suggested that the particularized accounts of travel offered by narratives like Smith's or Raleigh's more or less deliberately replaced arrival with the details of travel as a process. These details, of course, were not only substitutive but also served practical purposes of their own, guiding both future voyagers and investors in the voyages. Printed books like Richard Hakluyt's collection of voyage narratives or

Smith's *General History* were routinely carried by ships on voyages of trade and settlement. Observing this weight given to narratives, one might describe a shift in the center of value from things to be discovered to information about the terrain covered en route. When Hakluyt describes the capture of the Portuguese carrack *Madre de Deus* in 1592, among its spins was a 1590 treatise on China in Latin, found "enclosed in a case of sweet cedar-wood, and lapped up almost an hundred fold in fine calicut-cloth, as though it had been some incomparable jewel" (Hakluyt, 1598-1600, vol. 2, p. 88). Information itself becomes the priceless commodity. J. B. Harley (1988) links the censorship of cartographic information in early modern Europe to the economic transformations that accompanied the beginnings of overseas empires.

> In a period when the foundations of the European world economy and its overseas empires were being laid, absolute monarchs were also "merchant kings," pursuing economic objectives through the trade monopolies opened up by their navigations. As in the case of the nation-state, the essence of empire is control. For such com- mercial monopolies to survive and for the policies of *mare clausum* to be implemented, there had to be a monopoly of the knowledge that enabled the new lands and the routes to and from them to be mapped. (Harley, 1988, p. 61)

Christopher Columbus and John Smith withheld information on true distance traveled from the rest of their parties; Francis Drake was restrained from making charts or descriptions of his voyage, and his narrative was held back from publication for eight years. Raleigh's (1848) *Discoverie* broods over the impossibility of keeping any new knowledge secret, an impossibility that justifies his decision not to explore a potential gold mine:

> I thought it best not to hover thereabouts, least if the same had been perceived by the company, there would haue bin by this time many barks and ships set out, and perchance other nations would also have gotten of ours for pilots, so as both our selues might haue been prevented, and all our care taken for good vsage of the people been vtterly lost. (pp. 59-60)

Information itself became a valued commodity to be accumulated, withheld from circulation, and given out strategically.

HJ: When I watch my son playing Nintendo®, I watch him play the part of an explorer and a colonist, taking a harsh new world and bringing it under his symbolic control, and that story is strangely familiar. De Certeau reminds us that one traditional function of narratives is to define a people's relation to their spaces, to justify their claims upon a certain geography.

Cultures endlessly repeat the narratives of their founding as a way of justifying their occupation of space. What is interesting about Nintendo® is that it allows people to enact through play an older narrative that can no longer be enacted in reality—a constant struggle for possession of desirable spaces, the ever shifting and unstable frontier between controlled and uncontrolled space, the need to venture onto unmapped terrain and to confront its primitive inhabitants. This holds true for all players. For children, Nintendo® further offers the image of personal autonomy and bodily control that contrasts with their own subordinate position in the social formation.

MF: The notion of simulating this early colonial experience was not born with Nintendo®. The Victorian editor Edward Arber (1885) writes in his preface to *The Three Earliest English Books on America* that in them

> One is able . . . to look out on the New world as its Discoverers and first explorers looked upon it. Nowadays, this Globe has but few geographical mysteries; and it is losing its romance as fast as it is losing its wild beasts. In the following texts, however, the Wonderment of its Discovery in all its freshness, is preserved, as in amber, for all time. (p. v)

And if late 19th-century editions of American voyage narratives offered readers like Virginia Woolf a vicarious experience, America in the 16th and 17th centuries famously offered to the unlanded or disenfranchised youth of England an alternate arena of possible advancement and acquisition. But the offered autonomy was ambiguous. Advertised in some documents as a place where a young man's hands could be his lands, offering unique opportunities for social and economic mobility, America at other moments offers to England a place where potentially subversive elements—heterodox ministers or "masterless men"—can be sent, where the backbreaking labor that subdues the body will necessarily lead to a conformity of the exhausted spirit. The theory contemporaneous with the voyage, as well as the writings of colonists, represents America ambiguously as a place of acquiring mastery and of being mastered.

The time-honored representation of the English voyages has been a confident, masculine "thrust outwards" and expansion of, among other things, an enlightened English rule. The prestige that the voyages retrospectively acquired under Victoria was solidified by accounts that linked territorial expansion to the flowering of literary achievement represented, especially, by Shakespeare (also Marlowe, Sidney, and others). In contrast to this celebratory reception, the mastery of children playing Nintendo® is valued only within restricted circles and largely trivialized, if not stigmatized, within the larger culture. But if, as we argue, Nintendo® plays out in virtual space the same narrative of mastering new territory that these earlier texts repeatedly record, it has also been argued that Renaissance England was preoccupied with its own littleness, insularity, and triviality (Knapp, 1993). It also seems to be the case that most of England's early voyages and settlements were characterized less by mastery and success than by forms of incompetence, failure, and incomprehension. It is difficult to locate unambiguously in these narratives either what is masterful, prestigious, and monumental or what is trivial, disgraceful, and subordinate. Although our two subjects have acquired different cultural meanings, they are in important ways fundamentally the same narrative, the same kind of experience, one real, the other simulated.

HJ: Our purpose in talking about Nintendo® next to these older texts is not to make a claim about direct causal links between the two traditions nor to borrow cultural authority for Nintendo® by brushing it against works with a more prestigious status. A comparison against periods minimally allows us to think more creatively about forms of narrative that privilege space over characterization or plot development not as aberrations or failures to conform to aesthetic norms but as part of an alternative tradition of "spatial stories," a different way of organizing narratives that must be examined and evaluated according to their own cultural logic. Because all ways of organizing narratives presuppose ways of organizing social and cultural experience, there are ideological implications as well in seeing Nintendo® games as sharing a logic of spatial exploration and conquest with these earlier works. Nintendo® not only allows players to identify with the founding myths of the American nation but to restage them, to bring them into the sphere of direct social experience. If ideology is at work in Nintendo® games (and rather obviously, it is), ideology works not through character identification but, rather, through role playing. Nintendo® takes children and their own needs to master their social space and turns them into virtual colonists driven by a desire to master and control digital space.

Just as the earlier narratives played a specific role in relation to the economic and cultural imperialism of Renaissance Europe, Nintendo® games must also be positioned against the backdrop of a new and more complicated phase of economic and cultural imperialism. Critical theorists have often oversimplified this issue: American-based multinationals dump their cultural goods on the rest of the world, producing an international culture that erases indigenous cultural traditions. In this scenario, cultural power flows in one direction, from the West to the East—terms that provide a sharp reminder of how present a Renaissance geography still is, reaching Japan by traveling east, locating direction in relationship to the Old World and not the New. Nintendo®'s success complicates a unidirectional model, suggesting ways that the appropriation and rewriting of these cultural goods may become an alternative source of cultural and economic power.

Nintendo®'s much disputed bid to purchase the Seattle Mariners represented a public acknowledgment of the increasingly central role of Japanese popular culture in defining how Americans play. Japan's longtime adaption, appropriation, and reconstruction of Western cultural traditions enables it to sell its cultural goods in the American marketplace, much as in another age British pop stars ruled the American music scene. What exactly is the cultural status of a Nintendo® game, based partially on American generic traditions or adopted from specific Western texts, drawing some of its most compelling iconography from Japanese graphic art, licensed by Japanese corporations, manufactured and designed by corporations in both the Americas and Asia, and for sale to both Japanese and American marketplaces? What are the lines of economic and cultural influence when we see Bugs Bunny, Hulk Hogan, and Bart Simpson existing side by side with samurai, sumo wrestlers, and Mecha-men? Does Nintendo®'s recycling of the myth of the American New World, combined with its own indigenous myths of global conquest and empire building, represent Asia's absorption of our national imaginary, or does it participate in a dialogic relationship with the West, an intermixing of different cultural traditions that insures their broader circulation and consumption? In this new rediscovery of the New World, who is the colonizer and who the colonist?

References

Adventure Island 3. (1992). *Nintendo® Power*, 41, pp. 8-13.

Arber, E. (1885). *The three earliest English books on America.* Birmingham: 1 Montague Road.

Barlow, J. (1990, Summer). Being in nothingness. *Mondo 2000,* pp. 34-43.

Cortés, H. (1986). *Letters from Mexico* (A. Pagden, Trans. & Ed.). New Haven, CT and London: Yale University Press.

De Certeau, M. (1984a). *Heterologies: Discourse on the other* (B. Massumi, Trans.). Minneapolis: University of Minnesota Press.

De Certeau, M. (1984b). *The practice of everyday life.* Berkeley: University of California Press.

Hakluyt, R. (1598-1600). *Principal navigations.* N.p. London.

Harley, J. B. (1988). Silences and secrecy: The hidden agenda of cartography in early modern Europe. *Imago Mundi, 40,* 57-76.

Jenkins, H. (1993). 'x Logic': Repositioning Nintendo in children's lives. *Quarterly Review of Film and Video, 14,* 55-70.

Kinder, M. (1991). *Playing with power in movies, television and video games: From Muppet Babies to Teenage Mutant Ninja Turtles.* Berkeley: University of California Press.

Knapp, J. (1993). *An empire nowhere: England, America, and literature from Utopia* to *The Tempest.* Berkeley: University of California Press.

Lane, R. (1979). An account of the particularities . . . sent and directed to Sir Walter Ralegh. In D. B. Quinn (Ed.), *New American world* (pp. 84-119). New York: Arno Press and Hector Bye.

Page, E. (1973). *American genesis: Pre-colonial writing in the North.* Boston: Gambit.

Provenzo, E. F. (1991). *Video kids: Making sense of Nintendo.* Cambridge, MA: Harvard University Press.

Raleigh, Sir Walter. (1848). *The discoverie of Guiana . . .* (Sir Robert Schomburgk, Ed.). London: Hakluyt Society.

Rheingold, H. (1991). *Virtual reality.* New York: Simon & Schuster.

Smith, J. (1624). *The general history of Virginia, New-England, and the Summer Isles.* In P. Barbour, *Works of Captain John Smith* (pp. 214-261). Chapel Hill: University of North Carolina Press.

Walcott, D. (1986). Ruins of a great house. In D. Walcott, *Collected poems, 1948-84* (p. 79). New York: Farrar, Strauss, Giroux.

4

MAKING SENSE OF SOFTWARE: COMPUTER GAMES AND INTERACTIVE TEXTUALITY

Ted Friedman

Contemporary theories of literature and film have worked hard to "liberate the reader" from the shackles of authorial intent and textual determinism (see, e.g., Allen, 1992; Fish, 1980; Freund, 1987; Tompkins, 1980). Today, it practically goes without saying within the discourse of cultural theory that no text exists until it is engaged by a subject—that textuality is always an interactive, creative process.

But while critics in the humanities have grown more and more bold in proclaiming the reader's power over the images on a printed page or celluloid strip, few have paid much attention to the emergence of new media that call into question the very categories of author, reader, and text. (An important exception is the pioneering work of David Myers, to which I refer throughout this chapter.) Interactive software—computer games, hypertext, and even "desktop" programs and databases—connect the oppositions of "reader" and "text," of "reading" and "writing," together in feedback loops that make it impossible to distinguish precisely where one begins and the other ends. Recognizing a reader's changing expectations and reactions as a linear text unfolds is one thing, but how do we talk about textual interactions in which every response provokes instantaneous changes in the text itself, leading to a new response, and so on? The answer is not very clear yet, for whereas the humanities have theoretical accounts to explain the workings of literature, film, and television, as yet there is no "software theory."

Hypertext: A Limited Paradigm

The one form of interactive computer texts that has been explored in some depth by cultural theorists is hypertext (see, e.g., Barrett, 1989; Delany & Landow, 1991; Landow, 1992). Hypertext is software that allows many different texts to be linked, so that simply clicking a mouse on a key word brings up a new related document. It can be used to create fiction with myriad forking paths or to organize concordances and footnotes that do not simply supply page numbers but instantaneously call up whole documents, each of which in turn can be linked to other documents.

But emphasizing hypertext as the model for interactive computer texts traps software theory in traditional notions of textuality. The hypertext reader simply navigates through a network of choices, like a person flipping around in a book by consulting the index. Certainly, the possibility that this book may be thousands of pages and part of a series of thousands of volumes opens up incredible opportunities. But however great the database, the hypertext reader's choices are still limited by the finite number of links created by the hypertext author or authors. The constant feedback between player and computer in a computer game is a far more complex interaction than this simple networking model. And computers' graphics and sound capabilities along with joystick and point-and-click interfaces make reading an even more tenuous analogy. Whereas in one stage of development, computer games like Infocom's *Zork* series may have simply been "interactive fiction" in which players read sentences and typed responses, computer games today often need little or no written text at all.

This does not mean that computer game playing is a transparent activity—far from it, as any hapless Nintendo® novice can attest. Rather, like becoming teleliterate, learning how to play computer games is a process of learning a distinct semiotic structure. To some extent, this language, like that of classical Hollywood narrative, carries over from one text to the next; initiates can finish one game and comfortably move on to the next one, particularly if they remain in the same genre. But in some ways, every new computer game is its own world, a distinct semiotic system, and it is the very process of learning (or conquering) that system that drives interest in the game. Every game typically requires a "learning curve" while the user grows familiar with the new interface and the logic of the program. It is when the game's processes appear transparent, when the player can easily win the game, that the game loses its appeal.

Hypertext seems to me a transitional genre particularly appealing to literary academia because it dresses up traditional literary study with postmodern multimedia flash. Concentrating on an account of hypertext to explain interactive computer texts is like basing film studies on the genre of screenplays without looking at the movies themselves; what is needed is an analysis rooted in the distinct qualities of this new kind of interaction between viewer and text.

Computer Games

If we wish to move beyond familiar paradigms and look at software that has developed truly new forms of reader-text interaction, it seems clear to me the place to start is computer games.

Playing games on computers was first made possible by the introduction of minicomputers in the late 1950s. Freed from the IBM punch card bureaucracy, programmers for the first time were able to explore the possibilities opened up by hands-on interaction with computers. Games were among the first programs attempted by the original "hackers," undergraduate members of MIT's Tech Model Railroad Club. The result, in 1962, was the collaborative development of the first computer game: *Spacewar,* a basic version of what would become the *Asteroids* arcade game, played on a $120,000 DEC PDP-1 (Laurel, 1993; Levy, 1984; Wilson, 1992). Computer designer Brenda Laurel (1993) points out this early recognition of the centrality of computer games as models of human-computer interaction:

> Why was *Spacewar* the "natural" thing to build with this new technology? Why not a pie chart or an automated kaleidoscope or a desktop? Its designers identified *action* as the key ingredient and conceived *Spacewar* as a game that could provide a good balance between thinking and doing for its players. They regarded the computer as a machine naturally suited for representing things that you could see, control, and play with. Its interesting potential lay not in its ability to perform calculations but in its capacity *to represent action in which humans could participate.* (p. 1)

As computers became more accessible to university researchers throughout the 1960s, several genres of computer games emerged. Chess programs sophisticated enough to defeat humans were developed. The first computer role-playing game, *Adventure,* was written at Stanford in the 1960s: By typing short phrases the player could communicate commands to the computer to manipulate a character through various settings and solve puzzles. Then in 1970, *Scientific American* columnist Martin Gardner introduced Americans to *LIFE,* a simulation of cellular growth patterns written by British mathematician John Conway that became the first "software toy," an addictively open-ended model of systemic development designed to be endlessly tinkered with and enjoyed (Levy, 1984; Wilson, 1992).

The 1970s, of course, saw the birth of the video arcade, the home video game system, and the personal computer. By the early 1980s, computer game software production had become an industry (Wilson, 1992). And in the past 10 years, as personal computers' capacities have rapidly expanded, computer games have continued to develop, offering increasingly detailed graphics and sounds, growing opportunities for multiple-player interaction via modems and on-line services, and ever more sophisticated simulation algorithms.

According to the magazine *Computer Gaming World,* as of 1992 about 4,000 computer games had been published, not to mention thousands more public domain games (Wilson, 1992). These products range from arcade-style games emphasizing hand-eye coordination, to role-playing games adding graphics and sound to the *Adventure* formula, to simulation games in which players oversee the growth and development of systems ranging from cities to galaxies to alternate life-forms. *CGW* divides the contemporary field into seven genres: action/arcade, adventure, role-playing adventure, simulation, sports, strategy, and war. Within these categories, of course, there is much overlap. An empire-building game like *Civilization*™, for example, rests somewhere between a war game and a simulation, and many adventure games contain arcade-style interludes (see Myers, 1989, for a more extensive discussion of computer game genres).

The Computer Gaming Subculture

Of course, academia's neglect of computer games hardly means that games have gone untheorized. Among the people who design and play computer games, the poetics and possibilities of computer games have been a subject of continuous discussion. *Computer Gaming World* is the self-conscious organ of the computer game industry and subculture, publishing game previews, reviews, strategy tips, and periodic essays on the state of computer games. It takes its role as the connection between the hard-core computer game market and the computer game industry very seriously. It thoroughly covers the computer game industry and publishes abstracts from technical programming essays in the *Journal of Computer Game Design.* Every issue also ranks the Top 100 current games and Top 10 in each genre, based on continuous reader polling (each issue contains a ballot card). This interaction with readers continues not only through the mail but on-line as well. The Prodigy® service runs a daily column by the editors of *CGW,* and the editors regularly scan the gaming forum and respond to bulletins posted there.

The intense dialogue fostered by *CGW* and other forums within the computer gaming industry and subculture has led to the formulation of a computer game canon (a Hall of Fame printed in every issue of *CGW* and archived on Prodigy®) and several provisional theories of computer gaming. These discussions are, to my mind, the most successful theorizations to date of interactive computer texts.

Computer Games as "Interactive Cinema"

One prominent strand of thought within the computer gaming subculture is to describe the computer game industry as the "New Hollywood."[1] This analogy has its roots in the changing economics of entertainment production. Over the past few years, Hollywood studios have flocked to Silicon Valley to gain access to the latest computer-generated special effects techniques and to position themselves to be able to produce the kind of interactive entertainment to come in the 500-channel future.

The "New Hollywood" analogy serves as a helpful model for understanding the process of computer game design. Although in the industry's infancy it was possible for one programmer to write and market a game single-handedly, today computer game production is a complex, collaborative process among many specialists. The introduction screens for contemporary games read like movie credits, listing producers, programmers, artists, musicians, and even, in the newer games with digitized images and recorded dialogue, actors. At the top of the credits are the designers, the equivalent to movie directors. In the computer gaming world, designers like *Ultima®*'s Lord British, *King's Quest®*'s Roberta Williams, and *SimCity®*'s Will Wright are respected as artists with unique personal visions.

The difference between the New Hollywood and the Old, according to the analogy, is that computer games are "interactive cinema," in which the game player takes on the role of the protagonist. This model particularly fits adventure games such as Sierra On-Line's *Leisure Suit Larry*™ and *King's Quest®* series. And with the development of CD-ROM technology, the fit seems even closer: Much more data can now be stored on disk than ever before, so that what the game player sees and hears approaches movie quality. The newest CD-ROM games replace the traditional on-screen text with audio dialogue, often recorded by well-known actors. On the CD-ROM version of *Star Trek®: The 25th Anniversary*™, for example, the dialogue is spoken by the actual *Star Trek®* cast. It is not impossible to imagine the day when a computer game might look indistinguishable from a film.

Although production values may have vastly improved since the days of text-based "interactive fiction," the problem that designers of contemporary "interactive cinema" face remains the same: how to define "interactive"? How can one give the player a sense of "control" over the game while still propelling the player through a compelling narrative? The solution, dating back to *Adventure* and *Zork,* has always been to set up the game as a series of puzzles. The player must muddle through the universe of the game—exploring the settings, talking to the characters, acquiring and using objects—until she or he has accomplished everything necessary to trigger the next stage of the plot. In the process, the player is expected to regularly make mistakes, die, and restart the game in a previously saved position. (The film *Groundhog Day* perfectly captures this "Oh no, not again!" exasperation.) The flaws in this system have prompted the development of a cottage industry offering hint books, 1-900 numbers, and bulletin boards to help players stuck halfway through their adventures.

The idea of computer "role playing" emphasizes the opportunity for the gamer to *identify* with the character on the screen—the fantasy is that rather than just *watching* the protagonist one can actually *be* her or him. But whereas classical Hollywood cinema is designed in every way to allow one to "lose oneself" in the fantasy on-screen, the stop-and-go nature of the puzzle-solving paradigm makes it very hard to establish the same level of psychic investment. Although adventure games can be a lot of fun, even the best of them cannot really deliver what they promise. As *Computer Gaming World*'s adventure/role-playing game columnist Scorpia complained in 1992,

> There is an increasing undercurrent of dissatisfaction among game-players. Yes, the pictures are beautiful, the music is orchestral-quality, the interface simple and easy to use, but when the game is finished, there isn't so much feeling of satisfaction with it. Rather, one has the impression that the game was only a vehicle for displaying the virtuosity of artists and composers. (p. 56)

A second option in designing "interactive cinema" is to make the game more like hypertext: Rather than railroading the player through a predetermined story line, the game could simply present a series of choices, each branching out into new possibilities, like the children's book series *Choose Your Own Adventure.* Up until now, this approach has rarely been attempted in computer games, probably for economic reasons: It did not seem practical to create scenes and characters the player may never get around to seeing. A notable exception was Infocom's unsuccessful late-1980s *Infocomics* series (Wilson, 1992). Now that CD-ROMs open up the opportunity for far more data to be available in a game, it appears that this possibility is beginning to be explored again. The publicity for the most recent edition in the *King's Quest®* series, *King's Quest VI®*, emphasizes that "every choice you make affects your future options and the attitudes and actions of characters you encounter. Depending on your skills and the decisions you make, your adventure can follow dozens of different story lines, with nearly half of the possible events optional" ("News Notes," 1993, p. 16).

But a hypertext model of "interactive cinema" still does little to give the player a sense of real autonomy; the choices remain a limited set of predefined options.[2] This certainly increases the complexity of the game: The linear narrative becomes a web, giving the gamer the opportunity to explore the ramifications of various options and map out the game's network of forking paths. But whether a single plot or a network of choices, the world of the game remains as predetermined as that of any film or novel.

All of this is not to say that computer gaming is inherently a more distanced, alienating form of interaction than watching a movie—far from it, as we shall see. But, ironically, those games modeled upon cinema are likely to be the *least* involving. Hamstrung by the demands of traditional narrative, these games operate under a limited model of computer interaction as a series of distinct decisions. As a result, they do not begin to take advantage of the opportunities for constant interaction and feedback between player and computer in the way that other forms of computer games can. As science fiction writer and computer game critic Orson Scott Card (1991a) argues,

> What every good game author eventually has to learn . . . is that computers are a completely different medium, and great computer artworks will only come about when we stop judging computer games by standards developed for other media. . . . You want to do the rebuilding of Atlanta after the war? SimCity does it better than either the book or the movie of *Gone With the Wind.* The computer "don't know nothin' 'bout birthin' babies," but what it does well, it does better than any other medium that ever existed. (p. 54; reprinted by permission of Compute, © 1991, Compute Publications International, Ltd.)

SimCity®: The "Software Toy" Ideal

The game to which Card refers, *SimCity®*, is a simulation that allows the player to orchestrate the building and development of a city. The success of *SimCity®* demonstrates the surprisingly compelling power of a particular kind of human-computer interaction very different from either hypertext or "interactive cinema."

SimCity® actually did not start off as a simulation game. As the game's creator, Will Wright, explains,

> *SimCity* evolved from *Raid on Bungling Bay,* where the basic premise was that you flew around and bombed islands. The game included an island generator, and I noticed after a while that I was having more fun building islands than blowing them up. About the same time, I also came across the work of Jay Forrester, one of the first people to ever model a city on a computer for social-sciences purposes. Using his theories, I adapted and expanded the *Bungling Bay* island generator, and *SimCity* evolved from there. (quoted in Reeder, 1992, p. 26)

Nervous that the product Wright came up with would appear too "educational," distributors Broderbund took extra steps on *SimCity*®'s release in 1987 to make sure it would be perceived as a *game,* adding "disaster" options and prepackaged scenarios—earthquakes, nuclear meltdowns, even an attack from Godzilla. But as a 1989 *Newsweek* article on the game pointed out, such add-ons were "excess baggage" (Barol, 1989, p. 64). What turned *SimCity*® into a giant software hit, spawning numerous bootlegs, imitations, and spin-offs (including *SimEarth*®, *SimAnt*, *SimLife*, *SimFarm*™, *SimHealth*, and most recently the sequel/update *SimCity 2000*™), was the pleasure Wright discovered in the simulation process itself. A description of the original game comes from a Maxis catalog:

> SimCity makes you Mayor and City Planner, and dares you to design and build the city of your dreams. . . . Depending on your choices and design skills, Simulated Citizens (Sims) will move in and build homes, hospitals, churches, stores and factories, or move out in search of a better life elsewhere. (*Maxis Software Toys Catalog*, 1992, p. 4)

Beginning (in the basic scenario) with an undeveloped patch of land and an initial development fund, the player constructs a city by choosing where and what kind of power plants to build, zoning industrial, commercial, and residential areas, laying down roads, mass transit, and power lines, and building police stations, fire departments, and eventually airports, seaports, and stadiums, and so on. Although playing the game eventually comes to feel entirely intuitive, the system is quite complex, and the sequel *SimCity 2000*™ offers even more options. Every action is assigned a price, and the player can only spend as much money as he or she has in the city treasury. The treasury begins at a base amount and can be replenished yearly by taxes, the rate of which is determined by the player. As the player becomes more familiar with the system, she or he gradually develops strategies to encourage economic growth, build up the population of the city, and score a higher "approval rating" from the Sims. Which of these or other goals the player chooses to pursue, however, is up to the individual; Maxis likes to refer to its products as "software toys" rather than games and insists,

> When you play with our toys, you set your own goals and decide for yourself when you've reached them. The fun and challenge of playing with our toys lies in exploring the worlds you create out of your own imagination. You're rewarded for creativity, experimentation, and understanding, with a healthy, thriving universe to call your own. (*Maxis Software Toys Catalog*, 1992, p. 10)

Expanding on the "software toy" ideal, Card (1991b) argues that the best computer games are those that provide the most open-ended frameworks to allow players the opportunity to create their own worlds:

> Someone at every game design company should have a full-time job of saying, "Why aren't we letting the player decide that?" . . . When [designers] let . . . unnecessary limitations creep into a game, gamewrights reveal that they don't yet understand their own art. They've chosen to work with the most liberating of media—and yet they snatch back with their left hand the freedom they offered us with their right. Remember, gamewrights, the power and beauty of the art of gamemaking is that you and the player collaborate to create the final story. Every freedom that you can give to the player is an artistic victory. And every needless boundary in your game should feel to you like failure. (p. 58; reprinted by permission of Compute, © 1991, Compute International, Ltd.)

Computer Gaming as Demystification

Of course, however much "freedom" computer game designers grant players, any simulation will be rooted in a set of baseline assumptions. *SimCity®* has been criticized from both the left and the right for its economic model. It assumes that low taxes will encourage growth while high taxes will hasten recessions. It discourages nuclear power while rewarding investment in mass transit. And most fundamentally, it rests on the empiricist, technophilic fantasy that the complex dynamics of city development can be abstracted, quantified, simulated, and micromanaged.[3]

These are not *flaws* in the game—they are its founding principles. They can be engaged and debated, and other computer games can be written following different principles. But there could never be an "objective" simulation free from "bias"; computer programs, like all texts, will always be ideological constructions.

The fear of some computer game critics, though, is that technology may mask the constructedness of any simulation. Science fiction writer and *Byte* magazine columnist Jerry Pournelle (1990) argues,

> The simulation is pretty convincing—and that's the problem, because . . . it's a simulation of the designer's theories, not of reality. . . . [M]y point is not to condemn these programs. Instead, I want to warn against their misuse. For all too many, computers retain an air of mystery, and there's a strong temptation to believe what the little machines tell us. "But that's what the computer says" is a pretty strong argument in some circles. The fact is, though, the computer doesn't say anything at all. It merely tells you what the programmers told it to tell you. Simulation programs and games can be valuable tools to better understanding, but we'd better be aware of their limits. (on-line from Nexus)

Pournelle's warnings are well taken, but I think he overestimates the mystifying power of technophilia. In fact, I would argue that computer games reveal their own constructedness to a much greater extent than more traditional texts. Pournelle asks that designers open up their programs so that gamers can "know what the inner relationships are." But this is exactly what the process of computer game playing reveals. Learning and winning (or, in the case of a noncompetitive "software toy," "reaching one's goals at") a computer game is a process of demystification: One succeeds by discovering how the software is put together. The player molds his or her strategy through trial-and-error experimentation to see "what works"—which actions are rewarded and which are punished. Likewise, the extensive discourse on game strategy in manuals, magazines, bulletin boards, and guides like *The Official SimCity Planning Commission Handbook* and *The SimEarth Bible* does exactly what Pournelle asks, exposing the "inner relationships" of the simulation to help players succeed more fully.

Unlike a book or film that one is likely to encounter only once, a computer game is usually played over and over. The moment it is no longer interesting is the moment when all its secrets have been discovered, its limitations exposed. Game designer and author Chris Crawford (1986) describes the hermeneutics of computer games as fundamentally a process of deconstruction rather than simple interpretation. David Myers (1990a) observes, "According to Crawford, the best measure of the success of a game is that the player learns the principles behind that game 'while discovering inevitable flaws in its design. . . . A game should lift the player up to higher levels of understanding' " (p. 27, quote from Crawford, 1986, p. 16).

Simulation and Subjectivity

Playing *SimCity*® is a very different experience from playing an adventure game like *King's Quest*®. The interaction between human and computer is constant and intense. Game playing is a continuous flow—it can be very hard to stop because the player is always in the middle of dozens of different projects: nurturing a new residential zone in one corner of the map, building an airport in another, saving up money to buy a new power plant, monitoring the crime rate in a particularly troubled neighborhood, and so on. Meanwhile, the city is continually changing, as the simulation inexorably chugs forward from one month to the next (unless the player puts the game on pause to handle a crisis). By the time the player has made a complete pass through the city, a whole new batch of problems and opportunities have developed. If the pace of the city's development is moving too fast to keep up with, the simulation can be slowed down (i.e., it will wait longer in real time to move from one month to the next); if the player is waiting around for things to happen, the simulation can be speeded up.

As a result, it is easy to slide into a routine with absolutely no downtime, no interruptions from complete communion with the computer. The game can grow so absorbing, in fact, that players' subjective sense of time is distorted (see Myers, 1992). Myers (1991) writes, "From personal experience and interviews with other players, I can say it is *very* common to play these games for eight or more hours without pause, usually through the entire first night of purchase" (p. 343). You look up, and all of a sudden it is morning.

It is very hard to describe what it feels like when one is "lost" inside a computer game precisely because at that moment one's sense of self has been fundamentally transformed. Flowing through a continuous series of decisions made almost automatically, hardly aware of the passage of time, the player forms a symbiotic circuit with the computer, a version of the cyborgian consciousness described by Donna Haraway (1985) in her influential "Manifesto for Cyborgs." The computer comes to feel like an organic extension of one's consciousness, and the player may feel like an extension of the computer itself.

This isn't exactly the way the *SimCity*® user's manual puts it. The manual describes the player's role as a "combination Mayor and City Planner." In *Civilization*™, the player is referred to as "Chief," "Warlord," "Prince," "King," or "Emperor" (depending on the skill level) and can adopt the names of various historical leaders—Abraham Lincoln when playing the Americans, Genghis Khan when leading the Mongols, and so on. But while these titles suggest that the gamer imagines her- or himself playing a specific "role" along the lines of the "interactive cinema" model, the structures of identification in simulation games are much more complex. Closer to the truth is the setup in *Populous,* where the player is simply God—omnipotent (within the rules of the game), omniscient, and omnipresent. Whereas in some simulations explicitly about politics, like *Hidden Agenda* and *Crisis in the Kremlin,* the player's power and perspective is limited to that of a chief of state, in games like *SimCity*® the player is personally responsible for far more than any one leader—or even an entire government—could ever manage. The player directly controls the city's budget, economic and residential growth, transportation, police and fire services, zoning, and even entertainment (the Sims eventually get mad if you don't build them a stadium). While each function is putatively within the province of government control, the game structure makes the player identify as much with the roles of industrialist, merchant, real estate agent, and citizen as with those of Mayor or City Planner.

For example, in *SimCity*®, the way a new area of town is developed is to "zone" it. The player decides whether each parcel of land should be marked for residential, industrial, or commercial use. The player cannot *make* the zones develop into thriving homes or businesses; that is determined by the simulation on the basis of a range of interconnected factors including crime rate, pollution, economic conditions, power supply, and the accessibility of other zones. If the player has set up conditions right, an empty residential zone will quickly blossom into a high-rise apartment complex, raising land values, adding tax money to the city's coffers, and increasing the population of the city. If the zone isn't well-integrated into the city, it may stay undeveloped or degenerate into a crime-ridden slum.

Although the player cannot *control* the behavior putatively assigned to the residents of the city—the Sims—the identification process at the moment the player zones the city goes beyond simply seeing oneself as "the Mayor" or even as the collective zoning commission. The cost of zoning eats up a substantial portion of a city's budget—much more than it would cost a real city. This is structurally necessary to limit the player's ability to develop the city, so that building the city is a gradual, challenging process (something close to a narrative, in fact). The effect on game play is to see the process less as "zoning" than as *buying* the land. This is not to say that the gamer considers every building as owned by the government, but at the moment of zoning, the gamer is playing the role not of mayor but of someone else—homeowner, landlord, or real estate developer, perhaps, in the case of a residential zone.

One could see playing *SimCity*®, then, as a constant shifting of identificatory positions, depending on whether one is buying land, organizing the police force, paving the roads, or whatever. This, I think, is part of what's going on. But this model suggests a level of disjunction—jumping back and forth from one role to the next—belied by the smooth, almost trancelike state of game play.

Overarching these functional shifts, I think, is a more general state of identification: with the city as a whole, as a single organism. Even putting it this way, though, does not go to the root of the process because "the city" in question is a very different object from, say, the city of New York. Except for those cases when gamers choose to recreate real cities, no outside referent exists for the world on the computer screen. And while the game visuals are cleverly iconic—tiny little houses, factories, and mini-malls—they hardly evoke any "real" space the way a movie set or even a written passage can. It is unlikely, I think, that the player in the thick of the game takes the time to look at a residential district and imagine a "real life" city block.

Rather, for the gamer, the city exists in its own right, a substitute for nothing else—a quintessentially postmodern "simulation" in Baudrillard's (1983) sense, as "real" as any other representation and divorced from any need for a "real world" referent. In this case, attempting to map "roles" onto the player's on-screen identification misses the point. When a player "zones" a land area, he or she is identifying less with a "role"—Mayor, industrialist, or whatever—than with a *process.* And the reason why the decision, and the continuous series of decisions the gamer makes, can be made so quickly and intuitively is that the gamer has internalized the logic of the program, so that the gamer is always able to anticipate the results of his or her actions. "Losing oneself" in a computer game means, in a sense, identifying with the simulation itself.

Simulation as Cognitive Mapping

In *The Condition of Postmodernity,* David Harvey (1989) argues for the primacy of spatialization in constructing cognitive frameworks: "We learn our ways of thinking and conceptualizing from active grappling with the spatializations of the written word, the study and production of maps, graphs, diagrams, photographs, models, paintings, mathematical symbols, and the like" (p. 206). He then points out the dilemma of making sense of space under late capitalism: "How adequate are such modes of thought and such conceptions in the face of the flow of human experience and strong processes of social change? On the other side of the coin, how can spatializations in general . . . represent flux and change?" (p. 206). Representing flux and change is *exactly* what a simulation can do, by replacing the stasis of two- or three-dimensional spatial models with a map that shifts over time to reflect change. And this change is not simply the one-way communication of a series of still images but a continually interactive process. Computer simulations bring the tools of narrative to mapmaking, allowing the individual not simply to observe structures but to become experientially immersed in their logic.

Simulations may be our best opportunity to create what Fredric Jameson (1991) calls "an aesthetic of cognitive mapping: a pedagogical political culture which seeks to endow the individual subject with some new heightened sense of its place in the global system" (p. 54). Playing a simulation means becoming engrossed in a systemic logic that connects a myriad array of causes and effects. The simulation acts as a kind of map-in-time, visually and viscerally (as the player internalizes the game's logic) demonstrating the repercussions and interrelatedness of many different social decisions. Escaping the prison-house of language that seems so inadequate for holding together the disparate strands that construct postmodern subjectivity, computer simulations provide a radically new quasi-narrative form through which to communicate structures of interconnection.

Sergei Eisenstein hoped that the technology of *montage* could make it possible to film *Das Kapital.* But the narrative techniques of Hollywood cinema developed in a way that directs the viewer to respond to individuals rather than abstract concepts. A computer game based on *Das Kapital,* on the other hand, is easy to imagine. As Chris Crawford notes (paraphrased by David Myers), "Game *personalities* are not as important as game *processes*—'You can interact with a process. . . . Ultimately, you can learn about it'" (Myers, 1990a, p. 27, quote from Crawford, 1986, p. 15).

The Future: From Interactive Textuality to CMC

One criticism often made of simulation games like *SimCity*® is that they are solipsistic "power trips," gratifying the gamer's desire to play God. This is to some degree unfair—simulations are often played in groups, particularly in educational settings. (*SimCity*® is used as a pedagogical tool in many urban studies classes.) But it is true that the absorbing interaction between human and computer in simulation gaming tends to discourage collaborative play.

Adventure games, by comparison, have always been more conducive to collaborative playing because of the stop-and-go nature of the game play. When you cannot get any further in a game until you solve a puzzle, the more minds the better. Nonetheless, even the computer "role playing" adventures spun off from the *Dungeons & Dragons*® universe have always been designed primarily for solitaire play. (Theoretically, up to six players could each control a different character, but in practice there is very little for individual characters to do.) In part, this has been to take advantage of the particular power of human-computer interaction to substitute for interpersonal interaction—if you can't find anyone to play *D&D* with, the computer may be the next best thing. But it has also been the result of technical limitations. The bottom line has always been that when there is only one keyboard and one mouse, only one player at a time can actually interact with the computer. Only arcade games have actually developed interfaces to allow simultaneous play on a single set.

With the proliferation of modems and the growth of the Internet and other on-line services, all this is beginning to change. Sierra's ImagiNation, for example, allows players from across the country to join together to play both traditional games like chess and bridge, and a *D&D*-style role-playing adventure, *The Shadow of Yserbius.* How on-line interactivity will affect computer game development is hard to tell. Will the accessibility of human opponents make computer-generated opponents obsolete? Could it be possible to design an on-line simulation game that transcends the solitaire model, combining intense human-computer interactivity with computer-mediated collaboration? Or is playing a simulation, like reading a book, just something that has to be done alone?

These questions about a bunch of games may seem peripheral to the Big Issues rolling down the Information Highway. But we should remember that the first program the MIT hackers wrote on their new PDP-1 was *Spacewar.* Today, as we experiment with ways to better communicate on the Internet, many of the tropes of adventure gaming are being borrowed by new virtual spaces. The first "MUD," short for "Multi-User Dungeon," was invented in 1979 as an open-ended on-line fantasy world that role players could not only explore but help build by creating new objects and rooms (Rheingold, 1993, p. 151). Today, MUDs include not only Tolkeinesque lands and *Star Trek®*-based galaxies but also communities like MediaMOO, a virtual version of MIT's Media Laboratory where media researchers can get together for "virtual drinks" or attend panels in virtual ballrooms. The basic commands invented for text-based adventures—"move," "look," "talk," "ask," "get," and so on—provide visitors with a range of interactive opportunities. And the computer game traditions of thick textual description, playful role-playing, and persistent exploration remain powerful imaginative tools at MediaMOO for opening up computer-mediated communication beyond simply "chatting" in real time.

As data capacities increase and text-based virtual communities expand to include sound and graphics, it is likely that computer games will continue to have things to teach us about interacting both with software and with each other. Computer games, after all, are where we go to play with the future.

Notes

1. This widely quoted phrase was coined by Electronic Arts executive Trip Hawkins in the early 1980s (Wilson, 1992).

2. This version of "interactive cinema" is the most obvious possible application of computer gaming to Hollywood product as new interactive cable technology is introduced. It is the logical extension of the practice of filming multiple endings to show to test audiences. What better way to please *everybody* than to give *each viewer* the choice of a "happy" or "sad" ending? But again, to limit our notions of interactivity to this fixed-choice model—one that computers merely facilitate rather than make possible—is to fail to recognize the unique possibilities for interaction offered by computers. Perhaps a more exciting variation on the Hollywood scenario would be to give the viewer access to all the shot footage of a program, so that the viewer (with the facilitation of a computer interface) could choose how to edit it into a narrative. In this way, rather than being limited to a predetermined set of choices the viewer could have a sense of creative *control.*

3. Complaining about the pro-government "bias" of *SimHealth,* a new game simulating the economics of health care reform, one critic speculates, "Maybe what we really need is an economic simulator called SimAdam Smith: You turn it on and just leave it alone" (Moss, 1994). As we shall see, however, it is not a simple step to equate the gamer with the hand of government, even if she or he is putatively designated "SimMayor."

References

Allen, R. (1992). Audience-oriented criticism and television. In R. Allen (Ed.), *Channels of discourse, reassembled* (pp. 163-185). Chapel Hill: University of North Carolina Press.

Barol, B. (1989, May 29). Big fun in a small town. *Newsweek,* p. 64.

Barrett, E. (Ed.). (1989). *The society of text: Hypertext, hypermedia, and the social construction of information.* Cambridge: MIT Press.

Baudrillard, J. (1983). *Simulations* (P. Foss, P. Patton, & P. Beitchman, Trans.). New York: Semiotext(e).

Card, O. S. (1991a, February). Gameplay: Films can make lousy games. *Compute,* p. 54.

Card, O. S. (1991b, March). Gameplay: Games with no limits. *Compute,* p. 58.

Crawford, C. (1986). *Balance of power.* Redmond, CA: Microsoft Press.

Delany, P., & Landow, G. (Eds.). (1991). *Hypermedia and literary studies.* Cambridge: MIT Press.

Fish, S. (1980). *Is there a text in this class?* Cambridge, MA: Harvard University Press.

Freund, E. (1987). *The return of the reader: Reader-response criticism.* London: Methuen.

Haraway, D. (1985). Manifesto for cyborgs: Science, technology, and socialist feminism in the 1980s. *Socialist Review, 80,* 65-108.

Harvey, D. (1989). *The condition of postmodernity.* Cambridge, MA: Basil Blackwell.

Jameson, F. (1991). *Postmodernism, or, the cultural logic of late capitalism.* Durham, NC: Duke University Press.

Landow, G. (1992). *Hypertext.* Baltimore: Johns Hopkins University Press.

Laurel, B. (1993). *Computers as theater.* New York: Addison-Wesley.

Levy, S. (1984). *Hackers: Heroes of the computer revolution.* New York: Dell.

Maxis Software Toys Catalog (1992). Orinda, CA: Maxis.

Moss, C. (1994, February). From mold to penicillen and from moss to SimHealth. *Computer Gaming World.* Downloaded from Prodigy®.

Myers, D. (1990a). Chris Crawford and computer game aesthetics. *Journal of Popular Culture, 24*(2), 17-28.

Myers, D. (1990b). Computer game genres. *Play and Culture, 3,* 286-301.

Myers, D. (1991). Computer game semiotics. *Play and Culture, 4,* 334-346.

Myers, D. (1992). Time, symbol transformations, and computer games. *Play and Culture, 5,* 441-457.

News notes: Sierra and Dynamix sweep SPA nominations. (1993, Spring). *Interaction,* p. 16.

Pournelle, J. (1990, February). [Untitled column]. *Byte,* obtained on-line through Nexus.

Reeder, S. (1992, December). Designing visions. *Kids & Computers,* pp. 24-27, 66-67.

Rheingold, H. (1993). *The virtual community: Homesteading on the electronic frontier.* New York: Addison-Wesley.

Scorpia. (1992, October). Scorpion's view: What's in a game? The current state of computer adventure/role playing games. *Computer Gaming World,* pp. 54-56.

Tompkins, J. P. (Ed.). (1980). *Reader response criticism: From formalism to post-structuralism.* Baltimore: Johns Hopkins University Press.

Wilson, J. (1992, July). A brief history of gaming: Part 1. *Computer Gaming World,* obtained on-line through Prodigy®.

5

STANDARDS OF CONDUCT ON USENET

Margaret L. McLaughlin

Kerry K. Osborne

Christine B. Smith

A globe-spanning web of computer networks offers millions of users the opportunity to exchange electronic mail, transfer files, search databases, and retrieve information from remote libraries, take part in real-time conferences, run software on distant computers, and participate in discussion groups on topics from autism education to yacht design. Subscribers to these networks represent an eclectic mix of universities, government agencies, and commercial concerns, with the latter constituting the fastest growing user domain (Lazzareschi, 1993a). One of the largest networks in this web is the Internet (Arick, 1993; December, 1993; Electronic Frontier Foundation, 1993; Hardie & Neou, 1993; Krol, 1992; LaQuey, 1993; Rafaeli, Sudweeks, & McLaughlin, in press).

The growth of the Internet has been explosive in recent years and is likely to continue, given reports that communications industry giants Time-Warner and Tele-Communications are actively moving to bring Internet access and services to their millions of customers. Continental Cablevision expects to offer Internet connections to more than 300,000 of its current subscribers by the end of 1994 (Lazzareschi, 1993b), and Rupert Murdoch's News Corp. is reportedly acquiring Delphi Internet Services (Flanigan, 1993). Access to the Internet is currently offered by CompuServe and other proprietary on-line services. So addictive has network access become to recent college graduates that at least one observer has characterized the Internet as the MTV of the so-called Generation X (Herz, 1993).

The accelerating privatization of the net, as exemplified by the recent agreements between MCI and a consortium of regional networks, the active courtship of the cable companies by the regional Bells—most prominently the proposed acquisition of Tele-Communications by Bell Atlantic—and the construction of high-speed fiber-optic networks all suggest that the dream of a seamless, gigabit-speed network may be realized in the very near future, bringing vast communications resources to homes and businesses as well as to the traditional consumers in the educational and scientific communities.

Accompanying the revolution in communications will be an array of new social technologies (Harasim, 1993a, 1993b). The global reach of the Internet not only facilitates communication among members of existing distributed groups and teams but, perhaps more important, provides a medium for the formation and cultivation of new relationships by providing virtually instantaneous access to thousands of potential contacts who have compatible interests and spheres of expertise. Besides providing a hospitable environment for a host of new forms of relating ranging from long-distance gaming (Curtis, 1992) to remote collaboration (Carley & Wendt, 1991; Frederick, 1993), one of the major attractions of the Internet is that its users can turn to its many "newsgroups," or electronic bulletin boards, to ask for advice on researching their Irish ancestors or to express their opinions about the single life, to argue about Derrida or exchange references on Drosophilia, to compare notes on the soaps and the Simpsons (Baym, 1992), or to connect to others with compatible sexual tastes (Penkoff, in press). These bulletin boards, many of which are distributed through the Usenet store-and-forward network (Spafford, 1993b), represent a significant departure from communications media as traditionally understood, combining as they do aspects of both mass and interpersonal communication.

Usenet is a network of an estimated 75,000 computers that exchange "news" articles posted to more than 5,000 newsgroups (B. Reid, 1993c). Although many of the Usenet sites exchange articles via UUCP (O'Reilly & Todino, 1992) or Fidonet, Usenet traffic today is largely generated and carried on the Internet. Usenet is widely available not only at universities, libraries, government agencies and high-tech businesses but is also accessible through commercial entities such as Netcom, America Online, and GEnie, which are gatewayed into the Internet. An estimated 11 million users worldwide read, post, and/or reply to articles on topics ranging from Unix wizardry to recreational folk dancing (B. Reid, 1993c). Usenet news is available in read-only mode for walk-in traffic at many libraries, and available evidence suggests that, in fact, reading, or "lurking," as it is called, is the principal mode of participation in Usenet (B. Reid, 1993a, 1993b, 1993c, 1993d) for most people who have access to it.

Convenient interactive participation in Usenet is available to persons who have accounts on systems running "newsreader" software. The most sophisticated newsreaders (Wohler, 1993) organize the news by groups, by topic and subtopic, into a menu-driven user interface that makes it possible to select articles to read, save, reply to, or forward to others. Newsreaders may be customized to exclude groups, topics, or authors of no interest to the reader. Reply functions serve to organize posted messages with common subject headings into "threads" that create and sustain the topical macrostructure of the newsgroup's ongoing discussion. Topical continuity is enhanced by "reply including" features that allow responses to threads (called follow-ons) to include edited or unedited text of previous messages. Besides making contributions to ongoing threads, readers may initiate new topics as well. Many groups prepare FAQs that provide answers to "Frequently Asked Questions" and acquaint newcomers with newsgroup practices.

The Interplay of Discourse and Social Structure in Virtual Communities

B. Reid's data (1993a, 1993b, 1993c, 1993d) would seem to indicate that, at least for the most popular newsgroups, the ratio of readers to posters of messages on Usenet is extremely high. A comparison may be made between these readers and readers of newspapers and magazines in that a relatively minuscule number "post" responses to news items. While acknowledging that letters to the [magazine or newspaper] editor may create a fleeting sense of community, MacKinnon (1992) short-circuits further comparison by noting that this "emergent dialogue is not a dialogue at all, but a set of coincident monologues . . . possibly staged—selected—by the editor to represent a diversity of views" (p. 14). According to MacKinnon, newsgroup postings, by virtue of their spontaneity and uncensored state, are more representative of true dialogue. In his view, the frequency and regularity of contributions by a proportion of newsgroup readers further distinguishes this form of social interaction as a more stable and enduring aspect of community. The question then arises as to the authenticity of community fostered by mass consumption of dialogue produced by a relative few. Silent readers may feel that they are a part of the conversation; however, this vicarious participation raises the spectre of pseudocommunity.

Beniger (1987) argues that pseudocommunity represents the "reversal of a centuries-old trend from organic community—based on interpersonal relationships—to impersonal associations integrated by mass means" (p. 369). Even MacKinnon (1992) is careful to stipulate that on-line interactions are conducted by "personae" and that the actions and feelings expressed may not be mirrored either physically or symbolically by their creators. This prompts Rheingold's (1993a) concern:

> Individuals find friends and groups find shared identities on-line, through the aggregated networks of relationships and commitments that make any community possible. But are relationships and commitments as we know them even possible in a place where identities are fluid? The physical world . . . is a place where the identity and position of the people you communicate with are well known, fixed, and highly visual. In cyberspace, everybody is in the dark. We can only exchange words with each other—no glances or shrugs or ironic smiles. Even the nuances of voice and intonation are stripped away. On top of the technology-imposed constraints, we who populate cyberspace deliberately experiment with fracturing traditional notions of identity by living as multiple simultaneous personae in different virtual neighborhoods. (p. 61)

Nonetheless, it seems to be the case that most newsgroups have a small coterie of habitues, with consistently presented personae, who regularly initiate and contribute to message threads, and in the patterns of their posts and replies one can find the traces of what we have come to call virtual community.

Despite Peck's (1987) caution that we humans "are not yet community creatures," few writers bother to question their own assumption that computer-mediated communication virtually carves communities out of cyberspace. The use of the community analogy to describe social aspects of the medium is ubiquitous and seemingly arbitrary. For example, "community" may refer to attenuated networks of virtual strangers exchanging ideas and information (Sproull & Kiesler, 1991) or to virtual friends debating the finer points of gender-bending their on-line personae (E. Reid, 1991). Such diverse user groups as hackers (Meyer & Thomas, 1990), role-playing enthusiasts (Curtis, 1992; Serpentelli, 1992), bulletin board subscribers (Rheingold, 1993a; Smith, 1992), and USENET newsgroups (MacKinnon, 1992) have all been designated communities for equally diverse reasons. The question "What constitutes virtual community?" remains unexplored territory.

One apparent truth drives the metaphor: Computer-mediated communicators themselves see their activity as inherently social. Furthermore, this activity takes place in a conceptual, if not perceptual, space:

> Members of electronic virtual communities act as if the community met in a physical public space. The number of times that on-line conferencees refer to the conference as an architectural place and to the mode of interaction in that place as being social is overwhelmingly high in proportion to those who do not. They

say things like "This is a great place to get together" or "This is a convenient place to meet." (Stone, 1991, p. 104)

Justification for metaphoric use of the term "community" in the research literature stems from two fundamental approaches to research in CMC. One approach looks at discourse processes, another at social structures, and both seek cyberspace analogues to "real life" processes and structures. Discourse processes include the development of distinctive referent language, the virtual equivalent of jargon, such as "flaming" and "chat" (MacKinnon, 1992; E. Reid, 1991), "emote" and "mudding" (Carlstrom, 1992); truncated speech, the use of acronyms in place of common phrases (e.g., IMHO for "in my humble opinion"), and other electronic paralanguage (Carey, 1980); the use of "emoticons," such as ASCII-character smiley faces and other text-rendered non-verbal surrogates (Asteroff, 1987; Blackman & Clevenger, 1990; Danet & Reudenberg, 1992; Sherblom, 1990); face-saving mechanisms (Heimstra, 1982); and socioemotional content (McCormick & McCormick, 1992; Rice & Love, 1987; Smolensky, Carmody, & Halcomb, 1990; Thompsen, 1992a, 1992b; Walther, 1992; Walther & Burgoon, 1992).

Social structures include social and professional roles: for example, hackers, phreakers, and other "outlaws" (Barlow, 1990; Meyer & Thomas, 1990); moderators, sysops, chanops, and other "net police" (MacKinnon, 1992; E. Reid, 1991); sex roles (Herring, 1993; Kramarae & Taylor, 1993; Matheson, 1991); community boundary indicators, such as distinctive "neigborhood" addresses and domains, and "cultural" differences among communicative systems on the "net" (Serpentelli, 1992); rituals, such as weddings and funerals (Rheingold, 1993a); commitment to communal goals, such as development and maintenance of resources (Smith, 1992); and rules, norms, and community standards, such as "netiquette" (Spafford, 1993a, 1993c, 1993d; Taylor, 1993; Von Rospach, 1993).

Our approach in this chapter is to assume, a priori, the existence of analogic processes and structures in CMC. That said, we can also assume that virtual processes and structures function like their real-life counterparts. In brief, discourse processes generate social structures, which in turn affect discourse processes (Berger & Luckmann, 1967). A study of process yields evidence of the underlying structure (Toles-Patkin, 1986).

To be sure, there is evidence of community in Usenet (albeit community enacted on a public stage, with a substantial silent majority of onlookers). In no respect is this more apparent than in the discursive working out of community standards of behavior. There is no central authority to which activity on Usenet is subject (Spafford, 1993e); the existence and the character of newsgroups are shaped jointly by the decisions of individual site administrators, a widely disseminated set of rules for conduct (netiquette) (Spafford, 1993a, 1993c, 1993d; Taylor, 1993; Von Rospach, 1993), a set of guidelines for newsgroup creation, and the expectations of users. Examination of the on-line interactive management of conduct, as it emerges in patterns of posts and replies, has allowed us to formulate a preliminary account of Usenet community standards.

Any cursory reading of newsgroup postings will suggest, first, that conduct-correcting episodes are commonplace, reflecting the self-regulating nature of the network; further, that the type of conduct subject to remediating discourse ranges widely, from relatively innocuous errors in the use of news-reader software to actions characterized as "net terrorism"; and finally, that the sanctions invoked against such conduct also vary widely, from mildly admonitory private e-mail to active campaigns to deprive offenders of their net access. Using the notion of a reproach, as established in the literature on accounts and explanations (Cody & McLaughlin, 1990; McLaughlin, Cody, & Read, 1992), we make a preliminary approach to the questions of standards by looking at what is not allowed and present here a taxonomy of reproach-able conduct on Usenet. That is, we attempt to classify conduct sufficiently in violation of normative expectations that it prompts overt comment and sets discursive remedial sequences in motion.

A Taxonomy of Reproachable Conduct on Usenet

All articles posted to five newsgroups—comp.sys.ibm.pc.games (including comp.sys.ibm.pc.games.action, comp.sys.ibm.pc.games.adventure, comp.sys.ibm.pc.games.flight-simulator, comp.sys.ibm.pc.games.misc., comp.sys.ibm.pc.games.rpg, and comp.sys.ibm.pc.games.strategic); rec.sport.hockey; soc.motss; rec.arts.tv.soaps; and soc.singles—during the period May 17-June 7, 1993 were saved and analyzed for episodes of normative discourse: remedial or corrective sequences generated by an unacceptable post/reply or habitual pattern of the same. The groups selected were chosen for their wide propagation, popularity, heavy traffic volume, and low percentage of cross-posting. B. Reid's (1993c) readership summary for the immediately preceding month was consulted to select newsgroups that (a) had more than 25,000 estimated readers, (b) were received by at least 70% of surveyed sites, (c) had a traffic rate of at least 4,000 kilobytes per month, and (d) had cross-posting percentages at or near zero. With respect to the latter, we assumed that newsgroup identification and cohesiveness would vary inversely with the proportion of messages posted simultaneously to other groups. Readership data from January, February, and May of 1993 confirmed that the five groups had consistent patterns with respect to popularity, propagation, traffic volume, and cross-posting, although the soc.motss group had episodic spurts of cross-posting in the 15% range (B. Reid, 1993a, 1993b, 1993d). Data from UUNET Communications (1993) for the sampled period confirmed the readership and traffic standings of three of the five groups: soc.motss, rec. arts.tv. soaps, and comp.sys.ibm.pc.games.

Corrective episodes selected for analysis from postings to the five groups during the 3-week period made up a 3.09 megabyte message corpus, accounting for approximately 15% of all message traffic during the interval. Across the five groups, reproaches for conduct were leveled at 272 individuals. Many of these persons were reproached for more than one impropriety, and several were reproached in more than one newsgroup. We note that not all of the examples will apply in all newsgroups, and in fact we observed many cases where the putative offenses were committed without drawing comment. Also, that which gives offense in one newsgroup will be regarded as unremarkable in another (for instance, "for sale" announcements are welcomed in some quarters and treated with disdain in others). Further, those who issue reproaches may find themselves taken to task for nit-picking, bullying newcomers, or generalized nastiness.

Our analysis of the message corpus, supplemented by the widely posted "required reading" on netiquette (Spafford, 1993a, 1993c, 1993d; Taylor, 1993; Von Rospach, 1993) led to a seven-category account of Usenet offenses (see Table 5.1). Exemplars of reproaches in six of the seven categories are presented below with the permission of their authors. (Ethical considerations of our own obliged us to exclude specific examples of violations of community ethics standards.) Where included, text from the offending poster is indicated with an arrow (>) at the beginning of each line. Two arrows (> >) indicate an embedded quotation.

Category 1: Incorrect/Novice Use of Technology

Reproaches are given for making an apparent error or demonstrating lack of sophistication in the use of newsreaders, such as posting a message with a header identifying the author and origin of the message but with no lines (content) or inadvertently sending private e-mail to the newsgroup. For instance, a poster apparently having difficulty with the newsreader reply function posted a message containing a full header, quoting the entire lengthy text of a previous poster's message, but with no message lines of his own. Correctly using the same reply function, which conventionally begins "In a

Table 5.1 A Taxonomy of Reproachable Conduct on Usenet

1. Incorrect/novice use of technology
Message with header but no lines
Double signature
Confusing the "reply privately" and "reply to group" options
Confusing original and follow-on posts
Failing to use follow-on option (Re:)
Posting multiple copies of same article to group
Follow-on editing errors
Attributing quotes incorrectly
Word wrap errors
2. Bandwidth waste
Excessively long signatures (> 4 lines), particularly if attributable to product promotions, elaborate graphics
Multiple e-mail addresses
Surface mail address, telephone numbers
Selecting default (world) distribution for tests, "for sale," etc.
Quoted material longer than original in follow-on
Concatenating rather than summarizing private e-mail (surveys, polls, answers)
Posting answers to questions, rather than using private e-mail
Posting questions answers to which are readily available off-line
Posting a question which is covered in the FAQ
Posting "me too" follow-ons rather than private e-mail to poster
Debating a previous post point-by-point with quoted text
Indiscriminate cross-posting
Posting excessively long articles
3. Violation of networkwide conventions
Failing to encrypt offensive materials
Changing the subject line without apparent reason
Posting bulletins about major news events
Posting sensitive material more suitable for private e-mail
Failing to include a signature
Posting commercial announcements
Inappropriate subject line
Demonstrating lack of familiarity with recent threads; lack of regular reading
Failing to include text to which one refers in a follow-on
Reproaching others for minor violations (e.g., typos, spelling errors)
4. Violation of newsgroup-specific conventions
Failing to use "spoiler" warning for game solutions, TV/movie plots
Failing to observe group conventions for subject lines, abbreviations, etc.
Failing to observe group traditions as to appropriate message topics
Failing to conform to the group spirit or style
5. Ethical violations
Reposting/forwarding private e-mail without permission
Posting personal information about others (phone number, sexual orientation, etc.)
"Creative" editing of others' quoted posts
Playing pranks; intentional disruption
Failure to cite sources where appropriate

(*continued*)

Table 5.1 Continued

Harassment of individual posters
Posting "how to" articles on illegal activities
6. Inappropriate language
Flaming (except where encouraged, e.g., alt.flame)
Coarse or vulgar language
Personal attacks and insults
Ridicule
Hostile, intense language
Made-up or fey language (affecting a dialect or linguistic peculiarity)
7. Factual errors
Mistakes with respect to names, dates, places
Errors in summarizing others' posts
Spelling errors and/or typos

previous article, <postername> said:", one of the regulars posted this pointed reproach:

*In a previous article, <postername@ *************) says:*
Absolutely nothing.

Category 2: Bandwidth Waste

Reproaches are given for consuming more than one's fair share of network resources, such as unnecessarily increasing the costs of transport and storage of Usenet messages by indiscriminate cross-posting of the same message, failing to edit judiciously, or posting questions the answers to which are readily available elsewhere:

(1) *>[I'll go ahead and use the United States Senate, >Washington, DC 20515 until I get something more specific]*

This will probably work. But you can get the exact addresses in many ways:

— check in the phone book for their local offices, and call there. Many Senators have local offices in many cities in their states.

— call the League of Women Voters and ask.

— many (most) public libraries have directories of public officials and can give you the information over the phone

— there may be a "government" section in the white pages of your phone directory that lists the addresses

I'm not posting this to dump on you, <postername>. But lots of times people post requests for information to the net, when there are easy ways to get it locally.

(2) *Hey, <postername>, if you're going to post followups, perhaps you could "trim down the included article", as they say. At least delete the headers. It's common netiquette.*

(3) *nice signature, mind chopping it down a bit, bandwith costs some people money, which you wantonly waste with a signature which excedes your actual article.*

Category 3: Violation of Networkwide Conventions

Reproaches are given for not observing conventions common to all or most Usenet groups, such as neglecting to include a signature, failing to encrypt offensive materials, using an inappropriate subject line, failing to include text of a previous message to which one refers, or failing to follow the group discussion for a period of time before posting:

[question] >*Could someone out there settle a debate brewing in our*
>*department? We'd be interested to know the origins of the*
>*Montreal Canadiens nick-name the "Habs"? Where does the*
>*term originally come from, and what exactly does it refer*
>*to?*

[reply] *Myth #1: People read the FAQ before posting to a news group.*

Myth #2: People follow a news group for a period of a month before posting to that newsgroup.

If the poster had done either of these two, the answer would be there. Anyway, HABS is short for Habitants, which means inhabitant. The exact reason for this was the subject of some debate and I urge you look at articles posted last week to see what all the fuss is about.

Category 4: Violation of Newsgroup-Specific Conventions

Reproaches are given for demonstrating a lack of awareness of the practices of a specific newsgroup, such as failing to post a "spoiler" warning in the subject heading of a message in which a soap opera development will be revealed or posting a personal ad in a group devoted to discussion and debate about being single:

>*Hi, I'm a 23 year old graduate student and would like to* >*communicate with any females on this news net.*
>——*(Posted for a non-net friend)*——————————

Well, howdy! Finally, a request for a female that doesn't specify species — you wouldn't believe how many people on this net want a woman, which of course means a person.
giggle

*My name is Susa, and I'm a five-year old Lemur in the Philly Zoo. My measurements are 12-12-12, which is considered quite sexy for a lemur *giggle* we all fail the pencil test *giggle**
My hobbies include running around, climbing trees, and picking lice; I hope you have a nice thick head of hair!

*I only write to stupid people who post personals on soc.singles; the other ones are too smart for me — we lemurs may be very _cuddly *giggle* but we tend to be on the low end of the smarts scale. I know that with that post, you'll be really _dumb for a human, and perfect for me! *giggle**

Peter D. Smith

Category 5: Ethical Violation

Reproaches are given for perpetrating actions that violate the rights of individuals or have the potential to cause serious damage and disruption, such as posting someone else's telephone number/or address, forwarding private e-mail to the net, or playing pranks.

Category 6: Inappropriate Language

Reproaches are given for using language that is inflammatory—for example, it is demeaning, insulting, or sexist— or that in other ways is inconsistent with newsgroup standards—for example, it is imprecise, pretentious, or excessively whimsical:

In article < *****************************,
************************** writes:
> ** wrote:
> ->.... Look for me!!!!!
> you'll be the one in the dunce cap.
Soc.motss.nasty is back.

Category 7: Errors

Reproaches are given for posting messages that are demonstrably or patently incorrect in some regard—for example, contain spelling or typing errors or mistakes having to do with names, dates, or places:

*************************************** *writes:*
>MotssTangent: Saw >
<postername> at the symphony last night
>(final subscriber performance of the season, Bernstein and
>Motzart's Ninth - Full choir, including a Japenese [sic] choir from
>our sister city plus four soloists!) and explained the
>comparison to the muffin. He was flattered, but more than
>that, I think he was proud. Go figure.

BEETHOVEN, <postername>. It was BEETHOVEN's Ninth. Weren't you paying attention? Are there distractions up there in the balcony where you sit? Is that where they keep all the cute guys? There are none to see from my seat on the orchestra level.

Origins of Usenet Standards of Conduct

Although the presence of a set of standards for conduct might be construed as prima facie evidence for the existence of on-line communities, it is instructive first to consider an apparent paradox: that the medium through which the network of (virtual) relationships is constructed and made manifest is, by all accounts, particularly ill-suited for such a purpose. Rice (1993), in commenting on two complementary theoretic orientations in comparative media studies, social presence (Short, Williams, & Christie, 1976) and media richness (Daft & Lengel, 1986; Trevino, Lengel, Gerloff, & Muir, 1990; Trevino & Webster, 1992), notes that they share the fundamental assumption that effective use of a medium requires a good fit between its inherent characteristics and the communication activities it will be used to accomplish. Rice's (1993) reanalysis of data from six prior studies indicates that whereas electronic text-based messaging is generally regarded as appropriate for exchanging information, asking questions, or "staying in touch," this basic component of the Usenet news network regularly ranks at the bottom of the list of possible media choices with respect to most aspects of socioemotional relations. This effect is apparently attributable to the inability of the medium, in its current text-based incarnation, to convey the communicators' material presence and to reduce ambiguities.

Although some might argue that the net is well suited for organizing distributed communities of persons with specialized common interests, say, for example, the economies of the Caribbean Basin region, one is hard-pressed to accept that a worldwide, asynchronous, text-based bulletin board network is an ideal medium for singles or sports fans to develop meaningful interpersonal ties. Leaving for another time the argument that, in fact, communications media do not have inherent but only construed characteristics

(Fulk, Schmitz, & Steinfield, 1990) and the suspicion that, in fact, net users are attracted to the medium precisely because of its ambiguities, it is demonstrably the case that Usenet is regarded by at least the most vocal of its participants as a network of communities. Further, it is clear that its creative users have found strategies to mold the medium to suit their purposes. These strategies give Usenet rules for conduct a unique character that can best be apprehended as an overlay on a basic set of shared understandings about cooperative endeavor in human communities.

The discursively constructed nature of Usenet standards for conduct suggests that the "community" metaphor must be applied to these newsgroups with caution and that absolute adherence to the metaphor, in its face-to-face conceptualization, would be problematic. Clearly, there are similarities between the standards and structures of the evolving "communities" of the Usenet newsgroups and those of face-to-face communities. Some of those similarities are integral to this analysis. However, there are peculiarities of the newsgroup memberships that challenge the traditional understanding of "community." Particularly problematic is identifying a group's membership. In most of the Usenet groups, there is an enclave of frequent posters (Rheingold, 1993b). These posters often address each other in their public messages or refer to real-world meetings or the exchange of private e-mail. Readers (and scholars) may be confused as to whether these posters are a clique within the community or constitute the community itself. New contributors who address their messages to these frequent posters, sometimes expressing considerable trepidation in doing so, may experience a wide range of response: The frequent posters may issue a warm welcome, a rebuff, or ignore the newcomer altogether, in effect granting themselves something of an executive privilege or power with respect to entry into the community.

An interesting example of the fuzziness of a newsgroup's community membership occurred in a thread in which the original poster was ultimately classified as a "guest" in the newsgroup, even an "uninvited guest." Although "guest membership" was not overtly defined by the poster's detractors, interpretation of the thread reveals that "guest" membership was conferred when the rest of the thread participants found this poster's messages annoying. In this interaction, "guest membership" was a euphemism for a warning of imminent exclusion. In some groups, participation alone does not grant community membership.

Another peculiarity of the net newsgroups is the silent participation of the lurkers, or readers who do not post messages. The newsgroups themselves appear to be divided on the membership status of these lurkers. For instance, a poster who questioned what the vast readership would make of a particular thread was met with a number of replies discounting the membership status of anyone not actively engaged in the discussions. On the other hand, some posters clearly consider the silent readers in constructing their posts and in evaluating others': It is not uncommon to see appeals to flame-warring factions to "stop scaring the lurkers:"

> *As soc.motss seems to be descending into one of our periodic bouts of petty squabbling, we would like to remind the frequent posters here that what we say is going out to a potential readership of between 25,000 and 40,000 individuals. It is very easy to forget that there are a lot of people who read soc.motss but do not post; some choose not to, whereas others are restricted to "read only" accounts. Also, there are many people, ourselves included, for whom soc.motss is our main connection with the lbg world. So words do have meaning and what you write in haste or in anger may have more influence than you realize.*

(Of course, one could argue that lurker-conscious posters reflect not an inclusive view of the community membership but, rather, an alternative conceptualization of Usenet as a magazine or publication medium; that, however, is an argument our data do not currently allow us to resolve.)

Whatever determination we might make about the size and shape of the Usenet newsgroups as communities, it is apparent that the community to which these discussions apply is amorphous and possibly ephemeral. In addition to the lack of consensus over the degree and nature of participation as it applies to membership, we must also consider both the rapid growth rate of Usenet and the turnover patterns that co-vary with the academic calendar. In short, the newsgroup communities undergo a process of continuous membership evolution having few real counterparts in the life cycles of face-to-face communities.

One way to understand the forces that shape conduct in Usenet communities is to look at the network as subject to a set of external forces or constraints, both technological and pragmatic. Let us consider the pragmatic forces first. Some few of those who post to Usenet do so through bulletin boards or commercial on-line services to which they subscribe (and to which they pay a fee). Such persons are keenly aware that long hours spent cruising the net can be expensive. Most persons who currently take advantage of interactive access to Usenet do so at the pleasure of their employers or university administrators; consequently, always gnawing at the edge of the user's awareness is the knowledge that what is given can be taken away. Internet users generally have a notion that the access they enjoy is costly; further, many have heard talk that the forthcoming privatization of the network will increase costs to subscribers who may have been able to afford access only because of the current level of federal subsidy (DeLoughry, 1993a, 1993b;

Wilson, 1993b). Posters who rely on their employers' access to Usenet are constrained by lunch hours or lurking supervisors. Because the meter is running for these posters, bandwidth waste takes a personal toll. Sensitivity to the costs involved in transporting and storing Usenet messages seems to be the primary factor behind the habitual calls for conserving bandwidth. Although the avoidance of prolixity and redundancy are fundamental tenets of conversational interaction (see, e.g., Grice, 1975, on the "Quantity" maxim), concerns about preserving access for all (as well as conserving one's own disk space) undoubtedly drive much of the concern over bandwidth piggery.

Even more fundamental than preserving the affordability of Usenet access is maintaining its desirability in the eyes of those who pay for it. Users are aware of negative images of computer networks in the eyes of the public (and of some university and corporation executives): that it is the playground of adolescent malcontents and pranksters, that it caters to those with bizarre sexual preferences, that it is not a secure mode for the transport of proprietary information, and so on. One can interpret the proscriptions against flaming, prank playing, unauthorized forwarding of e-mail, unencrypted dirty jokes, and the like as high-tech variations of conversational "rules" as described in speech act theory (see, e.g., Grice, 1975, on the "Quality" maxim; Bach & Harnish, 1979, on the "Politeness" and "Morality" maxims), and to the extent that these rules represent standards for cooperative discourse in the larger community they are the generative mechanisms for Usenet standards of conduct. However, practical concerns for maintaining a profile of the network suitable for external consumption appear to give the rules their peculiar shape and force.

Bandwidth waste and language use violations can cause a newsgroup to self-destruct. A group plagued by excessively long articles, frequent postings of similar questions, or repetitious quotations can lose its capacity to interest its members and activity may diminish. Newsgroups with low levels of participation might see their propagation rates go down as individual site administrators decide to drop them. Language use violations can impact newsgroups similarly. Readers' or posters' weariness with flame wars may be reflected in declining traffic and readership statistics. Similarly, repeated ethical violations could result in a decline in propagation, and it is no great leap to speculate that certain kinds of misconduct could have legal consequences for posters, as well as transmitters, of offending messages (Turner, 1990; Wilson, 1993a).

A third factor that shapes the rules for conduct on Usenet is the nature of the technology, both with respect to electronic messaging generally and with regard to the newsreader software in particular. Although the examples of such influence are numerous, we restrict ourselves to two. First, in accounting for the relative frequency of flaming in net conversations, Fleck (1991) made causal attributions to two peculiar characteristics of the e-mail-based media generally: first, that the technology makes it easy to reply, and that one often does so in order to clear off the (virtual) desktop; and second, that feedback to posts can be slow, so that it may take some time for ambiguities or misunderstandings to be resolved:

> [An] analogy would be to suppose that the main linguistics journals had an instant reply service. That is, as you finish reading the latest spectacularly irritating article by [name your favorite bête noire], you could scribble down your thoughts and have them appear instantly in print, without editorial review. In real conversations, these problems are usually avoided by asking frequent questions. In journals, they are avoided by honing the prose into something that is difficult to misunderstand. (Fleck, 1991)

Beyond the distress it causes to individual recipients of inflammatory language, flaming has a peculiarly contagious quality in network newsgroups; one flame often generates a host of bandwagon insults, again, because it is easy to "follow on." As a series of posters join forces to belabor the original target (and, often, as a second clique forms in the target's defense), the degree of hostility expressed in the messages can escalate to the point that someone calls for someone else's expulsion from the community via an electronic cold shoulder or "kill file" (electronically blocking her or his messages) or by suggesting that someone's system administrator should deprive him or her of net access. It is not uncommon during such episodes to see voices of calm emerge as well as sharper reproaches to flame throwers. Just as the technology encourages flaming, so too does it encourage calls for restraint.

The availability of advanced software for reading the news creates an additional set of constraints on behavior. Virtual communities of interest can form only if everyone adheres to a common set of guidelines for organizing the millions of posted messages into a coherent set of groups, subgroups, and topics. Although some of the scorn directed at "newbies" who make errors in the use of the newsreaders may be attributable to the prevailing elitist sentiment on the net (see Sitkin, Sutcliffe, & Barrios-Choplin, 1992, on the symbol-carrying capacity of the new media), the requirements for technological competence are driven primarily by the need to bring order to chaos while simultaneously minimizing the costs of transport and storage. One of the most important features of the sophisticated netnews readers, for instance, is that they are able to present the reader with a menulike interface in which the various posts are organized into coherent threads. A message will be classified as part of an existing thread if the poster has correctly used the reply function and has a subject heading that indicates that the message is a follow-on. These subject headings are used not only to organize the threads but are widely employed to search the Usenet message corpus for topics of particular interest. In this latter regard, correct use of the technology saves time and bandwidth for everyone as well as assuring that messages find their proper audience.

Beyond the constraints imposed by the technology, the need to control costs, and other external factors, there are social-structural factors that favor users honoring established Usenet conventions and newsgroup idiosyncracies. By failing to adhere to the traditions of appropriate topic introduction—for instance, posting personal ads to the discussion-oriented newsgroup soc.singles—posters could threaten the identity of the newsgroup as a distinct virtual community. More to the point, the interests of the regular posters (or those who "got there first," the squatters of the virtual community) are threatened. FAQs are prepared, periodically posted, and promoted by the regulars not only to prevent posting the same questions again and again but also to serve as a sort of articles of incorporation cum statement of purpose in which the group style and spirit are explicitly spelled out and newcomers are socialized into the group ways. Admonishing offenders who stray from the specific newsgroup's norms is clearly an attempt to preserve the integrity of that community's raison d'être. For example, individuals who post unannounced "spoilers" (game solutions or upcoming story lines) can rob the community members of the guessing and anticipation that attracts discussion and thereby the foundation for the community. As newsgroups are discussion forums for particular topics and newsgroup communities are founded on a common interest in those topics, any impediment to discussion of the community's topic or any attempt to alter the norms that preserve such discussion are necessarily threats to the community itself, as it is constituted for the interests of the regular posters.

Usenet-wide conventions about appropriate content can be enforced with an equal degree of fervor. In the current configuration, Usenet discussion groups are not generally considered the appropriate place to post bulletins about breaking news events or product announcements, although there are certain groups where such posts are allowed. One of the most interesting examples of violent reaction to Usenet norm violations occurs when someone posts a blatantly commercial advertisement to a noncommercial newsgroup. Usenet was designed to provide discussion forums, and some newsgroup communities are outraged when their territory is invaded by profiteers. Although, as Rheingold (1993b) points out, no net.police will arrive to arrest the commercial poster, newsgroup members often respond to advertisers by calling upon fellow group members to boycott the advertiser in an effort to protect the integrity of the net. The high degree of intolerance for commercial postings indicates that if Usenet were to become exploited as a marketing arena the character of the net would be so drastically altered that it might lose its appeal entirely.

The rules of conduct on Usenet as currently constituted can be understood as a complex set of guidelines driven by economic, cultural, social-psychological, and discursive factors both within and outside the network. As CMC continues to evolve, and as particular applications of network communications undergo technological transformations, the use of the "community" metaphor in characterizing network discussion forums may prove to be only a starting point in analysis, and new and more appropriate concepts may emerge as a way of understanding this exciting frontier of communication.

References

Print Sources

Arick, M. R. (1993). *The TCP/IP companion: A guide for the common user.* Boston: QED Publishing Group.

Asteroff, J. F. (1987). *Paralanguage in electronic mail: A case study.* Unpublished doctoral dissertation, Columbia University, New York.

Bach, K., & Harnish, R. M. (1979). *Linguistic communication and speech acts.* Cambridge: MIT Press.

Baym, N. (1992, November). *Computer-mediated soaptalk: Communication, community and entertainment on the net.* Paper presented at the annual meeting of the Speech Communication Association, Chicago.

Beniger, J. (1987). Personalization of mass media and the growth of pseudo-community. *Communication Research, 14,* 352-371.

Berger, P., & Luckmann, T. (1967). *The social construction of reality.* Garden City, NY: Anchor.

Blackman, B. I., & Clevenger, T., Jr. (1990, June). *On-line computer messaging: Surrogates for nonverbal behavior.* Paper presented at the annual meeting of the International Communication Association, Dublin.

Carey, J. (1980). *Paralanguage in computer-mediated communication.* Proceedings of the 18th Annual Meeting of the Association for Computational Linguistics, Philadelphia.

Carley, K., & Wendt, K. (1991). Electronic mail and scientific communication: A study of the Soar extended research group. *Knowledge: Creation, Diffusion, Utilization, 12,* 406-440.

Cody, M. J., & McLaughlin, M. L. (Eds.). (1990). *The psychology of tactical communication.* Clevedon and Philadelphia: Multilingual Matters Ltd.

Curtis, P. (1992). Mudding: Social phenomena in text-based virtual realities. *Intertek, 3,* 26-34.

Daft, R. L., & Lengel, R. H. (1986). Organizational information requirements, media richness, and structural design. *Management Science, 32,* 554-571.

Danet, B., & Ruedenberg, L. (1992, October). *"Smiley" icons: Keyboard kitsch or new communication code?* Paper presented at the annual meeting of the American Folklore Society, Jacksonville, FL.

DeLoughry, T. (1993a, May 19). NSF plans for the future of the Internet. *Chronicle of Higher Education,* p. A17.

DeLoughry, T. (1993b, June 23). A "meeting of minds" on Internet's future. *Chronicle of Higher Education,* p. A15.

Flanigan, J. (1993, September 2). Murdoch set to buy Delphi Data Services. *Los Angeles Times,* pp. D1, D3.

Frederick, H. H. (1993). Computer networks and the emergence of global civil society: The case of the Association for Progressive Communication (APC). In L. M. Harasim (Ed.), *Global networks: Computers and international communication* (pp. 283-295). Cambridge: MIT Press.

Fulk, J., Schmitz, J., & Steinfield, C. (1990). A social influence model of technology use. In J. Fulk & C. Steinfield (Eds.), *Organizations and communication technology* (pp. 117-140). Newbury Park, CA: Sage.

Grice, H. P. (1975). Logic and conversation. In P. Cole & J. Morgan (Eds.), *Syntax and semantics: Vol. 3. Speech acts.* New York: Academic Press.

Harasim, L. M. (Ed.). (1993a). *Global networks: Computers and international communication.* Cambridge: MIT Press.

Harasim, L. M. (1993b). Networlds: Networks as social space. In L. M. Harasim (Ed.), *Global networks: Computers and international communication* (pp. 15-34). Cambridge: MIT Press.

Hardie, E.T.L., & Neou, V. (1993). *Internet: Mailing lists.* Englewood Cliffs, NJ: PTR Prentice Hall.

Heimstra, G. (1982). Teleconferencing, concern for face, and organizational culture. In M. Burgoon & N. E. Doran (Eds.), *Communication Yearbook 6* (pp. 874-904). Beverly Hills, CA: Sage.

Herz, J. C. (1993, September 30). Internet addiction launching Generation X into cyberspace. *San Diego Union-Tribune,* p. E5.

Kramerae, C., & Taylor, H. J. (1993). Women and men on electronic networks: A conversation or a monologue? In H. J. Taylor, C. Kramerae, & M. Ebben (Eds.), *Women, information technology, and scholarship* (pp. 52-61). Urbana: University of Illinois Center for Advanced Study.

Krol, E. (1992). *The whole Internet: User's guide and catalog.* Sebastapol, CA: O'Reilly & Associates.

LaQuey, T., with Ryer, J. C. (1993). *The Internet companion: A beginner's guide to global networking.* Reading, MA: Addison-Wesley.

Lazzareschi, C. (1993a, August 22). Wired: Businesses create cyberspace land rush on the Internet. *Los Angeles Times,* pp. D1-D2, D4.

Lazzareschi, C. (1993b, August 25). Cable firm to offer Internet data network to subscribers. *Los Angeles Times,* pp. D1-D2.

MacKinnon, R. C. (1992). *Searching for the Leviathan in Usenet.* Unpublished master's thesis, San Jose State University.

Matheson, K. (1991). Social cues in computer-mediated negotiations: Gender makes a difference. *Computers in Human Behavior, 7,* 137-147.

McCormick, N. B., & McCormick, J. W. (1992). Computer friends and foes: Contents of undergraduates' electronic mail. *Computers in Human Behavior, 8,* 379-405.

McLaughlin, M. L., Cody, M. J., & Read, S. J. (Eds.). (1992). *Explaining one's self to others: Reason-giving in a social context.* Hillsdale, NJ: Lawrence Erlbaum.

O'Reilly, T., & Todino, G. (1992). *Managing UUCP and Usenet* (10th ed.). Sebastapol, CA: O'Reilly & Associates.

Penkoff, D. (in press). Sex in cyberspace: Why people engage in risky CMC. In M. L. McLaughlin & L. C. Miller (Eds.), *Intimate decisions: Accounting for risk-taking in sexual behavior and courtship.* Newbury Park, CA: Sage.

Peck, M. S. (1987). *The different drum: Community-making and peace.* New York: Touchstone.

Rafaeli, S. R., Sudweeks, F., & McLaughlin, M. L. (Eds.). (in press). *Network and net-play: Virtual groups on the Internet.* AAAI/MIT Press.

Reid, E. (1991). *Electropolis: Communication and community on Internet Relay Chat.* Unpublished bachelor's honors thesis, Department of History, University of Melbourne, Australia.

Rheingold, H. (1993a). A slice of life in my virtual community. In L. M. Harasim (Ed.), *Global networks: Computers and international communication* (pp. 57-80). Cambridge: MIT Press. Also available by anonymous ftp to ftp. eff.org from directory /pub/EFF/papers/cyber.

Rheingold, H. (1993b). *The virtual community: Homesteading on the electronic frontier.* Reading, MA: Addison-Wesley.

Rice, R. E. (1993). Media appropriateness: Using social presence theory to compare traditional and new organizational media. *Human Communication Research, 19,* 451-484.

Rice, R. E., & Love, G. (1987). Electronic emotion: Socioemotional content in a computer-mediated communication network. *Communication Research, 14,* 85-108.

Sherblom, J. C. (1990). Organizational involvement expressed through pronoun use in computer mediated communication. *Communication Research Reports, 7,* 45-50.

Short, J., Williams, E., & Christie, B. (1976). *The social psychology of telecommunications.* London: Wiley.

Sitkin, S. B., Sutcliffe, K. M., & Barrios-Choplin, J. R. (1992). A dual-capacity model of communication media choice in organizations. *Human Communication Research, 18,* 563-598.

Smith, M. A. (1992). *Voices from the WELL: The logic of the virtual commons.* Unpublished master's thesis, Department of Sociology, University of California, Los Angeles.

Smolensky, M. W., Carmody, M. A., & Halcomb, C. G. (1990). The influence of task type, group structure and extraversion on uninhibited speech on computer-mediated communication. *Computers in Human Behavior, 6,* 261-272.

Sproull, L., & Kiesler, S. (1991). *Connections: New ways of working in the networked organization.* Cambridge: MIT Press.

Stone, A. R. (1991). Will the real body please stand up? In M. Benedikt (Ed.), *Cyberspace: First steps* (pp. 81-118). Cambridge: MIT Press.

Thompsen, P. A. (1992a, November). *An episode of flaming: A creative narrative.* Paper presented at the annual meeting of the Speech Communication Association, Chicago.

Thompsen, P. A. (1992b, February). *A social influence model of flaming in computer-mediated communication.* Paper presented at the annual meeting of the Western States Communication Association, Portland.

Toles-Patkin, T. (1986). Rational coordination in the Dungeon. *Journal of Popular Culture, 20,* 1-14.

Trevino, L. K., Lengel, R. H., Gerloff, E. A., & Muir, N. K. (1990). The richness imperative and cognitive styles: The role of individual differences in media choice behavior. *Management Communication Quarterly, 4,* 176-197.

Trevino, L. K., & Webster, J. (1992). Flow in computer-mediated communication: Electronic mail and voice mail evaluation and impacts. *Communication Research, 19,* 539-574.

Turner, J. A. (1990, January 24). Messages in questionable taste on computer networks pose thorny problems for college administrators. *Chronicle of Higher Education,* pp. A13-A14.

Walther, J. B. (1992). Interpersonal effects in computer-mediated interaction: A relational perspective. *Communication Research, 19,* 52-90.

Walther, J. B., & Burgoon, J. K. (1992). Relational communication in computer-mediated interaction. *Human Communication Research, 19,* 50-88.

Wilson, D. L. (1993a, May 12). Censoring electronic messages. *Chronicle of Higher Education,* p. A2.

Wilson, D. L. (1993b, September 1). Bitnet struggles to survive. *Chronicle of Higher Education,* p. A23.

On-Line Sources

Barlow, J. P. (1990). *Crime and puzzlement.* Electronic manuscript. Available by anonymous ftp to ftp.eff.org from directory pub/cud/papers. Also published in *Whole Earth Review,* Fall, 1990, 45-57.

Carlstrom, E. (1992). *The communicative implications of a text-only virtual environment.* Electronic manuscript. Available via anonymous ftp to parcftp.xerox.com from directory pub/MOO/papers.

December, J. (1993, August 28). *Information sources: The Internet and computer-mediated communication.* Available by anonymous ftp to ftp.rpi.edu from directory /pub/communications.

Electronic Frontier Foundation. (1993). *Big dummy's guide to the Internet.* Available by anonymous ftp to ftp.eff.org from directory /pub/EFF/papers.

Fleck, M. (1991, June 14). *Flaming.* LINGUIST Discussion List. 41153.AA25273@mcsun.EU, net. From the document /archives/Linguist/Vol-2-0200-0299.

Herring, S. C. (1993). Gender and democracy in computer-mediated communication. *Electronic Journal of Communication, 3.* Order from LISTSERV at RPITSVM.

Meyer, G., & Thomas, J. (1990). *The baudy world of the byte bandit: A postmodern interpretation of the computer underground.* Electronic manuscript. Available via anonymous ftp to ftp. eff.org from directory pub/cud/papers. Also published in F. Schalleger (Ed.). (1990). *Computers in criminal justice* (pp. 31-67). Bristol, IN: Wyndham Hall.

Reid, B. (1993a, February). *Usenet readership summary report for January 93.* Personal communication.

Reid, B. (1993b, March). *Usenet readership summary report for February 93.* Personal communication.

Reid, B. (1993c, April 7). *Usenet readership summary report for March 93.* Usenet newsgroups news.groups, news.lists, news.admin.misc. ptj0d$2h1@usenet.pa.dec.com.

Reid, B. (1993d, June2). *Usenet readership summary report for May 93.* Usenet newsgroups news.groups, news.lists, news.admin.misc. uibjb$8de@usenet.pa.dec.com.

Serpentelli, J. (1992). *Conversational structure and personality correlates of electronic communication.* Electronic manuscript. Available via ftp: parcftp.xerox.com:pub/MOO/papers.

Spafford, G. (1993a, April 25). *Rules for posting to Usenet.* USENET newsgroups news.announce.newusers, news.answers. <spaf-rules_735800472@cs.purdue.edu>. Available by anonymous ftp to rtfm.mit.edu from directory /pub/usenet/news.answers/posting-rules.

Spafford, G. (1993b, April 26). *Answers to frequently asked questions about Usenet.* USENET newsgroups news.announce.newusers, news.answers. <spaf-questions_728545554@cs. purdue. edu>. Available via anonymous ftp to rtfm.mit.edu from directory /pub/usenet/news.answers/usenet-faq.

Spafford, G. (1993c, April 26). *Emily Postnews answers your questions on netiquette.* USENET newsgroups news.announce.newusers, news.answers. <spaf-emily_728545564@cs.purdue. edu>. Available by anonymous ftp to rtfm.mit.edu from directory /pub/usenet/news.answers/emily-postnews.

Spafford, G. (1993d, April 26). *Hints on writing style for Usenet.* (original author A. Jeff Offutt VI). USENET newsgroups news.announce.newusers, news.answers. <spaf-style_ 735800508 @cs.purdue.edu>.

Spafford, G. (1993e, April 26). *What is Usenet?* USENET newsgroups news.announce.newusers, news.admin.misc., news.answers. <spaf-whatis_735800479@cs.purdue.edu>. Available by anonymous ftp to rtfm.mit.edu from directory /pub/usenet/news.answers/what-is-usenet.

Taylor, D. (1993, April 25). *A brief guide to social newsgroups and mailing lists.* USENET newsgroups news.announce.newusers, news.groups, news.answers. <spaf-social_735800549

@cs.purdue.edu>. Available by anonymous ftp to rtfm.mit.edu from directory /pub/usenet/news.answers/social-newsgroups.

UUNET Communications. (1993, May 9). *Top 25 news groups for the last two weeks.* USENET newsgroups news.lists.

Von Rospach, C. (1993, April 26). *A primer on how to work with the Usenet community.* USENET newsgroups news.announce.newusers, news.answers. <spaf-etiquette_735800490@cs.purdue.edu>. Available by anonymous ftp to rtfm.mit.edu from directory /pub/usenet/news.answers/usenet-primer.

Wohler, B. (1993, May 21). *NN frequently asked questions (FAQ) with answers.* USENET newsgroups news.software.nn, news.answers faq_737956805@GZA.COM. Posted monthly or e-mail to wohler@sap-ag.de.

6

SEARCHING FOR THE LEVIATHAN IN USENET

Richard C. MacKinnon

The purpose of this chapter is to identify signs of Thomas Hobbes's *Leviathan* in the Usenet computer conferencing network. Defined as "that mortal god, to which we owe under the immortal God; our peace and defence" (Hobbes, 1651/1962, p. 132[1]), Leviathan in a computer conferencing network is the institution of censorship or moderation of the messages written by the network's users. According to Hobbes, living in fear of death or wounds disposes men to obey a common power (p. 82). Certainly nothing that the Usenet users can experience can compare to the Hobbesian scenario in which persons are forced to give up the right to govern themselves in exchange for personal safety. This is certainly true on the surface, but there is another level of interaction within Usenet other than user-to-user. It is the level of the users' "personae," and it is at this level of understanding that the fear of vanishing from existence is ever present and near. For personae within Usenet, life can be described as "solitary, poor, nasty, brutish, and short" (p. 100). And it is for their sake that this researcher has searched for and found a Leviathan in Usenet.

To argue this work, this chapter is organized into short sections designed around major points. The first section introduces the reader to Hobbes, *Leviathan,* and Usenet. The argument itself consists of seven points and a survey of 200 randomly selected Usenet articles. The survey was conducted to find measurable signs of the Leviathan as described in the argument. The findings show the degree to which Leviathan is present in Usenet. Each section states its purpose in the opening paragraphs and is concluded with a summary of the points covered therein. In this way, it is possible to lead the reader through the theoretical worlds of *Leviathan* and the Usenet persona. At the end of the argument is a summary of all seven points, with a focus on the most difficult ones. The chapter concludes with a short discussion of future research considerations.

Hobbes, *Leviathan,* and Usenet

Hobbes's *Leviathan* was selected for this analysis primarily because it is a system of knowledge developed for the purpose of understanding the genesis of government. This system of knowledge for understanding the "matter, forme and power" of society, originally advanced during Cromwell's tenure, was published in 1651. The controversial title implied that the monarchy was the political manifestation of the Biblical beast and the work was considered scandalous.

Hobbes scholar Herbert Schneider explains that the choice of the title is curious because the mythological Leviathan is consistently the symbol of the "powers of evil" (Ross, Schneider, & Waldman, 1974, p. 86), rightfully upsetting the supporters of the Crown. Yet it is clear when Hobbes describes the Leviathan as the "mortal god" (p. 132) on earth that he does not share the common diabolical connotation. Certainly, Hobbes was aware of this discrepancy, and it is likely he intended for the discrepancy to further define his concept of a Leviathan rising from the people. It is possible that Hobbes selected the Leviathan symbol in part to convey that government is a necessary evil given humans' inclination to destroy one another without it.

Because his endeavor was intentionally comprehensive, Hobbes's treatise is unusually suitable for examining any and all societies—including those that did not exist in his time and, as in the case of Usenet, arguably do not exist now. This is possible because the treatise is presented mostly in general terms, giving it broad applicability and timelessness. While it is true that *Leviathan* is a product of troubled times, Hobbes's sparing references to Britain merely illustrate his points and do not confine them to that island. Additionally, his masterful understanding of philosophy beyond the realm of politics is useful in the establishment of personae and their virtual society of Usenet.

Despite its size, Usenet has no central authority that monitors access or content. All control, if any, is exercised at the site level. Sites determine whether to provide access to users or whether they want to provide a "feed" or connection to a potential site. Users and sites may remain on the net as long as the sites that provide them with access continue to do so.

Usenet articles are distributed using a "store and forward" method. This means that when a user writes an article, the original article is stored at his or her site and a copy is forwarded via telephone or leased line to neighboring sites. Because the associated costs of storage and forwarding can become very high, economics may have more of an impact over local control than anything else. A company, for example, may decide to restrict users from participating in any of the recreational newsgroups because the volume in those groups is high and their business value is low. Still, some organizations may opt to control content for other reasons. For example, a high school may decide to block participation in sexually-oriented newsgroups. However, thousands of users around the world enjoy unrestricted access to newsgroups containing articles from the technologically informative to the obscene. Depending on the user consulted, Usenet can be an anarchic or a highly regulated medium of communication.

Usenet as a Distinct Society

Before applying Hobbes's political philosophy to Usenet, it is important to establish the distinctness of the Usenet society. Distinctness assures that Usenet differs enough from the external world—the reality outside Usenet—to provide a unique laboratory to cultivate new insights and new conclusions. The argument for distinctness consists of Usenet's two-dimensional nature, its creation of an explicit language to describe its "physical" reality, its interference in the transfer of the social structure from the external world, and its ability to compensate for the lack of a complete social structure by developing a parallel or alternate structure to that of the external world.

Lacking physical reality, Usenet users must create an explicit, written language to convey meaning as well as emotion, physical qualities, and action. As a society based in language, it relies heavily on symbol, analogy, and metaphor to recreate or transfer physical matter and actions from the external world. But as these recreations are merely metaphors for, or "analogs" of, their physical counterparts, Usenet can never be a mirror image of the external world.

Usenet users are unable to "bring" with them their respective social structures because the limitations of written communication deconstruct their external world social structure. These social structures consist of the norms, mores, and traditions that guide the users' interaction as members of the external society. The computer medium inhibits computer users from transferring these social structures to Usenet. This inhibition resulting from the absence of, or limitations on, physical proximity, "face-to-face" interaction, and nonverbal cues is discussed and analyzed at length in Elizabeth Reid's (1991) *Electropolis: Communication and Community on Internet Relay Chat.* Reid exposes the failings of computer-mediated (i.e., written) communication as follows:

> Words, as we use them in speech, fail to express what they really mean once they are deprived of the subtleties of speech and the non-verbal cues that we assume will accompany it. . . . It is not only the meanings of sentences that become problematic in computer-mediated communication. The standards of behavior

> that are normally decided upon by verbal-cues are not clearly indicated when information is purely textual. (lines 495-505)

The deprivation of the "subtleties" is exactly what makes communication and interaction among Usenet users different from a room full of computer users. Computer users, as do all persons, learn standards of behavior from their respective social structures. As Reid suggests, these standards are reinforced by "subtleties of speech and non-verbal cues." But within Usenet, users limited to written communication are denied the full range of verbal and non-verbal cues customary to interpersonal communication and required for reinforcing behavioral standards. In the external world, behavioral standards dictate that one should not provoke a visibly angry man, but in Usenet the absence, or at least the distortion, of visible anger interferes with that standard of behavior.

Despite the limitations of a society based on written communication, Usenet users are able to compensate. The "interference" or distortion caused by the written medium forces Usenet users to confront what Reid calls the deconstruction of the "traditional methods for expressing community" by developing "alternate or parallel methods" (lines 200-206). In this way, Usenet has become an alternate or distinct society from the external world.

Usenet's parallel method or analog for conveying mores, norms, and traditions is known as "netiquette." As the term implies, it is literally "network etiquette" and it helps to reinforce the standards of behavior that users might miss from the lack of nonverbal cues. Several attempts have been made to summarize the norms of netiquette. The most widely cited is Gene Spafford's series of documents, which he compiled and edited from the suggestions of Usenet users. Either heeded or ignored by many, the estimates of the validity of Spafford's guidelines vary, but they are often invoked to resolve a dispute or to "advise" one another. In the following example, "Jack" from the University of California at Irvine advises "Bill" from the Netherlands of a breach of netiquette:

> *Your reply to my post gave me mixed messages. Some of your comments are cruel. Your flame should have been sent directly to me via e-mail.*[2]

Because enforcement of netiquette begins with the individual users, consensual interpretation by the Usenet public determines the "law." If a user's action offends one person in 10 million, that action is probably a slight breach but nothing of wider concern; however, if an action results in 30 complaints, then it usually is treated more seriously. Netiquette, then, is the Usenet analog for the external world's system of mores, norms, and tradition. While not a precise duplication of the external world's social structure, netiquette provides Usenet users with guidelines or standards of behavior. Chuq Von Rospach (1987), author of *A Primer on How to Work With the USENET Community*, writes,

> For USENET to function properly those people must be able to interact in productive ways. This document is intended as a guide to using the net in ways that will be pleasant and productive for everyone. This document is not intended to teach you how to use USENET. Instead, it is a guide to using it politely, effectively and efficiently. (lines 14-16)

It will be recalled that Reid (1991) suggests that nonverbal cues reinforce the standards of behavior in the external world. Just as netiquette developed into the Usenet analog for standards of behavior, a system of written cues has developed as an analog to reinforce those standards. These cues, known as "emoticons" make use of nonstandard punctuation, spelling, capitalization, and special keyboard characters to convey action, emotion, and emphasis. An excerpt from Spafford's guidelines follows:

> The net has developed a symbol called the smiley face. It looks like ":-)" and points out sections of articles with humorous intent. No matter how broad the humor or satire, it is safer to remind people that you are being funny. (Von Rospach, 1987, lines 112-114)

This guideline emphasizes the use of emoticons to convey humor so as to avoid the consequences of ambiguous or sarcastic statements but does not show the variety of possibilities, as in the following examples:

Al,
hahahahahahahhahahahahahahahahahahahahahaa
**sniff* waaaaaaaaaaaaaaaaaaaaaaaahhhhhh*
I laughed, i cried. . . . that post was GREAT! :-)
Amusedly,
-Mirth-

In this message, "-Mirth-" from the Massachusetts Institute of Technology, has no difficulty sharing his or her amusement with an earlier "post" or message of Steve's. Note the use of the asterisks in "*sniff*" to convey action as opposed to simply saying "I sniffed," as is done later. Of course, the capitalization of "GREAT" indicates emphasis, presumably enthusiasm given the presence of the "smiley." Consider the next example from a user at Dalhousie University in Halifax, Canada:

> *You know, I agree with everything you said. However, you looselyfall into the dweeb category by admitting you actually READ most of the damn thing. It brings no fame to its creator, but only humiliation to the human species (or does Kibo not fit into the homo sapien sapien category? Maybe there is a better division for an individual who's life is overwhelmed by USENET? homo sappy postus?) *shakes his head, almost embarassed that he has a 4 line .sig, let alone a 950 line one**

This article is an excerpt from a discussion on whether having a "950 line" signature on an article is a violation of netiquette. The Canadian user agrees that a lengthy signature is a violation and becomes embarrassed when he realizes that his own "4 line .sig" is considered too long by most interpretations of netiquette. He conveys this realization by using asterisks to simulate the shaking of his head.

To summarize, it is important to establish the distinctness of Usenet from the society of the external world so that new insights and new conclusions may be cultivated from the application of Hobbes's political philosophy. Although Usenet users are able to compensate for the lack of a physical reality, their parallels or "analogs" with the outside world have resulted in a distinct reality of their own.

The Notion of Persona

Usenet is distinguished from other written media by the level of interaction among its users. A printed newspaper, for example, offers its readers a one-way medium. Generally, a newspaper is a medium for the writers to communicate to their readers, not with them; however, the op/ed (opinion/editorial) page does provide for selected reader response. There the opinions expressed are personal and not necessarily the view of the newspaper's staff. These opinions may be compelling or inane, but it is the names attached that remind one that there are individuals at the source. These individuals, through the interaction of their opinions, briefly create a sense of community. Granted, such a community is a fleeting one at best, for often the emergent dialogue is not a dialogue at all but a set of coincident monologues submitted in reaction to a piece of news. Any repartee is unintentional and possibly staged —selected—by the editor to represent a diversity of views. In Usenet, dialogue is spontaneous and unedited, and the individuals at the source are users who frequently contribute on a regular basis. The most active users contribute over 50 articles per week each (UUNET Technologies, Inc., 1992). This high level of interaction among Usenet users creates a more permanent sense of community than among a newspaper's readership. Accordingly, this high level of interaction among users provides opportunities to develop relationships.

It has been established that the medium of written communication interferes with the transfer of the users' external world social structures into Usenet. By the same means, written communication interferes with the transfer of the users' personalities and unique qualities as well. The result is the creation of "personae," which are as distinct from the users as Usenet society is distinct from the external world. The external world of the users is a world of what Hobbes calls myriad objects to be sense-perceived ultimately to be desired or avoided (p. 48). The nature of the users' known universe possesses physical characteristics that can be sense-perceived either directly or indirectly via technological extension of the senses or a combination of these accompanied by scientific deduction. Words, for Hobbes, signify the memory of sensory experience and thought (p. 33), but the physical things of the external world exist independently of the words that describe them. Although important, words are not required for the existence of the things to which they refer. But within Usenet, words are the sole means of characterizing the network's universe. Thus wordsmanship in Usenet is a far more valued skill than it is in the external world. Consequently, possession or lack of this skill can inadvertently give the Usenet user a radically different persona from him- or herself. Accordingly, a command of written language can empower a persona in Usenet beyond the relative strength of its user in the external world.

The degree to which Usenet users resemble their personae seems to vary. The representation of a user within Usenet is the attempted transfer of the user's individuality into a Usenet persona. The user has some control over the representation and the extent to which the persona resembles himself or herself. A representation is transparent when the user attempts to represent him or herself as he or she is; a representation is translucent when the Usenet persona is only a shadow of the user; and accordingly, a representation is opaque when the persona does not resemble the user at all.

A user can spend a great amount of energy wondering about the "real" users behind the personae with which he or she interacts. In all cases where there is no direct knowledge of another user, if one cares, one must rely on the word of that user as to whether that persona is an accurate representation. Because it is, in effect, that user's word that is in question, relying on it offers little relief. Without direct or revealed knowledge, the pursuit of the true nature of representations is a matter for speculation. Therefore, until the full truth is known, it is a common and expedient practice to "forget" about the users behind the personae so that any purported resemblance or dissimilarity of personae to users can be treated as if it does not matter.[3]

It is the high level of interaction among Usenet users that gives their personae "life." In fact, a single response to one's statement is sufficient to generate a persona. That response, although minimal, is the foundation of existence within Usenet. It is obvious that a response implies a cause or stimulus worthy of reaction; however, it is less obvious that by implication it signifies an acknowledgment of that cause. In terms of "cause" and "effect," a characteristic of the effect is the substantiation of its cause's existence. In terms of Usenet, a response substantiates the existence of a statement. This may seem trivial until it is recalled that Usenet personae are created as a result of the interaction among Usenet users. This interaction consists of the cycle of statement and response. The existence of the personae, therefore, is tied to that cycle.

One may wonder why interaction is a prerequisite for a persona's existence. In a written world such as Usenet, there is a stricter burden of proof for existence than Descartes requires in the external world. A user can read and contemplate the words of another user, but unless there is a visible (i.e., written) response via his persona, the action of reading and contemplating goes unnoticed. If a user is unnoticed, then he or she is not interacting with other users. Because personae are created as a result of interaction, reading and contemplating alone are insufficient to generate or maintain the existence of a persona. As shown, "Cogito ergo sum" is an insufficient measure of existence within Usenet. If all users kept their thoughts to themselves, they certainly would be assured of their own existences, but Usenet would be reduced to a noninteractive, indistinct, written medium. Without some sort of response beyond interior cogitation there is nothing to be perceived by other Usenet users. "Network existentialism" is therefore more skeptical than Decartes' externalism can account for.

However, a dialectical approach can be used to establish a measure for existence within Usenet. Whereas "I think, therefore I am" is insufficient for this purpose, so too is "I write, therefore I am." Again, without a visible response, a written statement remains isolated and apparently unperceived—a persona's existence is neither generated nor substantiated. A further modification to the premise results in "I am perceived, therefore I am." Suddenly the Usenet user is no longer alone, for to be perceived requires another. The visible response "I hear you" generates and substantiates the existence of the first user's persona, whereby a reply would perform the same function for the second user's persona. The visible response is evidence of perception. Without that response the perception remains as an interior cogitation of the would-be respondent and does nothing to substantiate the existence of either user's persona. The visible cycle of cause and effect, the users' statements, responses, restatements, and correspondence, ensures the viability of the personae of both users. When extended beyond them to the multitude of the personae within Usenet, the existence of all of them is assured.

Where the parallel between dialectical existence in Usenet to independent existence in the external world might be difficult to follow, the parallel for the quality of life is more apparent. As in other aspects of the comparison of Usenet to the external world, persona existence is distinct from user existence. Users require air, food, water, and other essentials for basic existence. Personae, lacking physical form, do not require physical sustenance; nonetheless, they are dependent on three essential conditions for existence.

The first condition is the continued association between the user and the persona. The loss of the user's access to Usenet severs the association to his or her persona. Once Usenet loses its utility to the user, the continued association to the persona is threatened. In other words, a persona's existence is dependent on a user's access to Usenet, and a user maintains access to Usenet so long as it remains useful.

The second condition is the visible demonstration of presence. While Usenet may have great utility to a passive user,[4] the lack of interaction with other users does not create a persona that exists in a way previously defined as existence within Usenet. The passive user remains outside the boundary of Usenet existence and his or her actions are unnoticed to "life" within. This study concerns itself with those users who choose to participate.

The third condition is that the participation is continuous. A persona belonging to a user who is prevented, unable, or unwilling to continue to participate will continue to exist until the memory of that existence is forgotten by the other users.[5]

Personae Are Persons

Having established the distinctness of Usenet's society and its persona population, it is possible to proceed with a preliminary parallel to *Leviathan.* Establishing the parallel between persons and personae will allow for the subsequent application of Hobbes's political philosophy to Usenet. This parallel is established in the following discussion of Hobbes's definition of "person," the actions of personae, and the special form of representation known as "impersonation." Hobbes writes,

> A person is he, *whose words or actions are considered, either his own, or as representing the words or actions of another man* . . . When they are considered his own, then is he called a *natural person*: and when they are considered as

representing the words and actions of another, then is he a *feigned or artificial person*. (p. 125)[6]

According to Hobbes, a persona represents the "words or actions of another man." Indeed, a persona represents the words and actions of a user. Further, Hobbes defines "personation" as "to act or represent oneself" (p. 125). This being the precise purpose for personae in Usenet, "personation" is alternately definable as the "generation of a persona." Therefore, in terms of Hobbes, Usenet users must "personate" themselves via personae because written communication prevents the users from acting and representing themselves in person.

While it is true that a persona's actions represent the actions of a user, the distinctness of the persona from the user allows for the distinctness of the persona's actions. Recall that all persona actions must necessarily be derived from the written responses of the users. When a user writes a hostile message to another user, his or her persona in effect "attacks" the persona of the recipient. Whether a persona is actually responsible for or "owns" the "attack," Hobbes writes, "Of persons artificial, some have their words and actions *owned* by those whom they represent. And then the person is the *actor*; and he that owneth his words and actions, is the AUTHOR: in which case the actor acteth by authority" (p. 125).

Strictly interpreted, personae are "artificial persons" because their words and actions are owned by the users whom they represent, but since it is common and expedient to "forget" that personae are representations of users, it is possible to understand how a persona's actions can be interpreted as the persona's own. Although Hobbes does not say specifically, he suggests that accountability for one's own actions is the consequence of acting as "owner" of the actions or with "authority" (p. 126). Accordingly, the expedience of "forgetting" may lead one to treat a persona as the author of its actions, thereby expecting accountability from the persona for the actions. This is an unrealistic expectation, given that a persona is but a representation of a user who is the owner of its actions. From this it follows that a user seeking to evade accountability for his actions might attempt to exploit the expedience of "forgetting" by acting through another user's persona. By impostering or "impersonation," he or she can create a persona that appears to represent the personality and unique qualities of another user. Because of the expedience of "forgetting" and the uncertainty regarding the degree of representation (transparent, translucent, or opaque) between users and personae, "impersonation" is a more serious violation of trust in Usenet than it is in the external world. Reid (1991) writes, "The illegitimate use of [personae] can cause anger on the part of their rightful users and sometimes deep feelings of guilt on the part of the perpetrators" (lines 1139-1141).

"Impersonation" is classified as an opaque representation since the persona is intended to represent someone other than the user behind it; however, not all opaque representations are impersonations. A user seeking complete anonymity for personal privacy reasons might consider an opaque representation; however, a translucent representation is more common. A translucent representation is typified by the user who wishes to interact via a pseudonym. For the same reasons that an author would elect to use a pen name a translucent representation is useful in masking the user's identity in certain situations. When the user is not seeking to evade accountability for his or her actions he or she is not "impersonating."

The Powers

Given the preliminary parallel between personae and Hobbes's "persons," it is possible to establish a further parallel between *Leviathan* and Usenet. Hobbes explains that persons possess certain powers. The discussion continues with the consideration of these powers and development of their Usenet analogs. On the subject of power, he begins, "Natural power, *is the eminence of the faculties of body, or mind*: *as* extraordinary strength, form, prudence, arts, eloquence, liberality, nobility. *Instrumental* are those powers, which acquired by these, or by fortune, are means and instruments to acquire more" (p. 72).

Three of these natural powers are severely limited in their transfer to Usenet society because Usenet personae lack physical form. They are strength, form, and arts. Obviously, physical strength is irrelevant in any environment devoid of physical things, but a Usenet persona can have strength relative to other personae. In terms of Usenet, strength is one's ability to "execute an attack." It will be recalled that the action of "attack," like all actions in Usenet, must be derived from the cycle of statement and response. Therefore, "strength" in Usenet is one's ability to write a potent or even vehement statement.

The power of "form" comes from one's physical makeup. In essence, it is the effect that one's appearance has on others. According to Hobbes, "Form is power; because being a promise of good, it recommendeth men to the favour of women and strangers" (p. 73). Like "strength," it transfers poorly into Usenet because personae lack physical form. Yet it has an analogous counterpart: "Form" in terms of Usenet, comes from the impression one makes on others not with one's physique but with one's words. Even a pseudonym can convey form, as "Spartan" brings to mind images of frugality and warriors and "Damsel" connotes femininity and distress. "Form" can extend to actual word choice when academic language can make a persona "appear" more scholarly, or when language laden with scientific jargon might bring to mind images of laboratory coats and measurement instruments. Granted, while these images are not the clear, consistent images conveyed by "form" in the external world—in fact, they probably vary depending on the perceiver—they do serve to add a "face" to a name and a personality to the words. It is only natural to want to "fill in the blanks" that Usenet's analog for form leaves empty.

Regarding the power of arts, Hobbes writes,

> Arts of public use, as fortification, making of engines, and other instruments of war; because they confer to defence, and victory, are power: and though the true mother of them, be science, namely mathematics; yet, because they are brought into the light, by the hand of the artificer, they be esteemed, the midwife passing with the vulgar for the mother, as his issue. (p. 73)

Because Usenet is a nonphysical environment, the notion of defense, like that of strength, must be derived from the cycle of statement and response. Having established that "strength" in Usenet is one's ability to write a potent statement, then it follows that "arts" in Usenet, because they "confer to defence," must be one's ability to write a rebuttal.

In contrast, the powers of prudence and liberality are transferred to Usenet almost completely. Liberality is intended by Hobbes to mean "generosity." He writes, "Also riches joined with liberality, is power; because it procureth friends, and servants: without liberality, not so; because in this case they defend not; but expose men to envy, as a prey" (p. 72). "Liberality" can be combined with things other than riches to produce the same effect. Consider the act of restraining oneself from easily humiliating a subordinate in public or the act of freely and genuinely offering one's assistance to the uninitiated. These acts of kindness bolster one's liberality. Additionally, they are actions easily transferred to written form. On the subject of prudence, Hobbes writes,

> When the thoughts of a man, that has a design in hand, running over a multitude of things, observes how they conduce to that design; or what design they may conduce unto; if his observations be such as are not easy, or usual, this wit of his is called PRUDENCE; and depends on much experience, and memory of the like things, and their consequences heretofore. (p. 61)

Here Hobbes explains that prudence comes from "much experience" leading to "unusual observations" or insight. A person's prudence transfers to his or her persona because they share one and the same mind and experiences, despite the fact that expedience may permit one to "forget" this fact. Only when one's writing ability interferes with one's attempt to communicate prudently does a persona seem less prudent in Usenet than the user does in the external world.

Unlike the previously discussed powers, where it is clear that some have more exact Usenet analogs than others, the transferral of nobility to Usenet presents difficulty. Hobbes explains, "Nobility is power, not in all places, but only in those commonwealths, where it has privileges: for in such privileges, consisteth their power" (p. 73).

One's privileges come from the recognition by others of one's rank or nobility. Unless one conveyed one's nobility through a pseudonym or name such as "Dr. Oakeshott" or by the use of revealing information such as "My father, Senator Kennedy, says . . . ," it is not likely that external world nobility will have relevance to Usenet society. Additionally, in cases where external world nobility is transferred, the privileges and respect are not as forthcoming as expected. Perhaps this is because persons of nobility, accustomed to the "trappings" of the elite, find that without these "trappings" in Usenet, their nobility is nothing more than words. However, nobility does exist in Usenet. Users such as Spafford, the frequently cited authority on netiquette, seem to enjoy much deference when "making appearances" in Usenet. For example, because Spafford is famous, other users may be less visibly critical of his statements while he is "present."

Eloquence is possibly the most important power in Usenet. Hobbes probably included eloquence among the powers because it enables one to communicate not only functionally but with finesse. Hobbes writes, "Eloquence is power, because it is seeming prudence" (p. 73). The skill of writing enables one to have "a way with words" or eloquence. Moreover, in a world where words are primary to existence and serve as the sole mode of communication and activity, their importance cannot be exaggerated. In *Emily Postnews,* author Brad Templeton (1991) reminds the uninitiated user that "sloppy spelling in a purely written forum sends out the same silent messages that soiled clothing would when addressing an audience" (lines 241-245). On the other hand, actually wearing soiled clothing while accessing Usenet has absolutely no effect on one's persona. The premium that Usenet places on spelling, and writing skills in general, inflates the Usenet analog for eloquence beyond its relative worth in the external world.

Hobbes discusses additional powers which rely on or operate in conjunction with those already considered. Among those additional powers are affability and united power.

The power of affability seems similar to that of liberality, which was described earlier with the examples of public restraint with subordinates and generosity with the use of one's powers. Strictly speaking, these qualities of graciousness more accurately describe the power of affability. If one reviews Hobbes's definition of liberality, one will notice that "liberality" is power when "joined" with riches. Clearly, Hobbes is concerned with "riches" when he writes of liberality because "it procureth friends, and servants." Hobbes believes that "liberality" or generosity with one's riches is a power because friends and servants contribute to one's defense.

The external world concept of riches does not easily translate into a world without physical or material wealth, but the development of the analog is possible nonetheless. In the external world, money is used to barter for goods and services. In Usenet, goods do not exist. On the other hand, services are abundant: Sharing one's knowledge is a service; assisting a new user is a service. These services may be traded in Usenet analogously to their trade in the external world. Therefore, the Usenet analog for riches is "services." This conclusion returns one to the original observation that liberality and affability appear to share the same definition. With respect to Usenet, indeed they do.

Finally, the power of united power or power "united by consent" is described by Hobbes as follows: "The greatest of human powers, is that which is compounded of the powers of most men, united by consent, in one person, natural, or civil, that has the use of all their powers depending on his will" (p. 72). It is premature to discuss why persons would want to unite their powers in a single person before it has been considered why they would want to pursue powers for themselves. But since Hobbes includes this power with the rest, it is important to note that a power "which is compounded of the powers of most men" is the "greatest of human powers." While this may be true in the external world, the nature of Usenet's written medium may subordinate united power to the power of eloquence, as it is eloquence that enables users to create the environment where unity takes place.

The Pursuit of Powers

Given the discussion of Hobbes's "powers" and the development of their respective analogs in Usenet, it is possible to discuss and develop the pursuit of powers in the external world and in Usenet. With respect to the benefits of power, Hobbes writes, "[Powers] . . . are the means and instruments to acquire more: as riches, reputation, friends, and the secret working of God, which men call good luck" (p. 72). One will discover that these benefits are, in some instances, powers themselves and that the pursuit of power appears to be an end in itself.

Riches are perhaps the most difficult of the benefits of power to transfer to Usenet society. In the external world, riches are clear—they are the signs and objects of material wealth, such as money and possessions. Given that Usenet lacks a physical environment, an analog for material wealth, money, or possessions is nonsensical. However, it has been established that services, as in sharing one's knowledge, is the analog for riches.

Reputation is significant in both the external world and Usenet. It is the most important benefit of power in Usenet society. Hobbes does not provide a simple definition with which one can grasp the full meaning of reputation; in fact, he defines reputation contextually in the definitions of other powers. Consider the following passage:

> Reputation of power, is power; because it draweth with it the adherence of those that need protection. So is reputation of love of a man's country, called popularity, for the same reason. Also, what quality soever maketh a man beloved, or feared of many; or the reputation of such quality, is power; because it is a means to have the assistance, and service of many. Good success is power; because it maketh reputation of wisdom, or good fortune; which makes men either fear him; or rely on him. . . . Reputation of prudence in the conduct of peace or war, is power; because to prudent men, we commit the government of ourselves, more willingly than to others. (p. 72)

Broadly defined, reputation is the publicly held estimate of one's worth. With that in mind, Hobbes's definition of reputation in the context of other powers make more sense. This being the case, reputation is the publicly held estimate of one's powers. For example, one may be an excellent cook known only within the private circle of one's friends, but once one establishes a reputation outside that private circle the estimate of one's excellence may be held publicly. In this case, the power of one's prudence in cooking is amplified by one's reputation, and Hobbes tells us that in the first line of the preceding passage when he says, "Reputation of power, is power." It is in this sense of power begetting power that the importance of reputation is heightened in the external world. To the extent that reputation is the most important power in Usenet, the following discussion of the Usenet analog for reputation is critical.

In Usenet, one's powers, such as strength and eloquence, are expressed by participating in the cycle of statements and responses. Only in this way can one's powers be perceived, substantiated, measured, and ranked by others.

The resulting comparisons made among personae establish the public estimation of one's worth. This reputation-making process of comparison and worth is supported with the following two quotations from Hobbes: "Virtue generally, in all sorts of subjects, is somewhat that is valued for eminence; and consisteth in comparison" (p. 59) and "For let a man, as most men do, rate themselves at the highest value they can; yet their true value is no more, than it is esteemed by others" (p. 73). Indeed, Hobbes makes it clear that reputation serves to set a "market price" for one's worth. He implies that although reputation can amplify one's strengths it can expose one's weaknesses to greater scrutiny, thereby devaluating others' personal estimate of those strengths. With respect to Usenet, reputation is the collective memory of the comparisons of past cycles of statement and response.

Hobbes believes that the possession of friends is a benefit of power. The Usenet "public" that forms one's reputation consists of many personae, some of which are one's friends. During the cycle of the statement and response the participants and the observers rate and compare the participants' expressions of their powers. This comparison reveals degrees of affinities among personae; that is, they may "take sides" on an issue. These affinities are guided by what is described by Hobbes as passions (p. 47), which include but are not limited to appetite, desire, love, aversion, hate, joy, and grief (p. 50). Those personae whose passions move them together out of common affinity become friends, supporters, and allies. Those whose passions disassociate them may become enemies. A persona's friends enable it to establish and build its reputation, thereby increasing its power, whereas its enemies seek to discredit it, thereby reducing its power. There is no inherent quality such as "good" or "evil" that distinguishes one's friends from one's enemies; what is knowable is only that the former seek to support and increase one's power and the latter seek its attenuation.

To acquire the benefits of power, it is necessary to continuously participate in the cycle of statement and response. Although reputation is a benefit of power and a power (because it amplifies the other powers), the duration of that effect becomes important. If one's reputation is held by the public in collective memory, it follows that one's reputation is recalculated after each participation, with the readjusted reputation replacing the older reputation in the collective memory. Thus one's reputation lasts until it is forgotten. As one's reputation fades from memory so does one's power. However, to fade completely violates the condition of existence for continuous participation; therefore, to avoid the fading of one's power and the cessation of existence one must continuously participate in the cycle of statement and response.

Death

The possession of certain benefits of power, such as reputation, is power in itself; however, possession of power alone seems not to be enough. In revisiting the following passage on power, it is important to focus on Hobbes's use of "more": "[Powers] . . . are the means and instruments to acquire more: as riches, reputation, friends, and the secret working of God, which men call good luck" (p. 72). Hobbes does not say, for example, that powers are the means to acquire riches, reputation, friends and good luck. He says that powers are the means to acquire "more." This suggests that Hobbes believes that the simple acquisition of powers is not enough. In fact, it is clear from the following passage that there is no limit as to how much can be acquired:

> And the cause of this, is not always that a man hopes for more intensive delight, than he has already attained to; or that he cannot be content with a moderate power: but because he cannot assure the power and means to live well, which he hath present, without the acquisition of more. (p. 80)

As can be seen, the acquisition of more assures one's present power and "means to live well." This implies an active life of acquisition, not a leisurely life where one waits for power to come to him or her. Hobbes is saying that if one wants the assurance of one's "present means to live well," one must acquire more. Hobbes is very clear on this point when he uses the word "restless" in the following passage (note that "restless" should not be interpreted as "fidgety" but more literally as "without rest"): "So that in the first place, I put for a general inclination of all mankind, a perpetual and restless desire of power after power, that ceaseth only in death" (p. 80). This indictment of "mankind" clears the way for a discussion of death. According to Hobbes, death in the external world is the cessation of all movement, for men consist of a complex combination of motions ranging from one's limbs to one's dreams (pp. 23-27). These motions, "begun in generation, and continued without interruption through their whole life" (p. 47) distinguish the living from the not.

The Usenet analog for life is also derived from motions, the motion of the cycle of statement and response, and it is predicated upon the satisfaction of the three conditions for a Usenet persona's existence: enough utility to assure the continued association between the user and the persona, the visible demonstration of one's presence via a persona, and continuous participation in the cycle of statement and response. Without the satisfaction of these conditions, a persona cannot exist. It is clear from the conditions that utility and participation are essential: Usenet must remain useful to the user and the user must continuously assert the existence of his or her persona by participating in the cycle of statement and response.

The effect of participation in this cycle is the creation and development of one's reputation. Those personae whose reputations are highly valued attract a sufficient number of responses with which to perpetuate additional cycles for statement and response. Those personae with poorly valued reputations may at first generate an intense cycle based on criticism of another and defense, but often come to be ignored and forced to face exclusion, obscurity, and thereby "death." For example, well-regarded personae only need to participate occasionally to insure that they are not forgotten because the resultant cycle of statement and response will generate enough interest to maintain their reputations and thereby their existence. It is also possible that little-known personae may establish temporary notoriety for themselves by making outrageous statements before returning to obscurity after their cycle has run its course.

By far, the great majority of personae enjoy neither fame nor ignominy, for their participation merely consists of "skirmishes" and banter. To illustrate this case, it is common for one to state an opinion, draw criticism, and rebut it. The participants in this short cycle are then compared, rated, and their respective reputations adjusted in the collective memory. But consider the case where one is subjected to an undue amount of criticism. If the "assault" is without merit, as in the second illustration, one may choose to ignore it, but if the criticism is based on truth, one may feel compelled to defend his or her reputation. Hobbes explains this compulsion as a "right" when he says,

> THE RIGHT OF NATURE, which writers commonly call *jus naturale*, is the liberty each man hath, to use his own power, as he will himself, for the preservation of his own nature; that is to say, of his own life; and consequently, of doing any thing, which in his own judgment, and reason, he shall conceive to be the aptest means thereunto. (p. 103)

As it has been shown, reputation is the "tote board" of a persona's existence within Usenet; therefore, to defend one's reputation is to exercise one's natural right to self-preservation in Usenet. But even relatively minor "skirmishes" can lead to larger "battles" because the drive to acquire "more" can accelerate the cycle of statement and response into a reputation-making machine. Consider the effect of the "perpetual and restless desire of power after power" and the lengths that Hobbes believes a person will go to assure the acquisition of more. In Usenet, the analog for an attack designed for quick reputational gain is called a "flame." Perhaps named for their inflammatory nature, "flames" tend to be ad hominem, argumentative, and often have little to do with the original discussions in which they develop. The extremely personal nature of "flames" often draws one to respond reflexively with a statement even more insulting or offensive than the original. Again, the motivation to participate in such an exchange is to publicly defend one's reputation. A cycle containing ad hominem exchanges can gain momentum very quickly, attracting outside attention to its participants. As the number of observers increases, the reputational stakes of the participants increase. This has the effect of luring some of the observers from the "sidelines" into the cycle as well, causing the spread of the "war." Sometimes compared to storms because they appear without warning, wreak havoc, and subside just as unpredictably, "flame wars" can start over spelling, grammar, semantics, or any seemingly trivial issue.

Because flame wars can dominate or otherwise interfere with the discussion of nonparticipants, the wars tend to diminish the utility of Usenet to those nonparticipants. As utility is among the conditions of existence within Usenet, if enough nonparticipants feel the utility of their participation in Usenet is substantially threatened by a flame war, the warring participants have nothing to gain reputationally and much to lose. In fact, once a flame war loses its audience, the participants not only lose those who would judge and compare their actions but, more important, a war offensive, annoying, or useless enough to drive away its observers will probably cause a net loss to the reputations of its participants.

Although flame wars are generally discouraged because they are so disruptive, they persist and are commonly found in newsgroups oriented toward social issues and controversy. However, the relatively sedate technical discussion newsgroups have their share. The notoriously disruptive and futile cycle of "Macs are better than PCs" is a recurring flame war that many users try to extinguish as quickly as it begins by refusing to participate. It should be noted that a special newsgroup, alt.flame, exists for the specific purpose of being a place where one can participate in a flame war without being disruptive to the discussions in the rest of the newsgroups, a sort of "O.K. Corral." It is common to see someone write, "Let's take this discussion to alt.flame."

The following passage from *Leviathan* may shed light on why "flaming" and contention in general occur:

> Love of contention from competition. *Competition of riches, honour,* command, or other power, inclineth to contention, enmity, and war: because the way of one competitor, to the attaining of his desire, is to kill, subdue, supplant, or repel the other. (p. 81)

Here, Hobbes suggests that persons engage in lethal competition in order to acquire powers and their benefits. In terms of Usenet, "flaming" allows them to increase their reputations at the expense of others.

Living in Moderation

How contentious can the Usenet environment for participation become before the conditions to maintain the existence of one's persona become so difficult to meet that one is driven to surrender his powers to a single authority? The following discussion prepares one to answer by first considering the alternatives to the outright surrender of one's powers. For this purpose, the following passage from *Leviathan* is useful:

> Civil obedience from love of ease. From fear of death, or wounds. Desire of ease, and sensual delight, disposeth men to obey a common power: because by such desires, a man doth abandon the protection that might be hoped for from his own industry, and labour. Fear of death, and wounds, disposeth to the same; and for the same reason. (p. 81)

From this passage it is clear that Hobbes recognizes that the "restless desire of power after power" takes its toll on persons who are as inclined to ease as they are to contention. The balance between these opposing desires appears to be the "fear of death, and wounds." It follows, then, that it is the fear of death and wounds that persuades persons to abandon their pursuit of powers and surrender themselves to the power of another. This notion is apparent in Usenet, but it appears that there are other alternatives short of complete surrender. As discussed, one may ignore a user who interferes with the utility of one's access to Usenet. Additionally, to solve disputes and facilitate the interaction, one may voluntarily adhere to the general principles described as netiquette, as outlined by Spafford.

Sometimes, the situation arises where a user will offend or annoy another so severely that simply ignoring the user runs the risk of encountering him and being offended and annoyed at a later date. To remedy this situation, Usenet users have at their disposal a utility known as a "kill file." Basically an electronic filter, a kill file allows a user to screen out or block the message of another user. A kill file can contain the names of several users and sites as well as offensive words, effectively preventing the display of potentially unwanted messages. Note that a kill file does not actually destroy Usenet articles but merely shields the owner of the file from their existence. Kill files are an extreme method of self-censoring because they take the power of decision away from the kill file owner. Many users still prefer to run the risk of re-encountering annoyances than to subjugate themselves to an automatic censor.

As the amount of clutter or "noise"[7] increases, more and more users voluntarily submit to "moderation." A moderated newsgroup prevents unapproved statements from being distributed. All statements are submitted to a moderator who screens the messages for content, posts the appropriate ones, and rejects the ones he feels are unfit for the discussion. In the case of a moderated newsgroup, the moderator has tremendous control of one's network existence.

The price or reward for such restraint is the decrease of noise and the increase of relevant information. Moderated newsgroups are not without problems and as one user, "David," reminds us, "One person's 'clutter' may be another's insight." Additionally, the degree of censorship varies from moderator to moderator. In the case of comp.dcom.telecom, a moderated newsgroup dedicated to telecommunications issues, many individuals are unable to tolerate its highly opinionated moderator, Patrick Townson. As a result, they have created an alternative or unrestricted newsgroup called alt.dcom.telecom. To this day, Pat's group remains very popular while the much smaller alternative group is commonly cluttered with articles critical of him. This offers little choice for users who desire the volume of messages in the moderated group but deplore Pat's degree of restraint.

Looking for the Leviathan

If one were to search for a Leviathan in Usenet, one would obviously begin with the moderated newsgroups because the discussions therein consist of articles previously approved by a "common power." However, there are other less obvious indications of restraint, such as conformity to or compliance with netiquette as a general guide to behavior and conformity to or compliance with Spafford's more specific set of guidelines.

A survey was conducted on a randomly selected sample of 200 Usenet articles. The articles were selected from a list of 3,971 existing newsgroups, with each group having an equal chance for selection. A computer program was written to select at random a newsgroup from the list from which it randomly selected an article. The selected article became part of the sample population. If the newsgroup did not contain any articles, the computer program selected another newsgroup until the sample population was equal to 200.

After the sample population was determined, each article was examined for signs or indication of a Leviathan. These indicators were operationalized

Table 6.1 The Operationalization of Leviathan

Leviathan Factor	*Description*
0	No signs of coercion to conform or self-restraint
1	Unmindful conformity to/compliance with netiquette, such as the use of emoticons or other characters to convey physical actions
2	Reference to netiquette as means of conformity/compliance
3	Reference to Spafford's guidelines, more specific than LF 2
4	Article is from a moderated newsgroup or is otherwise censored

Table 6.2 Articles Containing Progressive Signs of Leviathan

Leviathan Factor	*Frequency*	*Percentage*
0	162	81.0
1	14	7.0
2	3	1.5
3	2	1.0
4	19	9.5
Total	200	100.0

as Leviathan factors (LF), with each increase in factor representing a greater sign or indication of coercion. Each LF is described in Table 6.1.

The factors are at the ordinal level of measurement such that LF 4 means "more Leviathan" than LF 3, but it does not mean than LF 2 represents twice as much as LF 1. Given the operationalization of Leviathan as factors, it was possible to read each article and ask "Does this article contain any signs of coercion to obey a common power?" If an article contained more than one indicator, then it was coded with the greatest LF for which it satisfied the requirements. The findings help one to conclude "how much" of a Leviathan is present in Usenet. A survey of the sample population produced the data shown in Table 6.2.

Based on the data, 9.5% of the articles surveyed showed the greatest amount of Leviathan (LF 4), and 81% showed no signs of Leviathan (LF 0). It was expected that there would be progressively fewer articles with each increasing factor of Leviathan, but the unusual distribution for LF 1 through 3 suggests possible operationalization problems. In retrospect, it was not correct to identify emoticons as a form of Leviathan because they are signs of compensation for the medium of written communication and not necessarily signs of compliance to or conformity with netiquette. The unexpect-

Table 6.3 Articles Showing Signs of a Leviathan

Leviathan Factor	*Frequency*	*Percentage*
0-1	176	88
2-4	24	12
Total	200	100

edly high number of observations coded LF 1 bear this out. Additionally, the sample did not support a five-way breakdown with any degree of accuracy between the extremes of LF 0 and LF 4. This resulted in a negligible difference between the number of observations coded LF 2 and LF 3 from which a meaningful conclusion can be drawn. To account for operationalization and sample size problems, the data in Table 6.3 are presented in such a way as to emphasize the measured extremes.

Presented in this way, the articles are divided into two consolidated categories. The first category, LF 0 and 1, consists of articles with no measured signs of a Leviathan, including emoticons, which are indicators of compensation and not coercion. The second category, LF 2 through 4, consists of articles that do contain signs of a Leviathan, including those in which someone asks another to observe netiquette to articles submitted under moderation. Based on the findings, some measure of Leviathan is present in 12% of the articles surveyed.

Conclusion

This chapter has sought to establish seven major points. First, Usenet is a distinct society because the exclusively written medium keeps much of the three-dimensional external world out. Second, personae are created by the interaction of Usenet users. A user always interacts with the personae of other users because it is impossible to interact *three-dimensionally* via a written medium. This always being the case, expediency allows one to "forget" that interaction is via personae. Third, Hobbes helps prove that personae are persons within Usenet. Fourth, like persons, personae have powers, although they may be different. Fifth, users participate in Usenet to maximize its utility; thus persona existence is tied to user participation and utility. Sixth, participation may become contentious or uninteresting, thereby decreasing Usenet's utility and threatening personae existence; however, users can increasingly subject their participation to restraint. Seventh, to maximize Usenet's utility and to maintain personae existence, some users may decide to allow another person to control or moderate the extent of their participation, thus controlling or moderating the existence of their personae.

The quantitative portion of this study raises provocative questions regarding trends toward moderation in a forum hailed by many as a "modemocracy" and a realization of the "global village." A future study could track the frequency of the Leviathan in Usenet over a period of several months. These data could be contrasted with the failure of a completely moderated alternate to Usenet formerly known as "InModeration." Perhaps the combination of moderated and unmoderated newsgroups in Usenet points to the utility of choice and freedom that "InModeration" might have underestimated. Additionally, refined operationalization and a larger sample size might provide more insight into the less obvious manifestations of the Leviathan in Usenet.

Although this analysis has been limited to the Hobbesian perspective on the origins of government, future researchers should be encouraged to employ other theoretical visions to the study of Usenet or of the Internet in general. The simple act of searching for proof within the Internet may more readily fasten the theories' nuances in a student's mind than traditional philosophical study. Where social studies were always possible, Internet studies present an equally complex but more easily observable self-documenting society.

I also recognize and encourage the need for more behavioral research. Although normative study is valuable in its own right, numerical analysis of Internet society is needed. It is important to know the distribution of the various degrees of representation of users by personae, how the number of users affects the generation of government, and the number and types of and reasons for selecting one polity over another. These lines of inquiry do not, of course, cover the entire range, but they do suggest that the entirety of political science can benefit from Internet studies.

Political scientists are not the first social scientists to explore this very new area. Current research in Internet studies reveals that insufficient ethical guidelines exist for guiding research and that there is considerable debate over how to proceed. For example, I was the sole political scientist on a large research team investigating computer-mediated communication. Due to the global distances between them, the researchers are represented by personae that include scholars of English, communication, linguistics, theater, sociology, and history. The qualitative portion of the research involves content analysis of the communication of a specific group of network individuals. Issues of privacy and intellectual property have arisen. It is still an unresolved question whether the research team should admonish the subjects and then seek their permission for further study to be conducted. It is still uncertain whether the study requires a human research waiver. It is still debatable whether this kind of analysis is closer to literary criticism than to behavioral science. It is still unknown whether published research should give the subjects credit for their statements or should withhold their names to protect their identities.

Despite these compelling questions, the computer allows one to cross traditional boundaries—it enables the writer to measure and the scientist to write—and to mix and combine elements from previously disparate fields. The problems described, of course, issue from the combination of scholars of literature with social scientists. A solution probably lies in acknowledging the unresolved nature of that combination once the interdisciplinary novelty subsides. The point, however, is that fertile ground for research has been uncovered and that the process of how it should be tilled has begun. To miss the opportunity to influence the process would be a major misfortune for political science.

Notes

1. All references to and quotations from Hobbes's *Leviathan* (1651/1962) are noted by page number(s) only. An earlier version of the present text with the same title is available at numerous sites on the Internet.

2. All such examples are excerpts from actual Usenet communication. The original spelling, punctuation, and spacing have been left intact to preserve the intent of the message. In the interest of privacy, the authors' surnames have been suppressed.

3. We commonly "forget" complications for the sake of simplicity. For example, it is simpler to think of the sun "rising" than it is to think of the earth turning.

4. A passive user is one who does not or cannot communicate with other users (e.g., while using a library's on-line catalog).

5. Prior to the "first cause," Participant A is isolated in silence and unaware of "self" and "other"—existence is undefined. Participant B, like A, is also alone and ignorant. Spontaneously, Participant A wonders aloud, "What is my purpose, if any?" B, surprised by the break in the silence and the presence of another, replies, "I don't know, but let's find out together." The phenomenon of mutual awareness implies the simultaneous awareness of the other and the self. This rudimentary confirmation of existence dependent on another (i.e., coexistence) is sufficient enough to allow A and B to pursue the purposes of their existence together.

6. Hobbes tends to emphasize with capitalization and italics. This emphasis is preserved in all selected passages and quotations.

7. The commonly used term for "clutter," which comes from the technical phrase "signal to noise ratio," which basically means that the less interference there is the cleaner the signal will be.

References

Hobbes, T. (1962). *Leviathan* (M. Oakeshott, Ed.). New York: Macmillan. (Original work published 1651)

Reid, E. (1991). "Electropolis: Communication and community on Internet Relay Chat." Unpublished master's thesis, University of Melbourne.

Ross, R., Schneider, H. W., & Waldman, T. (Eds.). (1974). *Thomas Hobbes in his time.* Minneapolis: University of Minnesota Press.

Templeton, B. (1991). *Dear Emily Postnews.* Part of a series of documents compiled and distributed by Gene Spafford, news.announce.new.users Usenet newsgroup.

UUNET Technologies, Inc. (1992, July 24). *Top 25 news submitters by user by number of articles for the last 2 weeks.* Falls Church, VA: Author.

Von Rospach, C. (1987). *A primer on how to work with the Usenet community.* Part of a series of documents distributed by Gene Spafford, news.announce.new users Usenet newsgroup.

7

THE EMERGENCE OF COMMUNITY IN COMPUTER-MEDIATED COMMUNICATION

Nancy K. Baym

Usenet is an extremely popular network that links an estimated 3 million users (Grimes, 1992) in an enormous stream of topical chatter. Usenet reaches an estimated 90,000 sites (B. Reid, 1993b) spanning five continents. The sites are primarily universities but also include research laboratories, computer engineering and telecommunication companies, government sites, and, increasingly, private individuals as well as others. Usenet carries almost 5,000 hierarchically organized "newsgroups" that operate as open forums for discussion of specific interests. As of July 1993, Usenet carried a daily average of 27,479 messages (B. Reid, 1993b). People access newsgroups through their accounts at sites that are linked to Usenet. Users "subscribe" to those groups that appeal to them and then use one of a number of programs called "newsreaders" to read the messages, or "posts," and to write their own.

For the past two years, I have been studying and participating in rec.arts.tv.soaps (r.a.t.s.), a Usenet newsgroup that, as its name suggests, is devoted to the recreational discussion of daytime soap operas. The idea of soap opera fans using computers to gossip about their favorite (and least favorite) soap characters challenges conventional images of both soap opera fans and computer users. The challenge is magnified, considering that in July 1993, r.a.t.s. carried more messages than any other Usenet group. Indeed, r.a.t.s. consistently ranks as one of the 15 highest-traffic groups, carrying approximately 150 new messages each day (B. Reid, 1993b). What interests me in r.a.t.s. is that over the course of nearly a decade the thousands of people who have participated in r.a.t.s. have created a dynamic and rich community filled with social nuance and emotion. R.a.t.s. is far from the only social world created through computer-mediated communication (CMC). Creating and participating in new communities is one of the primary pleasures people are taking in CMC, generating thousands of computer-mediated groups on countless networks and bulletin board systems (BBSs). Despite the popularity of computer-mediated community and the growing body of work on CMC, there has been little work addressing computer-mediated community directly. This chapter integrates a range of work on CMC in order to articulate a framework through which to view this process of creating community through CMC.

I begin by addressing task-oriented research on CMC. The first researchers intrigued by CMC focused on its applications in organizational contexts, a natural focus given the domains into which CMC was being introduced. The earliest of this work (e.g., Hiltz & Turoff, 1978) explored how work groups' behavior was affected by computer mediation as they collaborated on the accomplishment of tasks. Task-oriented applications of CMC remain the focus of most research. Sorted and sifted, the task-oriented work reveals a number of factors that influence communication patterns and social organization in CMC. After examining these preexisting structural factors, I turn to work addressing the social dimensions of emergent CMC communities, addressing how those dimensions might be influenced by those preexisting factors. This research on the social uses of CMC has demonstrated, in a variety of CMC contexts, ways in which participants form group-specific forms of expression, identities, relationships, and normative conventions. Throughout the chapter, I offer description and analysis of r.a.t.s. to refine and further the framework proposed here. My argument is that the distinct cultures that emerge in CMC are grounded in communicative practice. Community is generated through the interplay between preexisting structures and the participants' strategic appropriation and exploitation of the resources and rules those structures offer in ongoing interaction.

Preexisting Influences on CMC

Computer Determinism

Too much of the work on CMC assumes that the computer itself is the sole influence on communicative outcomes. This is sometimes called the "cues filtered out" approach (e.g., Walther & Burgoon, 1992) because, in this perspective, the computer is assumed to have low social presence and, therefore, to deprive interactants of salient social cues. Because computer-mediated interactants are unable to see, hear, and feel one another they cannot use the usual contextualization cues conveyed by appearance, nonverbal signals, and features of the physical context. With these cues to social context removed, the discourse is left in a social vacuum quite different from face-to-face interaction. The presumed lack of contextual cues and feedback is seen as producing several interrelated communicative outcomes (Baron, 1984; Cheseboro & Bonsall, 1989; Kiesler, Siegel, & McGuire, 1984). Interactants gain greater anonymity because their gender, race, rank, physical appearance and other features of public identity are not immediately evident. As a consequence of this enhanced anonymity, participation is said to become more evenly distributed across group members. Researchers often equate this balancing of participation with egalitarianism (Walther, 1992) and go on to claim that computer mediation makes it difficult for people to dominate and impose their views on others (Baron, 1984). This egalitarianism is sometimes seen as an advantage of CMC, for it allows women and minorities who are not heard in face-to-face interaction to have their voices heard (Baron, 1984). On the other hand, when everyone voices opinions it often takes longer to reach a decision, complete a task, or reach consensus (Sproull & Kiesler, 1991). To summarize, the computer creates anonymity, and anonymity grants all participants equal status. This evens out participation but impedes resolution.

While participant equality may be seen as a benefit of CMC, these researchers' view of CMC as socially impaired leads to an overwhelmingly negative characterization of the CMC social climate. The anonymity and lack of socioemotional information, for instance, is taken to erase norms for interaction (Kiesler et al., 1984; Rice, 1984, 1989; Sproull & Kiesler, 1991). Because people cannot see or hear others laugh, wince, or indicate other immediate reactions to their performances they become less socially inhibited and more likely to be rude (or, as it is called within the CMC subculture, to "flame") (Baron, 1984; Kiesler et al., 1984). The upshot of these findings for the social potential of CMC is well summarized by Baron (1984), who writes that "computer-mediated communication—at least as currently used —is ill-suited for such 'social' uses of language" (p. 136).

The research leading to this view of CMC has been severely criticized on numerous grounds. In the typical cues-filtered-out research design, small groups are brought into experimental research facilities equipped to facilitate computer conferencing. The subjects are given a task to accomplish and a time period in which to do it. Differences in the research design include the characteristics of the group and its members, the communication systems, the specific functions or tasks around which the groups were organized, and the groups' temporal structures (Hollingshead & McGrath, in press; Walther, 1992; Walther & Burgoon, 1992). However, these variations are rarely addressed within the work. As a consequence, many of the studies confound the experimental designs with findings (Hollingshead & McGrath, in press). Treating the combination of all of these factors as a single factor—the computer

—greatly oversimplifies the forces that affect CMC and renders the results neither generalizable nor comparable. Given the existence of CMC phenomena like r.a.t.s., one of many groups in which hundreds of participants have voluntarily created communities rich in social information, prominent personalities, valued relationships, and behavioral norms, it is clear that a more flexible and dynamic approach to CMC is called for.

Sources of Influence on CMC

Other researchers interested in task-oriented uses of CMC have avoided this media-deterministic approach, arguing instead that CMC patterns emerge unpredictably out of complex interactions between five factors. Those factors are the external contexts in which the use of CMC is set, the temporal structure of the group, the infrastructure of the computer system, the purposes for which CMC is used, and the characteristics of the group and its members (Contractor & Seibold, 1993; Hollingshead & McGrath, in press; Seibold, Heller, & Contractor, in press; Steinfeld, 1986). I address each of these factors in turn.

External Contexts

All interaction, including CMC, is simultaneously situated in multiple external contexts. The preexisting speech communities in which interactants operate provide social understandings and practices through and against which interaction in the new computer-mediated context develops. CMC use is always nested in the national and international cultures of which its participants are members. From this they draw a common language, usually but not always English, common ways of speaking, and a good deal of shared understandings. A more specific external context is found in the generally well-educated and economically comfortable substrata of the population with access to and knowledge of computers. The immediate situations through which participants come to have their computer network access can also influence the interaction. When the participants in a computer-mediated group are all employees of the same organization or all undergraduates at a large state university, the influences of those subcultures on communication will inevitably remain strong. In short, participants' communicative styles are oriented around common social practices before they even enter into CMC, practices that are unlikely to be supplanted by computer mediation (Contractor & Seibold, 1993).

A sense of the ways in which contexts may affect interaction can be gained from a glance at three contexts surrounding r.a.t.s. These are the Usenet environment, the environments through which the participants gain Usenet access, and the external environments from which participants draw group-relevant resources, especially the culture of soap opera fans. The Usenet environment provides a terrain in which the paths of individual participants may cross outside the group. It also provides some of the group's vocabulary. This vocabulary includes an extensive catalogue of acronyms, among them IMHO for "in my humble opinion" and BTW for "by the way." Many of these acronyms first appeared in collaborative amateur presses run within fan cultures as early as the 1920s (H. Jenkins, personal correspondence, October 13, 1992). R.a.t.s. also adapts behavioral norms from Usenet culture, including conventions about when to quote previous messages when responding to them and how to edit those quotes. I will return to norms and vocabulary in the discussion of social dimensions of computer-mediated community below.

Participants access r.a.t.s. through personal accounts that they almost always obtain through student status or through their places of employment. This work context influences some of the shared significances in the group. Responses to funny posts, for example, often refer to the work environment, as with "I was laughing so hard everybody knew I wasn't working." Even though it is nearly impossible to determine the demographics of Usenet participants, they seem to be predominantly male. R.a.t.s. participants, in contrast, are overwhelmingly female, due, no doubt, to the fact that they are also participants in soap opera fan culture (or fandom), a predominantly female subculture.

This external subculture of soap opera fandom is of fundamental importance to the interaction on r.a.t.s. It provides a wealth of resources and practices with which participants organize their talk. Being a soap opera fan involves more than faithful viewing. Soap fans are especially involved viewers—many have watched the same shows for over 20 years. They support an entire soap opera industry including not just the production of the soaps but also several magazines, merchandising operations, dozens of fan clubs, prime-time awards shows, celebrity public appearances, charity events across America, and even cruises with the stars. Fans vary in the extent to which they take advantage of all of these options. When hundreds of these fans are brought together, as they are on r.a.t.s., information drawn from all these sources is pooled. One communicative practice on r.a.t.s. that emerges as a direct consequence of soap fandom is the sharing of news culled from these many resources. Another informative communication practice on r.a.t.s. that is directly related to soap operas is the daily "updates" that retell in extraordinary detail what happened on the shows.

Besides providing informative practices, the context of soap opera fandom provides interpretive practices that are central to the communication in r.a.t.s.

These include identifying with characters, bringing the real world to bear on interpreting story lines, speculating on the meaning of soap opera events, and criticizing the show. Interpretation of the characters' behavior and psyches is the most common activity on r.a.t.s. (Baym, in press-a). Soap operas present communities of as many as 40 characters, many of whom have been on the shows for years. The fans find most characters interesting; they identify with some, hate others, and love hating some. Importantly, they come to care what happens to the characters, and they see and interpret the story through characters' perspectives (Livingstone, 1990). To interpret character psyches and see things from their perspectives, participants must draw on their own interpersonal and emotional experiences as well as other areas of expertise. Because soap characters live in a world where life is focused always on the personal, the familial, the relational, and, above all, the emotional, viewers must bring their own knowledge of these realms to bear on interpretation. The viewers' relationship with characters, the viewers' understanding of socioemotional experience, and soap opera's narrative structure, in which moments of maximal suspense are always followed by temporal gaps, work together to ensure that fans will use the gaps during and between shows to discuss with one another possible outcomes and possible interpretations of what has been seen (Allen, 1985; Ang, 1985; Brundson, 1989; Geraghty, 1991; Nochimson, 1992). When fans use r.a.t.s. for such discussions they rely on preexisting practices of soap fandom.

Temporal Structure

Many researchers have pointed out that the temporal structure of CMC can be either synchronistic or asynchronistic. With synchronistic communication, all participants are on-line simultaneously and read and respond to one another immediately. This is the case in most of the cues-filtered-out research discussed earlier here (Hollingshead & McGrath, in press). With asynchronistic communication, participants need not be on-line simultaneously and can read and respond at different times. This is the case in the field studies of corporate uses of CMC discussed by Sproull and Kiesler (1991) and Steinfeld (1986). Hollingshead and McGrath (in press) expand this dichotomy to include three further ways the interaction can be temporally structured. First, the group may meet only once for a limited time, communicating either synchronistically or asynchronistically. Second, the group can carry out a series of meetings, again either synchronistically or asynchronistically. Third, the group can carry on a continual asynchronistic meeting over an extended time period. Differences in temporal structures influence the availability of immediate feedback, the opportunity to compose and rewrite messages before sending them, how many members of a group are participating at any given time, and other variables that directly affect a group's communication patterns.

The temporal structure of r.a.t.s., as with all Usenet newsgroups, is that of an ongoing asynchronistic meeting. Messages are stored at each site for a time period left to the system administrators to decide, usually no longer than a couple of weeks. Until the old messages are removed, readers can check in at their convenience to read or respond to what has arrived. This temporal structure provides both challenges and opportunities. Because messages arrive in chronological rather than topical order, it can be difficult to maintain topical coherence (although many newsreaders offer users strategies for overcoming this). On the other hand, the fact that things can be read and responded to at one's leisure makes it possible for more people to participate and for people to contemplate and edit their messages before sending them. It also allows people to respond to multiple messages at one time.

The temporal structure of r.a.t.s. is also affected by the fact that its use is situated in office environments. Because most r.a.t.s. participants access the group while at work, most messages are written during working hours Monday through Friday, with far less traffic generated during evenings and weekends. The temporal structure of participation is also influenced by the temporal structure of the soap operas. Because there are five new episodes of each soap opera each week and the stories continually evolve, it is only relevant to respond to posts for a few days. Most responses on r.a.t.s. are posted within 48 hours of the original post (Baym, in preparation). Temporal norms of relevance are an important dimension of temporal structure not previously addressed. The evidence from r.a.t.s. suggests that such norms may be related to the external contexts in which interaction is situated.

System Infrastructure

As the differences in possible temporal structures suggest, computer network infrastructures shape interaction in many ways. Seibold et al. (in press) argue that systems differ in three general ways: physical configurations, system adaptability, and level of user friendliness. Physical configuration includes such subvariables as how many computers there are, how they are spatially dispersed, and the speed of the system. System adaptability includes variables like the capacity for anonymous entries and the system's programmability. User friendliness incorporates the dimensions of ability to support multiple tasks, flexibility and ease of learnability, and others. A difference in any one of these many features modifies the possibilities available to users as they develop organized communicative systems.

R.a.t.s. is highly influenced by the structure of Usenet and the newsreaders through which it is read and written. It is beyond the scope of this chapter to fully explain the structure of Usenet or newsreaders; the reader is referred to Kehoe (1992), Gene Spafford's monthly postings in the newsgroup news.announce.newusers, and Rapaport (1991) for more detailed description. Here I want to address a few salient features of Usenet and of the newsreaders that influence emergent social patterns in Usenet groups. Usenet shapes both the temporal structure and the participant structure of interaction. It shapes temporal structure, as I have suggested, because it is a continual asynchronous medium. Another element of the temporal structure attributable to Usenet infrastructure is the fact that most posts are distributed to the other sites within a matter of minutes or hours, although some sites may not receive messages for days. Responses to messages may thus come within minutes or take as long as days. At some sites, replies may arrive before the original posts do. Coherent threads of conversation spans days or weeks. Usenet also shapes the participant structure of its interaction. Usenet links almost 3 million people, any of whom can read anything posted to any group received at their site. Because anyone can read or participate, all Usenet interaction is fundamentally multiparty and public. People never know who all the readers of their messages are.

The interaction on Usenet is also shaped by the many newsreader programs that are used to read and post to the groups. Three especially significant features of newsreaders are the headers they automatically attach to the top of all posts, the quotation system they provide, and the possibility for readers to create "KILL files" to edit what they read. The headers convey information about the sender, the subject of the message, the time the message was sent, and more. This information can be, and is, used by participants to decide what to read and what not to read. The quotation system that most newsreaders provide makes it easy for posters to quote previous messages when they respond to them. Quoted material is automatically marked, usually with a > at the start of each line. Responses can then be embedded directly into the original message at relevant points. This system along with the use of subject identification in the headers allow posts to be explicitly linked. Without these features of newsreaders it would be difficult to navigate the flood of seemingly disconnected messages. Finally, many newsreaders allow users to create KILL files that recognize patterns in the headers and delete messages matching those patterns. People use KILL files to avoid topics or to avoid reading messages from particular individuals. For fuller discussion of these and other Usenet features' effect on practice in r.a.t.s., the reader is referred to Baym (in press-b).

Group Purposes

The purposes toward which group interactions are oriented also affect the discourse. The literature I have discussed thus far has limited its conceptualization of purpose to "tasks." Hollingshead and McGrath (in press) propose the most articulated perspective on tasks, arguing that task types have prior structures that affect communication processes. Drawing on an earlier formulation by McGrath (1984), they claim that tasks vary in whether they require that the group generate ideas or plans, choose among answers or solutions, negotiate conflicting views or conflicting interests, or execute performances in competition with opponents or external standards. These four task types differ in whether or not each requires "the transmission of information among members of the group, or also requires the transmission of values, interests, personal commitments and the like" (Hollingshead & McGrath, in press). The task at hand thus influences the extent to which the individuals are involved or invested in what they say in CMC as well as influencing more obvious factors, such as the topics that will be raised.

Although this is an important insight, it is limiting to view all CMC as task oriented because a good deal of CMC is primarily social. It is interesting that there has been very little work on recreational uses of CMC because there is good reason to believe that is CMC's most popular use. A tremendous amount of the traffic on Prodigy®, Compuserve, and other interactive commercial computer networks and on Usenet is recreational (Grimes, 1992). Furthermore, the social use of CMC is expanding rapidly as the number of modems in use grows and as commercial networks, Usenet, and independent BBSs continue to offer a growing range of forums to increasing numbers of participants. As was the case with Usenet, originally designed so that software could be exchanged between North Carolina and California (Raymond, 1991), often participants in CMC have taken a system that was not intended to be fun and transformed its usage despite the intentions of the networks' founders. In one of the earliest pieces on commercial CMC networks, Carpenter (1983) observed that "what Compuserve and the Source apparently didn't realize when they first put together their potpourri of consumer goods is that people are not crying for airline schedules and biorhythms, but to talk to one another" (p. 9). If this was true in 1983, it is even more so now.

A glance at Usenet illustrates the popularity of recreational and social CMC use. In the 20 most-read discussion groups in March 1993 (B. Reid, 1993a), 25% (4,629 messages) of all messages were in groups organized to discuss social issues ranging from political activism to Indian culture. Almost 20% of the messages were in groups that discuss sex. If readership taps the users' curiosities, the number of messages each group generates taps the users' creative investments. In the highest-volume discussion groups, 50% (24,983 messages) of the messages were about social issues, including Indian culture, abortion, homosexuality, and guns. Another 40% (20,025 messages) of the messages in these high traffic groups were in fan groups that discussed sports, television shows, and movies. (For current figures, the reader is referred to the monthly and biweekly rankings of Usenet use posted by Brian Reid and Rick Adams, respectively, to the newsgroup news.lists.) In short, Usenet is used, above all, for social interaction on topics of personal rather than professional interest. Forcing the purposes of categories as broad as "discussing homosexuality" into a typology of tasks is clearly more limiting than clarifying. A general model of CMC requires a more flexible understanding of group purposes.

Analysis of the communicative practices on r.a.t.s. reveals that the talk is aimed toward several purposes. Some of these purposes are influenced by the external context of soap opera fandom. Others emerge within the group's interaction. A common finding in work on soap opera fans is that the opportunity to discuss soap operas with others is a valued incentive to watch (Rubin & Perse, 1987), and having others with whom to discuss the soap opera increases the extent to which people expect to gain pleasure from soap opera viewing (Babrow, 1989). The primary goal around which interaction is constructed on r.a.t.s. is to enhance the pleasure of soap opera involvement. As I suggested in my discussion of the context of soap fandom, enhancing soap opera pleasure through talk, whether computer mediated or not, involves practices of collaborative interpretation and distributing information. The fact that collaborative interpretation of soap operas involves sharing perspectives on socioemotional issues creates non-soap-opera concerns toward which participants orient. Discussion often evolves beyond the soap opera to tackle these socioemotional issues more directly. At these times, r.a.t.s. serves as a forum for the discussion and negotiation of private issues difficult to discuss publicly. The topics addressed in these extended discussions range from corporal punishment, sexual abuse and assault, wife beating, and racism to engagements, weddings, and pregnancies. The use of r.a.t.s. as a forum for talking about issues beyond the soap opera, issues which are often highly personal and emotionally charged, shows that while some purposes are predetermined, others can emerge within a group's interaction. For those who engage in this personal talk over extended periods of time, maintaining friendships and acquaintances becomes another purpose of the interaction. Some of the purposes of r.a.t.s., then, are to provide information about what has happened and what will happen on the shows, to interpret the shows, to negotiate private issues in a public space and to sustain relationships.

Although some purposes of a CMC group are givens, this discussion shows that the complete list of purposes is a question for empirical analysis.

Participant Characteristics

Group and member characteristics are the final factor that has been argued to affect CMC outcomes. One important group characteristic is size, which can vary from fewer than 10 to thousands. Other important group characteristics are composition, members' joint interactional history, and whether or not the group is hierarchically structured (Baron, 1984; Hollingshead & McGrath, in press; Seibold et al., in press). Individual members differ in their degrees of training in the medium, ability and task experience, experience with new technologies, and attitudes toward technology (Hollingshead & McGrath, in press; Seibold et al., in press). Participant perceptions in particular are privileged as particularly important determinants of communicative outcomes. Steinfeld (1986), in his study of social and task-oriented uses of e-mail in an organizational setting, found that participant perception of the medium was a major determinant of whether or not people used it socially. Those most likely to use the computers socially did not perceive computers as low in social presence. I have already argued that this is true of the participants in r.a.t.s., who are involved in the group voluntarily and many of whom work on computers daily and are quite adept at using them for interpersonal communication. R.a.t.s. participants, like the millions of others who use computers socially, often view the computer as a "playground" (E. Reid, 1991).

R.a.t.s. is a large group. Several hundred people write in r.a.t.s. each month, and as many as 41,000 may read it at least once each month (B. Reid, 1993b). Participants are distributed geographically throughout the United States and Canada. A handful of people participate from Europe, Australia, and New Zealand. Their jobs are diverse. There are nurses, secretaries, engineers, scientists, teachers, students, and more. The group thus brings together people who would not otherwise interact and who have no preexisting social structures. Several interactants, however, enter r.a.t.s. with preexisting acquaintances from other Usenet groups.

The participants on r.a.t.s., as I have said, are mainly women, although many men are involved. The gender balance of the group affects the communication in several ways. The personal topics broached, for example, are often those that particularly affect women. There is also a social taboo against insulting one another, a consideration that, in light of other Usenet interaction, seems gendered, a point I return to shortly.

Because r.a.t.s. participants have diverse experiences, each brings unique resources to the group. The relevance of those resources depends, of course, on the twists of soap opera story lines. Those with knowledge of law, for instance, were able to debate whether it was wise for an attorney on *All My Children* to seek an "order of protection" rather than a "restraining order" against the client's psychotic ex-husband. Those who read the soap opera press are able to bring the resources of inside information. Those who watch daily and have time may post regular updates of the shows. As the soap operas cover a range of personal topics, participants differ in what relevant life experiences they can bring to the interpretive process. Finally, participants span a wide range of writing skill, wit, and insight. Together their knowledge, opinion, experience, and skill provide more than enough resources to transform soap opera viewing into a collaborative communal enterprise.

Summary

Clearly, it is a mistake to view patterns in CMC as direct effects of the medium. As the work discussed above shows, there are at the least five different sources of impact on CMC. Each of those sources—external contexts, temporal structure, system infrastructure, group purposes, and participant characteristics—is itself composed of subvariables. Furthermore, these already complicated factors affect one another in ways that may not be expected, as when the external context of soap operas impacts on norms of temporal relevance or on purposes in the group. Finally, the discussion of purposes in r.a.t.s. demonstrates that which aspects of the five categories of impact are relevant in a group may be emergent rather than predictable. It may not be possible to specify in advance of actual interaction what specific factors in what combination will be relevant to CMC outcomes in a particular group, let alone what their impact will be. Research on CMC must attend to the areas of impact raised in this section if the findings are to be comparable with those of other studies.

Appropriation

The idea that communicative outcomes in CMC are emergent is shared by Contractor and Seibold (1993), who draw on Giddens to argue in their work on group decision support systems (GDSS) that the outcomes of CMC use depend on how the participants appropriate the rules and resources from these preexisting sources of influence through their social interaction. Contractor and Seibold base appropriations in members' perceptions of the group's rules for structuring discussion and in the content and pattern of group interaction. Drawing on structuration theory and self-organizing systems theory, they argue that the group members' interactive appropriation of the preexisting rules and resources creates structure beyond that which already exists. The generative mechanism of a group's structure, they argue, lies in the recursive interplay between structure and interaction. The patterns of appropriation that emerge in computer-mediated groups may attain stability, may occur cyclically, or may fluctuate, depending on the fit between the factors of temporal structure, external contexts, communicative purposes, and participant characteristics. The notion of "appropriation" is apt. Rather than seeing participants in CMC as operating in ways dictated by the available resources or rules, appropriation implies that participants pick and choose from what is available, at times using things in unexpected ways, at times not using some of the possibilities.

However, Contractor and Seibold leave the specifics of appropriation vague. The scholar looking to see how, in general, groups appropriate what is offered and transforms possibilities into social structures is left without precise pointers about where to look or what to look for in search of "appropriation." Answers to these questions can be found in the growing body of work in many of the social sciences that approaches culture as a system dynamically recreated through the interplay between preexisting structures and the practices of everyday life (Ortner, 1984). This practice perspective runs through the work of the French sociologist Bourdieu (1977) and many recent scholars of language socialization, including Ochs (1988), Schieffelin (1990), and Miller and Hoogstra (1992). These scholars have used ethnography to record and interpret the concerns toward which members of a culture orient their interaction and the ways in which they use cultural resources, especially language, to achieve and validate cultural meanings. This work has shown that even the most mundane interactions require that people draw upon preexisting resources that have meaning within a community to create and invoke event types, identities, relationships, and norms. It is through the use of resources to invoke social meanings that culture is continually recreated and modified.

This thumbnail sketch of the practice approach to culture suggests that the researcher interested in computer-mediated groups' appropriation of resources needs to view the creation of social meanings as central to the appropriation process. Social meanings are found in communicative practice. The work I discussed in the first section focused on preexisting structures. Those structures do not make a group. Social organization emerges in a dynamic process of appropriation in which participants invoke structures to create meanings in ways that researchers or system designers may not foresee. Those innovative uses may, in turn, impact the structures. In the next section, I turn to the creation of social meaning through everyday computer-mediated interaction.

Emergent Social Dynamics

All interaction, including that which is task oriented, conveys social meaning and thus creates social context (Goodwin & Duranti, 1992; Watzlawick, Beavin, & Jackson, 1967). The social meanings created in CMC have been the focus in studies of Internet Relay Chat (IRC), a mode of interaction on the Internet in which people are able to communicate synchronistically on different "channels" from disparate locations (E. Reid, 1991), BBSs in single cities which cater to specific interests including software distribution and role-play games (Myers, 1987a, 1987b), and a universitywide network populated primarily by computer students (Hellerstein, 1985), as well as in my work with r.a.t.s. These researchers show that, rather than being constrained by the computer, the members of these groups creatively exploit the systems' features so as to play with new forms of expressive communication, to explore possible public identities, to create otherwise unlikely relationships, and to create behavioral norms. In so doing, they invent new communities. I review each of these four facets of the creation of community in more detail and suggest how each might be related to the factors of external context, temporal structure, system infrastructure, group purposes, and participant characteristics discussed above.

Forms of Expression

The computer medium is often used to diffuse forms of expressive communication usually associated with face-to-face communication (Dorst, 1991; Fox, 1983). Fox (1983) found that computerized networks in a high school were quickly taken over as a way to share jokes and riddles. The success of the Usenet group rec.humor also shows this transmission of expressive communication via CMC. However, Fox went beyond arguing that CMC was used for expressive purposes to propose that eventually the medium could lead to the development of new forms of expressive communication. Bakhtin (1986) is among those who argues that as groups develop over time they generate group-specific meanings. Eventually, new forms of speech, or genres, unique to that community evolve. Indeed, countless new forms have been created and conventionalized as part of the interactive process in computer-mediated communities. A few of these innovations are ways to express affect, new vocabulary, new kinds of jokes, and new categories of talk all together. In what follows, I discuss each of these.

Rather than accepting the filtering out of social cues, CMC users invented, and continue to invent, new ones. Smiley faces, graphic icons built out of punctuation marks, are used for a variety of purposes often served by facial expressions or vocal intonations. They smile (:-)), wink mischievously (;-}), and frown (:-(). They may indicate that a comment is to be taken as humorous or sarcastic. They may indicate good spirits, disappointment, surprise, and a range of other emotions. They may also suggest general friendliness. Creative ones may be used to indicate the identity of the user, as when an "8" is substituted for the colon to show that the poster wears glasses. These "emoticons" are collected in "smiley face dictionaries." Compiled by users, the dictionaries catalogue those emoticons actually in use as well as dozens of purely silly ones meant to represent things as obscure as buck-toothed vampires. That the repertoire of smiley faces is codified into folk dictionaries and circulated informally among users indicates that users are aware that their cultures have group-specific forms of expression and take active roles in the codification of those expressions.

Smiley faces are only one of many expressive innovations in CMC. Others are personalized signatures, using asterisks or capital letters for emphasis and explicit verbal descriptions of behavior. Because people being funny in CMC cannot hear their audience's laughter (or lack thereof), the amused often describe themselves as "rolling on the floor laughing," sometimes abbreviated to ROFL. Movements in the fictional spaces of computer-mediated role-play games may be described in great detail (Danet & Reudenberg, 1992).

Users of r.a.t.s. adapt these communicative innovations from other CMC contexts and also create their own forms of expression. The response to humorous posts mentioned earlier—"I laughed so hard everybody knew I wasn't working"—is one such r.a.t.s.-specific convention. Another r.a.t.s.-specific expressive innovation is the acronym IOAS, meaning "it's only a soap" and repeated like a mantra at times when the show is particularly unrealistic or otherwise frustrating.

R.a.t.s. also invents a good deal of group-specific vocabulary that is loaded with expressive intentions. Soap opera characters are nicknamed, for example. *Days of Our Lives'* Marlena became "Big Bird" and Carly was renamed "Camel Lips." The day the character of Natalie on *All My Children* was fatally injured in a car accident her moniker was changed from "Nat" to "Splat." Like the smiley face dictionaries, lists of nicknames are often compiled and posted to the group or e-mailed to confused newcomers. Again, the active collection and codification of the group's expressive forms demonstrates the self-reflexivity of computer-mediated community.

R.a.t.s. has also developed unique forms of jokes. "Soap opera laws," for instance, enumerate common narrative devices, such as "if you only have sex once, you will get pregnant." The posing of "unanswered questions" in the *All My Children* discussion likewise finds its humor in drawing attention to the absurdity of the soap opera world and demonstrating competence in reading the soap opera genre. New categories of communication are also found in r.a.t.s., some borrowed from Usenet culture. These include the "updates," which retell the soap operas, "spoilers," which preview what will happen on the shows, "predictions," guesses as to what will happen on the show, and "TAN"s, discussions tangential to the topic of soap operas.

These innovative forms of expression that occur as part of the creation of computer-mediated culture are related to each of the factors discussed earlier. The external context of being "on the net" provides an extensive expressive vocabulary and repertoire of emoticons. External cultural norms about the expression of affect suggest when their use might be appropriate. The temporal structure of CMC groups allows them time to develop needs for forms of expression, needs that will be influenced by the group's purposes, and time to codify particular forms. The system infrastructure disables many conventional forms of expression but also offers the tools and links to build new forms. Finally, participant characteristics provide the creativity that generates and chooses among emergent forms of expressive communication.

Identity

The cues-filtered-out perspective argues that the computer creates anonymity, which leads to a decrease in social inhibition and an increase in flaming. In this way, anonymity is conceptualized as something both inevitable and problematic. The finding that people are more insulting when using anonymous CMC has also been found in fieldwork on BBSs and IRC (Myers, 1987a, 1987b; E. Reid, 1991). However, Myers and Reid have argued that, rather than being seen as a negative influence by CMC participants, anonymity is often valued because it creates opportunities to invent alternative versions of one's self and to engage in untried forms of interaction. Reid writes on-line that IRC "users are able to express and experiment with aspects of their personality that social inhibition would generally encourage them to suppress." Carpenter (1983) demonstrates this when she writes about trying "compusex," or interactive sex carried out via the Compuserve network. Given time, anonymous CMC users do build identities for themselves. However, even in systems that are not anonymous, identities are actively and collaboratively created by participants through processes of naming, signing signatures, role creation, and self-disclosure.

The obvious starting point in creating an identity is in the choice of a name. Myers (1987b) writes that names are "transformed into trademarks, distinctive individual smells by which their users are recognized as either friends or enemies within an otherwise vague and anonymous BBS communication environment" (p. 240). Anonymous CMC systems give people the chance to name themselves (Myers, 1987b; E. Reid, 1991). Other systems attach real names, as do many Usenet newsreaders, but users may still sign their messages with names they have chosen for themselves. Walther and Burgoon (1992), for example, studying a nonanonymous CMC system, found that participants still developed nicknames and used embellished signatures. Taking a social-information-processing perspective, Walther and Burgoon suggest that the creative enhancement of naming counteracts the inordinately high levels of uncertainty about one another in computer-mediated space. This is further supported by reports that names are also enhanced to define identity in other disembodied communication media, including citizens band (CB) radio (Dannefer & Poushinsky, 1977; Kalcik, 1985) and urban subway graffiti (Castleman, 1982).

The computer medium offers the chance not only to enhance one's name but to create fictional identities for one's self. Kalcik (1985), writing about the choice of a CB "handle," or on-the-air name, says, "In discussing handles and identities, then, some significant aspects of the CB community include the choice between . . . the possibility of fantasy and real identities and their separation, or the maintenance of both side by side" (p. 102). One of the users of the BBS who Myers (1987b) examined, a 14-year-old who named himself "the Professor," told him, "You can make the character behind the alias exactly like you, nothing like you, a combination of both, or even make it vary depending on the situation" (p. 256). Anonymous users can switch genders, appearances, and countless other usually integral aspects of the public self. People can also take on multiple identities (Carpenter, 1983; E. Reid, 1991).

Both Dannefer and Poushinsky (1977) and Myers (1987b) found that participants highly valued their anonymity and protected it by carefully guarding the release of private information. For Myers, this meant that none of his subjects would complete his surveys accurately. While initially frustrating, his further interviews and observations revealed the significance of this seemingly useless data. Such information, he concluded, is excluded from discussion because of the expressive freedoms that accompany anonymity. One active New Orleans BBS participant, who goes by the name "Andromeda X," told him, "I keep my identity secret not because I am afraid of the contact with the people I meet in BBS but because anonymity is part of the magic" (p. 259). Not all users of social CMC thrive on anonymity, however. E. Reid (1991) writes of "net romances" in which people meet and fall in love over the IRC. The CB users who Kalcik (1985) studied had chosen to meet face-to-face and had thus given up their potential anonymity. Hellerstein (1985) also discusses CMC interactants who seem to interact as "themselves."

In r.a.t.s., people usually use their own names. Some take on nicknames, but most who use nicknames also promulgate their real names within the same messages. One prominent r.a.t.s. personality, for instance, uses her initials as a name, but her full name appears in the headers. The use of real names is no doubt partly due to the general Usenet tendency toward using real names. However, participants on r.a.t.s. actively discourage anonymity, suggesting that the Usenet is not the only influence on the creation of r.a.t.s. identities. When a person's e-mail address is a seemingly random collection of letters and numbers and there is neither a name nor a signature, people will often ask for a name when they respond. I argue that this aversion to anonymity is related to the nature of soap opera discussion and the emergent purposes of the group. As I have suggested, r.a.t.s. functions in part as a public sphere in which people can discuss what are normally private socioemotional issues. The soap opera is continually assessed for socioemotional realism, which entails a good deal of self-disclosure from participants on highly personal topics. The use of real names helps to create an intimate environment in which this kind of disclosure can be voiced. This intimate environment also makes it appropriate for people to build identities through explicit self-disclosure, as when a much-beloved poster who calls herself "Granma" reveals that she is a grandmother, a college undergraduate, and, among other attributes, a former stripper. Granma even shared with the group her joy and excitement when the daughter she had given up for adoption years ago came, with her own daughter, to live with her. Participants also individualize themselves by taking on different roles within the group. As I discuss elsewhere (Baym, in press-a), only a few participants can take on the role of updater for a particular day's episodes. Some create roles for themselves by creating new genres of post, as with the man who invented the AMC "unanswered questions."

Another means of creating identity, one related to naming, is the creation of a "signature file," a possibility that some computer networks, including Usenet, offer. Signature files are attached automatically to the bottom of posts by the sender's newsreader. Signature files usually include a name and an e-mail address. Other components often included are quotations, company disclaimers, and illustrations created using punctuation marks and letters. Illustrations may show bicycles in the signature files of cyclists, longhorns in the case of University of Texas sports fans, or stylized representations of one's name. Signature files, because they appear in the body of each post from a given sender, are one of the most immediate and visually forceful cues to identity.

Through these practices, participants are able to interactively create identifiable personalities for themselves in this potentially anonymous terrain. The creation of social identities is clearly related to the interplay between the factors discussed in the previous section. The temporal structure of the group affects the ability to build identity. Without sufficient time, none of the practices of identity formation discussed here can occur. Individual identities must also be understood in terms of their own temporal structures; one of the most important distinctions between posters is the frequency with which they write. Most people write less than twice a month, a few several times each week (Baym, 1992). Furthermore, some who write only a few times each month may participate long enough that their cumulative contribution will forge them an individual role in the community. External contexts and group purposes also affect the formation of identity. This is seen in r.a.t.s. when anonymity is discouraged and self-disclosure encouraged as a result of the context of the soap opera and the practical goals that its discussion entails. The ability to be anonymous or to append signature files depends on the system infrastructure. Anonymous systems will offer a greater range of potentials. However, even in nonanonymous systems, identity is creatively constructed through the use of enhanced naming, signature files, self-disclosure, and role adoption. The personalities themselves come, of course, from the idiosyncratic qualities of participant characteristics. The extent to which people use CMC as a means to invent new personas, to recreate their own identities, or to engage in a combination of the two and the ways in which they do so are issues central to the construction of a computer-mediated social world.

Relationships

Not only can CMC participants have identities, they can have relationships with other participants. In some cases, people go into CMC with preexisting face-to-face relationships, as is the case when colleagues in the same office use CMC (Baron, 1984; Seibold et al., in press; Steinfeld, 1986). In other cases, people know one another from prior computer-mediated interactions in different contexts. Myers (1987b) found that many of the people on his BBS had already established relationships on other BBSs. Subscribers to multiple electronic mailing lists or readers of multiple Usenet newsgroups know that even in a network as vast as the Internet the same people cross paths repeatedly.

People also construct new relationships within computer-mediated groups. Walther and Burgoon (1992) argue that the problems that computers pose for the establishment of relationships are easy to surmount. The social information unavailable in the immediacy of the face-to-face context can be gained verbally through computer-mediated interaction; the "social penetration process" just takes longer. Using a factor-analytic approach to relational development, they found that participants' ratings of one another on the socially desirable dimensions of composure/relaxation, informality, receptivity/trust, and social (versus task) orientation increased over time while ratings of one an- other's dominance decreased. In other words, people came to perceive one another in ways that reflected a greater sense of social relationship.

The work of both Myers (1987b) and Hellerstein (1985) suggests that some of the heavier CMC users thrive on the relational possibilities of the medium. The heavy users of the University of Massachusetts system that Hellerstein studied said their primary use of the system was to communicate with friends. They reported spending more time in computer-mediated social interaction than on the phone or in face-to-face communication. Myers found two kinds of experts among his heavy users: one technologically astute and the other relationally astute, both of whom dominated the message flow. What he called the "social experts," those who focused on relational concerns within the group, gained their power from their ability to nurture and direct the flow of on-line relationships. They saw the computer as a community and the communication networks as based on social relationships. They interpreted the communication content as the expression of values and saw the result of communication as the creation of roles. My analysis of r.a.t.s. interaction demonstrates that the heaviest posters on the subject of *All My Children* were more likely than lighter users to attend to interpersonal alignment of the interaction. They are more likely, for example, to use people's names when they respond to their messages and to explicitly acknowledge others' perspectives (Baym, in preparation).

People who meet on-line may then take that relationship off-line if an opportunity arises, as was the case with the CB users Kalcik (1985) examined. Hellerstein (1985) found this relational movement off-line in her work as well. This has been the case on r.a.t.s., where people often arrange local get-togethers or meetings when one participant is visiting an area where others live. A few of the r.a.t.s. participants in my town, for instance, meet every few months for lunch to watch a few episodes of *All My Children* together or to meet a visiting r.a.t.s.ter.

Although it has always been treated as a negative consequence of CMC, even the seemingly antirelational practice of flaming can be reinterpreted as a kind of sporting relationship. Myers (1987a) describes flaming as a kind of play. Although he doesn't make the comparison, flaming might be compared to forms of ritual insults that are popular in children's peer groups and serve to define them as members of that group (Bronner, 1988). This is demonstrated by one of Myers's BBS users who wrote to a new user, "It is lots of fun to insult each other but don't get involved." Flaming occurs even when there is no anonymity and, as Myers's work suggests, might in some cases be better understood as a form of relationship to be enjoyed at an emotional distance than as a form of social paralysis caused by decreased social cues. Myers's description of this flaming as the "chest-thumping display of on-line egos" suggests that this kind of relationship may be gendered and that its prevalence in work on CMC may be related to the predominantly male composition of most CMC groups. The fact that flaming is discouraged far more vehemently than any other form of talk on r.a.t.s., a group composed predominantly of women, further supports this. R.a.t.s. participants with whom I have discussed this no-flaming norm have explicitly suggested to me that it is a consequence of the dominance of women in the group.

Relational development between CMC participants is also related to the five factors of external contexts, system infrastructure, temporal structure, group purposes, and participant characteristics. External contexts, such as the physical locations of the participants, clearly impact people's ability to meet or the likelihood that they are already acquainted. The external context of other networked interactions similarly affects whether or not participants may already know one another when they enter a group. System infrastructure provides the links across which relationships can form. As with the development of expressive communication and identities, relational development depends on the presence of a conducive temporal structure. In CMC, as in real life, relationships take time to build. Because the purpose of r.a.t.s. is to discuss soap operas, a process that, as I have shown, involves a fair amount of self-disclosure and discussion of private issues, creating friendly relationships becomes one of the emergent purposes of the group. The influence of participant characteristics on relational formation is seen in part in Myers's finding that the most relationally oriented users' perception of the computer was as a place on which relationships can thrive. The extent to which social relationships develop on-line seems to be influenced in part by the presence of a relatively few heavy users whose perceptions of the medium lead them to encourage the creation of interpersonal bonds in ways that may be quite subtle. CMC relationships may develop into face-to-face relationships, which can then play back into the computer-mediated relationships. The extent to which CMC groups appropriate the medium as a relational forum and the ways in which they do so are important issues in the social construction of computer-mediated societies.

Behavioral Norms

Many CMC groups create behavioral norms as well as the shared significances, personalities, and relationships I have discussed. Myers (1987b) writes that "there is widespread acknowledgment of a national BBS community—with both positive and negative norms of behavior" (p. 264). In the case of Usenet, some of these norms are codified into informational postings distributed across the network and summarized by Kehoe (1992). Usenet etiquette, or as it is called on-line, "netiquette," includes norms aimed at preventing others from having to read useless material, limiting the extent to which one can fictionalize identity, protecting other users' privacy, retaining attribution when following up on ideas, and remaining readable. The repertoire of emoticons used on Usenet also comes with a number of conventions about their appropriate use, including what kinds of messages should be marked and how many smiley faces is too many. Usenet groups that discuss television shows and movies often have a norm that the word "spoilers" should be included in the subject lines of posts that give away the story ahead of time. This enables those who don't want the show spoiled by this advanced information to avoid such posts. The system programmers and the participants in each subculture can also create unique normative standards (Hellerstein, 1985). IRC users, like the University of Massachusetts system users, continually reinforce the norms by creating structural and social sanctions against those who abuse the groups' systems of meaning (E. Reid, 1991).

In the course of this chapter I have mentioned a number of normative conventions that have developed in r.a.t.s. All of the Usenet netiquette is used in the group. Quotations are used, edited, and correct sources attributed, all in keeping with Usenet standards. Identities are represented relatively accurately. Emoticons are used to avoid misunderstandings. I have also discussed norms that have evolved within the group. The taboo against flaming others, I have argued, is one such norm. The group's temporal norm of relevance, which makes it inappropriate to post responses more than four or five days after the original message was posted, is another emergent norm.

The final norm I want to discuss in r.a.t.s. is also related to soap operas and represents a particularly organized innovation on the part of the participants. Because all soap operas are discussed in r.a.t.s., but few if any participants follow every soap opera, the need arose to identify which soap opera a post addresses. The group responded to this need by conventionalizing acronyms to designate each soap opera and using them at the start of every subject line. Participants can use these designations to construct KILL files that will delete messages on soap operas they don't follow. This rule of netiquette, more than any other on r.a.t.s., is systematically enforced. Those who omit the soap abbreviation in their subject lines, whether through ignorance or negligence, are likely to be chastised both publicly and through e-mail.

The norms that develop in r.a.t.s. and, I suggest, in any other group are directly related to the purposes of the group. It is to meet the needs of the community, needs both given and emergent, that standards of behavior and methods of sanctioning inappropriate behavior develop. The taboo on flaming in r.a.t.s., for instance, functions to keep r.a.t.s. a safe environment for the kinds of self-disclosures and expressions of opinion involved in interpreting soap operas. The system is clearly an influence on emergent norms; indeed, many of the norms revolve around the appropriate use of the system possibilities. Systems also provide different kinds of means to enforce norms. On systems like Prodigy, where posting is moderated, inappropriate messages can simply be yanked before they ever appear. In Usenet's unmoderated groups, in contrast, people turn, in effect, to shaming people into compliance by drawing attention to their violations. The external contexts influence norms both by providing preexisting standards and by providing the concerns around which normative systems develop. The r.a.t.s. norm of temporal relevance is related to the external context of soap opera fandom, resulting from the soap opera's continually evolving story structure. The temporal structure, as always, provides time to develop norms but also becomes subject to norms itself. In ongoing groups, norms will develop about how to use time, and these emergent temporal structures further structure interaction. Finally, participant and group characteristics, including gender, play a role in determining what behaviors people will and won't tolerate.

Conclusion

When Baron (1984) wrote that "computer-mediated communication—at least as currently used—is ill-suited for such 'social' uses of language" (p. 136), she assumed that the work she drew on (that of Sarah Kiesler and her associates) accurately reflected the current uses of CMC. This was not the case then and is certainly not the case now. If anything, the ways in which people have appropriated the commercial and noncommercial networks demonstrate that CMC not only lends itself to social uses but is, in fact, a site for an unusual amount of social creativity.

This discussion has shown that participants in CMC develop forms of expression which enable them to communicate social information and to create and codify group-specific meanings, socially negotiate group-specific identities, form relationships which span from the playfully antagonistic to the deeply romantic and which move between the network and face-to-face interaction, and create norms which serve to organize interaction and to maintain desirable social climates. As Dorst (1991) puts it, CMC "is an extremely active folkloric space, in which social and cultural forces operate and register" (p. 183). While the folk in CMC "may have little or nothing in common except access to a common computer and correlates of that access" (Fox, 1983, p. 15), together they appropriate the possibilities offered by commonality and individuality in ways that weave them into distinct communities. These communities, which span Internet Relay Chat, private BBSs, Usenet, commercial networks, and many in-house networks, create shared social realities through interactive negotiation. This chapter proposes that the creation of forms of expressive communication, identity, relationships, and norms through communicative practice in computer-mediated groups is pivotal to this process of creating community. Social realities are created through interaction as participants draw on language and the resources available to make messages that serve their purposes.

Interaction does not work on its own. The resources on which participants draw when they compose their messages and the rules that shape what they can do come from a variety of outside sources. The factors of temporal structure, external contexts, system infrastructure, group purposes, and participant and group characteristics have been put forward as the most salient preexisting forces on the development of computer-mediated community. I have tried to show the ways these forces affect one another as well as the ways they affect emergent social dimensions of the group. The emergence of pattern in a computer-mediated group is a complex and dynamic process. Rather than focusing on building predictive models of CMC, more naturalistic, ethnographic, and microanalytic research should be done to refine our understanding of both influences and outcomes.

References

Allen, R. C. (1985). *Speaking of soap operas.* Chapel Hill: University of North Carolina Press.

Ang, I. (1985). *Watching* Dallas: *Soap opera and the melodramatic imagination.* New York: Routledge.

Babrow, A. S. (1989). An expectancy-value analysis of the student soap opera audience. *Communication Research, 16,* 155-178.

Bakhtin, M. M. (1986). *Speech genres and other late essays.* Austin: University of Texas Press.

Baron, N. S. (1984). Computer mediated communication as a force in language change. *Visible Language, 18*(2), 118-141.

Baym, N. (1992, November). *Computer-mediated soap talk: Communication, community and entertainment on the net.* Paper presented at the annual meeting of the Speech Communication Association, Chicago.

Baym, N. (in press-a). Interpreting soap operas and creating community. *Journal of Folklore Research, 30.*

Baym, N. (in press-b). From practice to culture on Usenet. In S. L. Star (Ed.), *The cultures of computing.* London: Basil Blackwell.

Baym, N. (in preparation). *Communication, interpretation, and relationships: A study of a computer-mediated fan community.* Unpublished doctoral dissertation, University of Illinois, Urbana-Champaign.

Bourdieu, P. (1977). *Outline of a theory of practice.* Cambridge: Cambridge University Press.

Bronner, S. J. (1988). *American children's folklore.* Little Rock, AK: August House.

Brundson, C. (1989). Text and audience. In E. Seiter, H. Borchers, G. Kreutzner, & E. Warth (Eds.), *Remote control: Television, audiences, and cultural power* (pp. 116-129). New York: Routledge.

Carpenter, T. (1983, September 6). Reach out and access someone. *Village Voice,* pp. 9-11.

Castleman, C. (1982). *Getting up: Subway graffiti in New York.* Cambridge: MIT Press.

Cheseboro, J. W., & Bonsall, D. G. (1989). *Computer-mediated communication: Human relationships in a computerized world.* Tuscaloosa: University of Alabama Press.

Contractor, N. S., & Seibold, D. R. (1993). Theoretical frameworks for the study of structuring processes in group decision support systems: Adaptive structuration theory and self-organizing systems theory. *Human Communication Research, 19*(4), 528-563.

Danet, B., & Ruedenberg, L. (1992, October). *'Smiley' icons: Keyboard kitsch or new communication code?* Paper presented at the annual meeting of the American Folklore Society, Jacksonville, FL.

Dannefer, W. D., & Poushinsky, N. (1977). Language and community: CB in perspective. *Journal of Communication, 27,* 122-126.

Dorst, J. (1991). Tags and burners, cycles and networks: Folklore in the telectronic age. *Journal of Folklore Research, 27,* 179-190.

Fox, W. S. (1983). Computerized creation and diffusion of folkloric materials. *Folklore Forum, 16,* 5-20.

Geraghty, C. (1991). *Women and soap opera.* Cambridge: Polity.

Goodwin, C., & Duranti, A. (1992). Rethinking context: An introduction. In A. Duranti & C. Goodwin (Eds.), *Rethinking context: Language as an interactive phenomenon* (pp. 1-42). Cambridge: Cambridge University Press.

Grimes, W. (1992, December 1). Computer networks foster cultural chatting for modem times. *The New York Times,* p. B1.

Hellerstein, L. N. (1985). The social use of electronic communication at a major university. *Computers and the Social Sciences, 1,* 191-197.

Hiltz, S. R., & Turoff, M. (1978). *The network nation: Human communication via computer.* Reading, MA: Addison-Wesley.

Hollingshead, A. B., & McGrath, J. E. (in press). The whole is less than the sum of its parts: A critical review of research on computer-assisted groups. In R. Guzzo & E. Salas (Eds.), *Team decision and team performance in organizations.* San Francisco: Jossey-Bass.

Kalcik, S. (1985). Women's handles and the performance of identity in the CB community. In R. Jordan & S. Kalcik (Eds.), *Women's folklore, women's culture* (pp. 99-108). Philadelphia: University of Pennsylvania Press.

Kehoe, B. (1992). *Zen and the art of the Internet.* Electronic document.

Kiesler, S., Siegel, J., & McGuire, T. W. (1984). Social psychological aspect of computer-mediated communication. *American Psychologist, 39*(10), 1123-1134.

Livingstone, S. M. (1990). Interpreting a television narrative: How different viewers see a story. *Journal of Communication, 40,* 72-85.

McGrath, J. E. (1984). *Groups: Interaction and performance.* Englewood Cliffs, NJ: Prentice Hall.

Miller, P. J., & Hoogstra, L. (1992). Language as a tool in the socialization and comprehension of cultural meanings. In T. Schwartz, G. White, & C. Lutz (Eds.), *New directions in psychological anthropology* (pp. 83-101). New York: Cambridge University Press.

Myers, D. (1987a). A new environment for communication play: On-line play. In G. A. Fine (Ed.), *Meaningful play, playful meaning* (pp. 231-245). Champaign, IL: Human Kinetics Publishers.

Myers, D. (1987b). "Anonymity is part of the magic": Individual manipulation of computer-mediated communication contexts. *Qualitative Sociology, 19*(3), 251-266.

Nochimson, M. (1992). *No end to her: Soap opera and the female subject.* Berkeley: University of California Press.

Ochs, E. (1988). *Culture and language development.* Cambridge: Cambridge University Press.

Ortner, S. B. (1984). Theory in anthropology since the sixties. *Comparative Studies in Society and History, 26*(1), 126-166.

Rapaport, M. (1991). *Computer mediated communications: Bulletin board, computer conferencing, electronic mail, and information retrieval.* New York: John Wiley.

Raymond, E. S. (Ed). (1991). *The new hacker's dictionary.* Cambridge: MIT Press.

Reid, B. (1993a, April 7). *Usenet readership report for March, 1993.* Newsgroup: news.lists.

Reid, B. (1993b, August 6). *Usenet readership report for July, 1993.* Newsgroup: news.lists.

Reid, E. M. (1991). *Electropolis: Communication and community on Internet Relay Chat.* Electronic document.

Rice, R. E. (1984). *The new media: Communication, research, and technology.* Beverly Hills, CA: Sage.

Rice, R. E. (1989). Issues and concepts in research on computer-mediated communication systems. In J. A. Anderson (Ed.), *Communication yearbook 12* (pp. 436-476). Newbury Park, CA: Sage.

Rubin, A. M., & Perse, E. M. (1987). Audience activity and soap opera involvement: A uses and effects investigation. *Human Communication Research, 14*(2), 246-268.

Schieffelin, B. (1990). *The give and take of everyday life.* Cambridge: Cambridge University Press.

Seibold, D. R., Heller, M. A., & Contractor, N. S. (in press). Group decision support systems (GDSS): Review, taxonomy, and research agenda. In B. Kovacic (Ed.), *Organizational communication: New perspectives.* Albany: State University of New York Press.

Sproull, L., & Kiesler, S. (1991). *Connections: New ways of working in the networked organization.* Cambridge: MIT Press.

Steinfield, C. W. (1986). Computer-mediated communication in an organizational setting: Explaining task-related and socioemotional uses. In M. L. McLaughlin (Ed.), *Communication yearbook 9* (pp. 777-804). Beverly Hills, CA: Sage.

Walther, J. B. (1992). Interpersonal effects in computer-mediated interaction. *Communication Research, 19*(1), 52-90.

Walther, J. B., & Burgoon, J. K. (1992). Relational communication in computer-mediated interaction. *Human Communication Research, 19*(1), 50-88.

Watzlawick, P., Beavin, J., & Jackson, D. (1967). *Pragmatics of human communication: A study of interactional patterns, pathologies, and paradoxes.* New York: Norton.

8
VIRTUAL WORLDS: CULTURE AND IMAGINATION

Elizabeth Reid

Since William Gibson coined the term in his best-selling novel *Neuromancer,* "cyberspace" and virtual reality have been part of late-20th-century culture and have been infused with a variety of cultural and emotional meanings. Gibson himself envisaged a direct neural connection between humans and computers against a background of urban decay and personal alienation. The film *The Lawnmower Man* depicted a meld of mind-altering drugs and computer-controlled sensory stimulation that offered a new stage for the evolution of mankind toward both godlike wisdom and satanic evil. The popular media have posed cyberspace as the new frontier and the new promise of the 20th century. Gibson's "console cowboys"—virtuoso cyberspace users hacking at the edges of the law—have been incarnated in media coverage of groups such as the infamous Legion of Doom. Arcade games incorporating datagloves and headsets have become the latest fad in entertainment. *Business Week* filled its October 5, 1992, issue with features introducing virtual reality technologies and applications to its readers. Best-selling books such as *The Cuckoo's Egg* have promoted cyberspace as a stage for new levels of international espionage, betrayal, and tyranny acted on by glamorous foreign spies and dedicated heroes.

Technically speaking, the term "virtual reality" is most commonly used to refer to systems that offer visual, auditory, and tactile information about an environment that exists as data in a computer system rather than as physical objects and locations. This is the virtual reality depicted in *The Lawnmower Man* and approximated by the "Virtuality" arcade games marketed by Horizon Entertainment. This chapter is not about these kinds of systems. I do not wish to talk about cyberspace or virtual reality as technological constructs but as cultural constructs. Along with Howard Rheingold (1991) I do not see virtual reality as a set of technologies but as an experience. More than that, I believe that it is primarily an imaginative rather than a sensory experience. I wish to shift the focus of attention away from the gadgets used to represent a virtual world and concentrate on the nature of the user's experience of such worlds. I contend that technical definitions of virtual reality beg the question of what it is about such systems that sustains the illusion of reality in the mind of the user. A list of technical components cannot explain why users are prepared to accept a simulated world as a valid site for emotional and social response.

The virtual reality systems I discuss are technically very simple. I have chosen to refer to a family of computer programs known as MUDs. MUDs are networked, multiparticipant, user-extensible systems most commonly found on the Internet, the international network that connects many thousands of educational, research, and commercial institutions. Using a MUD does not require any of the paraphernalia commonly associated with virtual reality. There are no visors or gloves, let alone body suits. The MUD interface is entirely textual, and a simple PC can act as a gateway into this kind of virtual world. Instead of using sophisticated tools to see, touch, and hear a virtual reality, users of MUD systems are presented with textual descriptions of virtual locations.

MUD originally stood for Multi-User Dimension, the name given by Richard Bartle and Roy Trubshaw to the computer game they designed in 1979. The original system consisted of a database of textual descriptions of a fantastic world of the swords and sorcery genre. Through reading these descriptions players could journey through the virtual world. Players could communicate with one another, could cooperate on adventures together—or fight against each other—and could create new objects, or descriptions of objects, that others could then interact with. Since the original game was written, many similar programs have appeared, the names of which reflect their indebtedness to the original—MUCK, MUSH, and LPMUD, to name but three of at least a dozen. There are many hundreds of individual programs running on the Internet, each depicting a different virtual environment. The name MUD is now used to refer to the entire class of such text-based virtual world systems, and the original expansion to Multi-User Dungeon has been commonly replaced by the more generic Multi-User Domain or Multi-User Dimension.

As Pavel Curtis (1992) has commented, the virtual worlds within MUD systems have many of the social attributes of physical places, and many of the usual social mechanisms apply (p. 26). Users treat the worlds depicted by MUD programs as if they were real. However, it is not the technological interface itself that sustains the willingness of users to treat this simulated environment as if it were real. Rather, it is the degree to which MUDs act not only as a tool for the expression of each user's imagination but mediate between the user's imagination and the communication to others of what he or she has imagined. Cyberspace—the realm of electronic impulses and high-speed data highways—may be figured as a technological construct, but virtual reality is a construct within the mind of a human being. Within this construct a representation of a person can be manipulated within a representation of a real or imagined environment, both of which can be manifested through the use of various technologies, including computers. Virtual worlds exist not in the technology used to represent them nor purely in the mind of the user but in the relationship between internal mental constructs and technologically generated representations of these constructs. The illusion of reality lies not in the machinery itself but in the user's willingness to treat the manifestations of his or her imaginings as if they were real.

Certain technical attributes of these virtual places, however, have significant effects on social phenomena, leading to new modes of interaction and new cultural formations. The lack of actual physical presence, indeed the great physical distances between individual participants, demands that a new set of behavioral codes be invented if the participants in such systems are to make sense to one another. The problems posed by the lack of cultural cues that physical presence carries influence behavior in virtual environments. The solutions that participants devise constitute the culture of the virtual world in which they are played out. It is the tension between the manifestation of conventional social and cultural patterns, the invention of new patterns, and the imaginative experience of these phenomena as taking part in a virtual world that is the subject of this chapter.

Scenery: Making Sense of the MUD World

Human communication is never merely a matter of words; much less so is human culture. For words to have a shared meaning they must be given a context. The information on which we decide which aspects of our systems of social conduct are appropriate to our circumstances are more often physical than verbal. We do not need to be told that we are at a wedding and should be quiet during the ceremony to enact the code of etiquette that our culture reserves for such an occasion. "Being cultured" says Greg Dening (1988), "we are experts in our semiotics. . . . We read sign and symbol [and] codify a thousand words in a gesture" (p. 12). In interacting with other people we rely on nonverbal information to delineate a context for our own contributions. Smiles, frowns, tones of voice, posture, and dress tell us more about the social context within which we are placed than do the statements of the people we socialize with. Language does not express the full extent of our cultural and interpersonal play. Words themselves tell only half the story—it is their presentation that completes the picture.

This is something that we all take for granted in our everyday lives—yet the virtual environments that are the subject of this study are a product of pure language, pure text. Because of this these virtual places subvert many of our assumptions about the practice of interactive communication. Unable to rely on conventions of gesture and nuances of tone to make sense to one another, common sense dictates that MUD users ought to fail to make sense or, at the least, be able to convey only sparse unemotional messages. This is, however, not the case. On the contrary, MUD environments are extremely culturally rich, and communication between MUD users is often highly emotionally charged. The means of expression open to users are limited by the technology on which MUDs are based, but instead of allowing that to restrict the content of their communication, users have devised methods of incorporating socioemotional context cues into pure language itself. They use text, seemingly such a restrictive medium, to make up for what they lack in physical presence. On MUDs, social presence is divorced from physical presence, a phenomenon that refutes many of the assumptions made in the past about the ideal richness of face-to-face interaction. On MUDs, text replaces gesture and has even become gestural itself.

A MUD program is, in essence, a set of tools that can be used to create a sociocultural environment. It is this that sets MUDs apart from other textually based, computer-mediated communication tools. The latter merely provide an interface that separates what one person types from that of another and so allows a form of written conversation. MUDs, by contrast, allow the depiction of a physical environment that can be laden with cultural and communicative meaning. They allow imagination and creativity to furnish the void of cyberspace with socially significant indicators. It is this that makes a MUD system a form of virtual reality.

When a user connects to a MUD through the computer network, he or she is immediately provided with a textual manifestation of the MUD's virtual environment. On LambdaMOO, run by Pavel Curtis at the Xerox Corporation's Palo Alto Research Center, the user will seem to enter the coat closet in the sprawling house that is at the core of the LambdaMOO world:

> *The Coat Closet*
>
> *The closet is a dark, cramped space. It appears to be very crowded in here; you keep bumping into what feels like coats, boots, and other people (apparently sleeping). One useful thing that you've discovered in your bumbling about is a metal doorknob set at waist level into what might be a door.*

Don't forget to take a look at the newspaper. Type "news" to see it. Type "@tutorial" for an introduction to basic MOOing. Please read and understand "help manners" before leaving The Coat Closet.

This coat closet is a remarkable place. It may be small and cramped, but it provides an initial point of reference in the Lambda world and furnishes the newcomer with information about the cultural nature of the world he or she has entered. Most MUDs contain an anteroom. It is often a cramped, dark place and rarely an open space with a great many sights to distract or disorient the newcomer. Closets, cracks under bandstands, teleportation rooms, and hotel hallways—to suggest just a few of the anterooms I have seen—might not seem especially inviting places in the actual world, but on textually represented virtual worlds they provide a sense of safety and familiarity. These spaces are sparsely furnished and do not overload the newcomer with information. At the same time they provide the reassurance of others' virtual presence, most often in the form of sleeping bodies, and they allow the user to pause for orientation before stepping into the main area of the virtual landscape. Most important, MUD anterooms typically contain pointers to helpful information and rules. The LambdaMOO novice is directed to a newspaper, which will tell him or her about recent events on the Lambda scene, a tutorial, which will explain how to interact with the Lambda universe on a technical level, and a list of advice on etiquette, which offers advice about social interaction on LambdaMOO.

Once ready, the LambdaMOO newcomer may decide to open the closet door and venture into the greater part of the virtual world. The first port of entry is the living room (reached by typing "out" from the Coat Closet):

The Living Room

It is very bright, open, and airy here, with large plate-glass windows looking southward over the pool to the gardens beyond. On the north wall, there is a rough stonework fireplace. The east and west walls are almost completely covered with large, well-stocked bookcases. An exit in the northwest corner leads to the kitchen and, in a more northerly direction, to the entrance hall. The door into the coat closet is at the north end of the east wall, and at the south end is a sliding glass door leading out onto a wooden deck. There are two sets of couches, one clustered around the fireplace and one with a view out the windows.

You see Cockatoo, README for New MOOers, a fireplace, a newspaper, Welcome Poster, The Daily Whale, The Birthday Machine, lag meter, Power Elite Voting Machine, Helpful Person Finder, a map of LambdaHouse, and A band of the knights who say NEE! here.

Guinevere, jane, MadHatter, Fred, Obvious, Alex, jean-luc, tureshta, Bullet_the_Blue, Daneel, KingSolomon, lena, Laurel, petrify, Ginger, and Groo are here.

The importance of anterooms on MUDs becomes much clearer once one has been exposed to the quantity of information that entrance into more dynamic areas elicits. The LambdaMOO living room is a social and virtually physical nexus. From this point the user of the system may enter an ever increasing number of virtual places. The body of the living room's description details the places that can be visited from that room. Having come this far, most novice players are provided with a strong sense of physical context, which provides a sense of the conceptual limitations and possibilities of the virtual world. Physical context is a dimension of social context—place and time are as much loaded with cultural meaning as are dress and gesture. LambdaMOO provides the place and makes it a nonthreatening, comfortable place. With fireplaces and couches, books, sunlight, fresh air, and poolside views, the LambdaMOO house is definitely a desirable residence. It is a place to relax and chat in, and that is exactly what people do in it.

Along with geographic centrality the living room provides social centrality. It is the main meeting place for LambdaMOO's inhabitants. It is quite likely the first port of call for newcomers seeking to find a social niche in the virtual setting. Initially, the living room was presented in such a way as to offer a sense of social orientation to newcomers. Fixtures in the room included a simple map of the main areas of the ever growing Lambda house, a welcome poster and a device enabling the newcomer to get in touch with users designated as "Helpful People" willing to answer questions and provide aid to the confused. As LambdaMOO has evolved, its users have added to this list of fixtures. The more popular additions are a device for registering one's birthdate and finding out the birthdates of other players and the LambdaMOO newspapers, which are commonly filled with social notes, gossip, announcements, and opinions. All of these objects, and the functions they perform, create LambdaMOO as a space held together by interpersonal sociality. Birthdays are remembered and commemorated. Help is easy to find and clearly advertised. All newcomers are offered a welcome, and the day-to-day social lives of LambdaMOO denizens are reported and commented on.

Most if not all MUDs—I have been unable to find an exception—provide the user with both an anteroom and a nexus point, each room containing information about the physical and social context of the MUD. The nature of that context differs widely between MUDs. Some, such as LambdaMOO, give an impression of warmth and friendliness. Others might be competitive and dangerous or might offer adventure and challenge. The details may differ, but the method of transmitting those details does not. MUDs create their own context out of language. The cues normally associated with sight and sound and touch are provided through description. The information with which newcomers are met allows them to imaginatively place themselves within the virtual world and encourages them to treat these textual cues as if they were physical cues. This information provides a common basis for interaction between players.

Speech: Making Sense of Each Other

The MUD system provides players with a stage, but it does not provide them with a script. Given the context created by the MUD universe, players are free to act and interact as they please. They are not technically dictated to by the MUD but are, instead, provided with tools that enable them to act and speak virtually. Interaction on most MUDs is carried out through the use of four commands known as say, emote, whisper, and page.[1] Each of these commands allows communicative information to be channeled in different ways. The say, emote, and whisper commands are used between players in the same virtual space. If the player in the Living Room is named Fred and he types, "say Hi there!" then all the players in that room will see

Fred says, "Hi there!"

If Fred then types, "emote grins amiably" all those in the room will see

Fred grins amiably.

The emote command can also be used to mix actions and utterances together. If Fred were to type "emote hugs Ginger warmly and says, 'It's great to see you again!'" those in the Living Room, including the character named Ginger, would see

Fred hugs Ginger warmly and says, "It's great to see you again!"

If, however, Fred wishes to communicate only with Ginger, he might choose to use the whisper command. Typing "whisper Hi there! to Ginger" will cause Ginger, and only Ginger, to receive

Fred whispers, "Hi there!"

Even if Ginger were not in the same virtual room as Fred, he could still communicate with her. The page command functions similarly to say and whisper but allows messages to be sent to a person in another virtual location. The results of this command appear this way:

Fred pages, "Hi there!"

Described baldly, this series of commands seems simplistic. They are, however, the tools with which social presence is formed on MUDs and through which social interaction is made possible. They may be simple, but they are immensely flexible. A player can say, whisper, or page whatever he or she chooses to and may emote any desired action or feeling. There is no technical limit to what can be expressed, although as I shall describe, conventions have arisen on MUDs that delimit the acceptability of various kinds and subjects of communication.

It is tempting to draw a parallel between MUDs and novels or plays. Given the above commands, it would be possible for interaction between players to resemble a play and for the social dimension of MUDs to be viewed as multiauthored interactive literature. However, despite this possibility, MUD sessions rarely resemble scripts or books. The language is simply not the same. It is more dynamic, less carefully constructed. The language of MUD players is a hybrid one and contains elements of both written and spoken forms. Conversations on MUDs are, after all, synchronous and ephemeral. Although sessions may be recorded using computer programs designed for the purpose, MUD interaction is not intended for an audience uninvolved in it. MUD interaction is not enacted to be read but to be experienced. As would spoken interaction, virtual interaction loses meaning when transposed to a computer file and reread. The pauses, breaks, disjunctions, speed, and timing of virtual conversations are lost in such transposition, and such factors are a crucial signifier of meaning and context.

MUD users' language does not employ the same degrees of respect for textual conventions as does written language. MUD users have at their command a keyboard that allows them to employ a finite set of characters—the alphabet, numbers, punctuation signs, and symbols such as % and &. Written language ascribes various rules to the use of these characters and gives each character a certain place and meaning. Ampersands, percentage signs and exclamation marks all have their assigned tasks in written texts. Capitalized and lower case letters are called into action in various well-known circumstances. Few written texts break with these conventions. Most writers begin sentences with capital letters, end questions with question marks, and use percentage and number (#) signs only when referring to numeric cases. MUD users, in common with users of computer-communication systems, do not hold with these conventions. For them, the standard symbols and signs available on a computer keyboard are tools to be called into uses far removed from that known to traditional grammarians. Commonly known as "smileys" or "emoticons," these are alphanumeric characters and punctuation symbols combined by MUD users to create strings of highly emotively charged keyboard art:

:-) or :) *a smiling face, viewed side on (tilt your head to the left)*

;-) or ;) *a winking, smiling face*

:-(or :(*an unhappy face, or 'unsmiley'*

:-(*) *someone about to throw up*

8-) *someone wearing glasses*

:-P *someone sticking out their tongue*

:-O *someone screaming in fright, their hair standing on end*

:-& *someone whose lips are sealed*

*<| :-) *Santa Claus*

!#!^*&:-) *a schizophrenic!*

Smileys or emoticons are pictographs made up of keyboard symbols. They are at once extremely simple and highly complex. They provide a form of shorthand for the depiction of physical and emotional condition. In a few keystrokes, MUD users can provide their fellows with a far more graphic and dynamic depiction of their feelings and actions than a conventional textual description could have furnished. Emoticons are legion on MUDs. Although the most commonly used is the plain smiling face—used to denote pleasure or amusement or to soften a sarcastic comment—MUD users continually develop their own emoticons, adapting the symbols available on the standard keyboard to create minute and essentially ephemeral pieces of textual art to represent their own virtual actions and responses. This method of presenting textual characters as representations of physical action can be confusing to the uninitiated. Interpreting them demands not only familiarity but also skill and imagination. Many emoticons are easy to interpret with a little practice. Others are more obscure but at the same time all the more evocative and affective once their obscurity has been explained. The "schizophrenic" smiley, while at first seeming a jumbled mess, offers both humour and meaning to those in the know.

MUD users share not only a common virtual environment but also a common language and a common textuality. Within the context of the former, the latter two allow MUD users to make sense of one another despite the allegedly low social bandwidth of the medium in which MUDs exist. MUD players share both a stage and an understanding of the rules and ways of breaking rules that allow them to speak meaningful lines. They are able to read each other in far more than a textual fashion. With inventiveness and lateral thinking has come a set of tools and symbols enabling MUDs to become a social environment within which MUD users experience human dramas as strongly as they might in actuality.

"Culture," suggest Van Maanen and Barley (1985), "can be understood as a set of solutions devised by a group of people to meet specific problems posed by situations they face in common" (p. 33). Users of MUD systems are commonly faced by the problems inherent in the medium's reduction of experience to pure text and its annihilation of conventional models of social interaction based on physical proximity. The measures that users of MUD systems have devised to meet their common problems are the markers of their common culture. They have devised systems of symbolism and textual significance that enable them to achieve understanding despite the absence of conventional social context cues. With these tools MUD users are able to read between the lines of text that make up their virtual world, a skill that is all the more challenging and all the more crucial in such an environment. These shared abilities and strategies allow me to think of the users of a MUD as sharing a common culture, and this common culture allows MUD users to engage in activities that serve to bind them together as a community.

Plot: Social Experience on MUDs

If all computer-mediated communication (CMC) can be said to have one single unifying effect upon human behavior it is that users of such systems become less inhibited. Although they often disagree on the effects of such lack of inhibition, researchers of human behavior on these systems have often noted that users tend to behave more freely than they would in face-to-face encounters. Kiesler and Sproull (1986) state that computer-mediated behavior "is relatively uninhibited and nonconforming" (p. 1498). Kiesler, Siegel, and McGuire (1984) have observed that "people in computer-mediated groups were more uninhibited than they were in face-to-face groups" (p. 1129). The forms that this disinhibition take differ from one researcher's experience to that of the next. Some have seen an increase in examples of aggressive and disrespectful behavior; others have noted increases in friendliness and intimacy. Behavior on MUDs conforms to these observations. Players do seem to be less inhibited by conventions adhered to in everyday life. They can be seen to be both more intimate and more hostile with each other than would be socially acceptable in everyday life, particularly when considering that hostility or intimacy may be shown by players who are strangers to one another.

Rice and Love (1987) have suggested that disinhibition may occur on CMC systems and in virtual environments "because of the lack of social control that nonverbal cues provide" (p. 89). However, as I have shown, nonverbal or socioemotional cues are indeed present on MUDs. The contexts and atmospheres that we take for granted in regulating our behavior are very much present on MUDs, although not in the forms we are used to encountering in actuality. Descriptions, communicative commands, and specialized language and textual forms play much the same role on MUDs as do physical contexts and gestures in everyday life. Nevertheless, people are more likely to behave without inhibitions while using MUDs than they are if engaging in face-to-face interaction. The nature of MUDs and the particular social contexts created on MUD systems themselves encourage uninhibited behavior.

Crucial to the fostering of disinhibition is the fact that MUD users are essentially anonymous. They need not be known to others by their real, legal names. They may instead choose to be known by any variety of name or nickname. Many use conventional first names; many others adopt far more evocative and inventive pseudonyms, such as those seen in the description of LambdaMOO's Living Room quoted previously. The immediate effect of this anonymity is to provide users with a feeling of safety. There is nothing very mysterious about this. Protected by computer terminals and separated by distances of often thousands of kilometers, users are aware that there is little chance of a virtual action being met by an actual response. There are no sticks or stones to contend with, and although words may hurt, users can always resort to the "off" switch on their computer. This feeling of safety holds true for users of many Internet services, not all of which provide anonymity. The mere fact of distance offers protection; anonymity only strengthens this.

Feeling safe, MUD users also feel free. They are free to act in a context divorced from external measures of response, be they positive or negative. In a sense, what is said or done on a MUD doesn't matter, as the results of actions cannot affect the person behind the MUD character. This apparent lack of meaning to MUD interaction creates an atmosphere in which greater meaning can safely be expressed. MUD users feel free to openly express greater intimacy and greater hostility toward each other than might be acceptable in everyday life. Moreover, the existence of the MUD system itself depends on a richness of communication and creation of context. Like any other system, MUDs abhor a vacuum, and a vacuum on a MUD is seen in a lack of textual exchanges. The virtual universe functions only when players are willing to elicit text from the program and from each other and are willing to volunteer their own contributions. Communication is necessary to the existence of the MUD and successful systems are likely to see a great deal of communication between players, which cannot help but form a basis for familiarity.

Users of MUDs can form strong personal attachments. That this can be so depends on the degree to which players are willing to suspend the usual rules of social self-preservation and open up to each other. By accepting that the dangers associated with intimacy—the possibility of hurt and embarrassment —can be avoided on MUDs, users can allow themselves to become very close to one another. Ironically, the safety of MUD friendships increases their worth, and players can become extremely dependent on such relationships. Both the lack of factors inhibiting intimacy and the presence of factors encouraging it can induce deep feelings of attachment in players toward their virtual friends:

> *Subject: MUDs are NOT just games!*
> *I don't care how much people say they are, muds are not just games, they are *real*!!! My mud friends are my best friends, they are the people who like me most in the entire world. Maybe the only people who do . . . They are my family, they are not just some dumb game.*[2]

Some of these virtual friendships go beyond the platonic. MUD romances are a well-established institution held together by a number of tools and rituals. Virtual lovers use the commands with which the MUD system provides them to transform the virtual stage into a set designed to express and uphold their feelings for one another. The most common action taken by such partners is to set up virtual house together. They quite literally create a home together, using the MUD program to arrange textual information in a way that simulates a physical structure which they can then share and invite others to share. These relationships may even be consummated through virtual sex, enacted as cowritten interactive erotica. More technically gifted players may also create objects, which other players can interact with, that textually mimic the behavior of pets and children. Such creations act as a virtual affirmation and imaginative realization of players' emotions.

These relationships should not be thought of as emotionally inferior or invalid. It may be only virtual actions that are being played out, but real emotions are involved. The prevalence of the virtual wedding attests to both the extent to which players attempt to recreate the trappings of actual romances in their virtual interactions and to the ways in which the entire community of players on a MUD serve to act as witness for such attachments. MUD weddings are simple in conception. The virtual bride and groom are married by another player who virtually reads, and actually types, the wedding ceremony. Tokens are often exchanged, virtual representations of flowers and rings attached to a player's virtual manifestation through the manipulation of the textual description of the character. The wedding is usually attended by a number of fellow players, whose participation in the event bolsters its imaginative reality in the shared minds of the MUD community. The forthcoming nuptials are often publicized in the communications media internal to the MUD, such as the LambdaMOO newspaper. In some cases, the MUD romance may develop into a real-life relationship, and actual marriages have been formed from MUD romances:

Subject: MUD romances?
I met Mark, who I'm now married to, on a MUD [. . .] We spent a lot of time chatting and we got closer and closer. It was really good—I could tell him anything and he was really supportive. We ended up building this castle together and everyone on the MUD treated us like a couple. I could tell that he was interested in me, and at first I was reluctant to get involved but he was so nice and he said that he really loved me and in the end we had this MUD marriage. It was so beautiful - I burst into tears in real life half way through it! After a few months I had the chance to visit the East coast, and we met while I was there. He was different from what I'd expected, mostly in the way he looked, but we really got along well, and I decided that I really did love him. He ended up getting a transfer to near where I lived and we got married last year.

Romances and deep friendships display MUD relationships at their most idyllic, but the lack of inhibition seen on MUDs has another side. The lack of control over others' everyday lives can lead some MUD players to use the systems as a forum for the expression of hostility. MUD systems can reduce self-consciousness and promote intimacy, but they can also lead users to feel free to express anger and hatred. This can take the form of "flaming," a phenomenon of CMC that has been characterized as the gratuitous and uninhibited making of "remarks containing swearing, insults, name calling, and hostile comments" (Kiesler et al., 1984, p. 1129). Anonymity makes the possibility of everyday punishments appear to be limited. The safety of the medium causes the sanction of physical violence to appear irrelevant to virtual actions, although, as I shall describe, social sanctions are present and often in a textual form that apes physical violence. The safety of anonymous expression of hostilities and obscenities that would otherwise incur social sanctions encourages some people to air their resentment of individuals or groups in a blatantly uninhibited manner:

BlueWarrior says, "Fuck you all!!!! Everybody on this MUD is a lame pervy ass-licker."

In some cases, harassment of individual players occurs. Resentment seems equally at home with attachment on MUDs and can be equally well expressed. A harassed individual may face repeated messages from the harasser and be the object of derogatory descriptions written into objects created purely for that purpose—the virtual environment can be used to manifest an individual's feelings of hostility as easily as those of intimacy. These electronic monuments to hate can be as upsetting and hurtful as the more positive relationships can be sources of support and happiness. This kind of behavior is not, as friendships generally are, an accepted part of MUDs. Harassment and offensiveness, while they may be facilitated by the physical safety and anonymity of MUD worlds, are certainly not viewed by the majority of players as acceptable aspects of the game. A few players feel that because MUDs are "just games" offensive behavior is of no moment, but most do not agree:

> *Subject: Re: Obscene mudding*
> *Now sometimes, people make too much of it, but sometimes people also are quick to say, "Hey, it's only a game." Does that mean we can now throw all civilization to the winds and act like boors and idiots without the normal threat of ostracization or societal admonition? Poker is only a game; baseball is only a game; backgammon is only a game. Does that mean you can insult and harrass the other players with foul language? No! And people who do act this way should be punished!*

The threats of ostracism or societal admonition that this player alludes to are, despite the seeming safety of anonymity, present on MUDs. Both technical and social means of control are used, with the latter often dependent on the former.

All MUD systems have facilities that enable disruptive users to be silenced or banished. Users have the option of ignoring, or "gagging," another user, making them and all their actions invisible. By editing their personal virtual reality MUD players can negate attempted harassment by severing the links of communication between themselves and an harasser. Those who are a continual problem can be not only rendered invisible but actually banished from the system by the person running the MUD program. Such a person, commonly called a "wizard," can perform virtual magic—destroying the offending character or even editing the MUD program so as to disallow connections from the particular computer the offender is connecting from. In most cases, these technical measures are sufficient to discourage offenders. Those who persist in their disruptive behavior, or who counter it by other technical means, can be subjected to public rituals intended to humiliate and punish them.

Many MUD systems allow a form of public shaming that uses the facility of MUDs to redesign their reality. An offending player will be "toaded," a practice that traditionally involves the MUD's wizard using his or her special powers to change the name and description of the player to present an unpleasant appearance (often that of a warty toad) and moving the character to some very public area of the MUD to be taunted and chastised by other users. This public humiliation is usually sufficient to discourage the user from visiting that particular MUD world again, even if earlier attempts at ostracism had been unsuccessful.

The physical aspect of MUDs may be only virtual, but the emotional aspect is actual. MUDs are not "games" in any light-hearted sense for a great many of those who use them. Strong feelings are inspired by the social contexts realized within the system, and the emotional line between virtual and actual reality is blurred when imagination is allowed its greatest expression. Although the exercise of imagination is necessary for the creation of a social context within which to act, and as the basis for shared social understandings, it is clear that players' imaginings cease to be acceptable when they threaten the ties that bind the community together. Violation of each other's personal integrity is frowned upon by the majority of players and is dealt with through social and technical conventions that act to exclude and shame offenders. Offenders may be safe from actual physical violence at the hands of those they have victimized, but ostracism is common, and social admonition has taken the form of ridiculing and subverting the efforts of disruptive players to actualize their imagined selves within the virtual world.

Characters: Self-Made People

If anonymity on MUDs allows people to do and say whatever they wish, it also allows them to be whoever they wish. The MUD system does not dictate to users the form of their virtual persona. The characters that are initially created by users have no attributes other than a reference number in the MUD database. Users must give themselves names, describe themselves, and furnish themselves with a background.

In everyday life, our efforts at self-presentation usually assume that we cannot change the basics of our appearance. Physical characteristics, although open to cosmetic or fashionable manipulation, are basically unalterable. What we look like, we have to live with. This is, however, not the case on a MUD. How a MUD user "looks" to another user is entirely dependent on information each chooses to give. It is possible to bypass the boundaries delineated by cultural constructs of beauty, ugliness, and fashion. The changes that a user might make to his or her perceived identity can be small, a matter of realizing in others' minds a desire to be attractive, impressive and popular. Some descriptions match the owner's nickname in evoking fictional characters, but most are the products of the players' own imaginations and usually indicate the possession of attractive and even superhuman attributes:

> *Darklighter*
> *A lean Man standing a metre 73, weighing about 70 kilos. His hair is golden brown with hints of red, that frame his angelic face. Deep set are two emerald eyes that peer back at you. His vestige is all in black with a cloak concealing him. You see on his right hand an emerald colored ring of peculiar origin. You realize that it is that of a Green Lantern. You can tell he is the sort of man who can see the strings that bind the universe together and mend them when they break.*

Curtis (1992) describes this phenomenon in player description as simply being a case of wish-fulfillment—"I cannot count," he says, "the number of 'mysterious but unmistakably powerful' figures I have seen wandering LambdaMOO" (p. 29). In many cases, this may well be true—certainly the majority of people in everyday life are neither as extraordinary nor as powerful as many MUD characters present themselves. However, it must be remembered that their personal description is the only method open to users to substitute for what, in everyday life, would be a complex mixture of nonverbal social context cues such as accent, dress, and race. If many descriptions are exaggerated, even fantastical, attempts to indicate social acceptability, it may indicate not only that the players have the freedom to do this, and that they wish to, but also that it is necessary to do so as part of the effort to compensate for the lack of other nontextual communication channels. Information is concentrated into one channel and therefore exaggerated.

Of the cultural factors considered most important in encounters in Western society—gender, race, class, and age—gender is the only one always "hard coded" into MUD programs. Some systems do ask characters to choose a racial background, but the choices are more likely to be between Elvish, Dwarvish, and Klingon than between Caucasian, Black, and Asian, and the choices made do not stir the emotions that choices of gender can. All MUDs allow, and some insist, that players set their "gender flag," which controls which set of pronouns are used by the MUD program in referring to the player. Most MUDs allow only three choices—male, female, and neuter—which decide between the families of pronouns containing him, her, or it. A few MUDs demand that players select either male or female as their gender and do not allow those with an unset gender flag to enter the MUD. Other MUDs allow a great many genders—male, female, plural, neuter, and hermaphrodite being among the possibilities.

It is obviously easy, at least technically so, for users to choose to play a character with a gender different from their own, but it is not necessarily socially easy as there is a lively controversy surrounding the issue of cross-gendered playing. It is common lore among MUD users that most of their number are in fact male. This may well be so. Because MUD users are necessarily people who have access to the Internet computer network, they are most likely to live in industrialized countries and be either employed by an organization with an interest in computing or enrolled in an educational institution. Although the gap is slowly closing, the majority of people employed as or studying to be computer programmers and computer engineers are male. It is therefore quite likely that the folklore on the subject is correct and that the majority of MUD users are male.

Because female- and male-presenting characters are about equally common, it follows that some of those female characters are actually run by male players, and the ethics of this are subject to debate among MUD players. Opinion is sharply divided. Some players feel that cross-gendering, particularly in the case of males controlling female characters, is a despicable and even perverted thing to do. There appear to be two issues about which those who oppose cross-gendering are concerned. First, they feel that it is "cheating" for a male to take advantage of the favoritism and chivalry commonly showered upon female-presenting characters in order to get special privileges in the game. Second, and more important, many obviously feel very uncomfortable and at a disadvantage in interacting with others whose gender is unclear and feel even more discomforted on discovering that they have been interacting under false assumptions. Some go so far as to accuse those males who admit to playing female characters of various psychological, social, and sexual illnesses:

> *Subject: Re: Gender Issues: "Real World" Warning*
> *Well, I think it *is* sick for guys to play female characters. Most only do it to fool some poor guy into thinking he's found the lady of his dreams, and then turn around and say "Ha! Ha! I'm really male!" Real mature. I think if you get off on pretending to be female you should go and dress up and go to some club in San Fran where they like perverts—just don't go around deceiving people on muds.*

For many others, cross-gendered playing is a part of the game and, if anything, a positive aspect of it:

> *Subject: Re: Gender Issues: "Real World" Warning*
> *Um, I mud primarily to socialize. I also play female characters, despite being male. I don't think I'm the only person who's like this. I don't give my real gender to people very often.[. . .] I'm exploring aspects of human interaction that are denied me in real life because I am male.*

The same degree of controversy does not surround the idea of female players using male characters or of either sex playing neutrally gendered characters. A good many women have stated in USENET discussions that they choose to use male or neutral characters to avoid the very attentions that others seem to fear will end up being directed at people who are, in real life, of the "wrong" gender. Those opposed to cross-gendering on the part of male users seem indifferent to female users' practice of it. The cross-gendered users—whether they are doing it out of curiosity, in the spirit of role-playing, or even to get special treatment—have much to say about the supposed sexism, inhibitions, and desperation of men who want to know who the real women are, and many claim to sympathize with the offensiveness displayed by some males toward female characters:

> *Subject: Re: MUD practical jokes?*
> *I played a couple of muds as a female, one making up to wizard level. Other players start showering you with money to help you get started, and I had never once gotten a handout when playing a male player. And then they feel they should be allowed to tag along forever, and feel hurt when you leave them to go off and explore by yourself. Then when you give them the knee after they grope you, they wonder what your problem is, reciting that famous saying "What's your problem? It's only a game." I can see why some women say men are bastards.*

The structure of MUD programs destroys the usually all but insurmountable confines of sex. Gender is self-selected. This freedom opens up a wealth of possibilities, for gender is one of the more "sacred" institutions in our society, a quality whose fixity is so assumed that enacted or surgical reassignment has and does involve complex rituals, taboos, procedures, and stigmas. This fixity, and the common equation of gender with sex, becomes problematic when gender reassignment can be effected by a few touches at a keyboard. MUDs become the arena for experimentation with gender specific social roles and debate over the ethics of such experimentation. Some find the lack of fixity intimidating; others show a willingness to exploit this phenomenon and to join in the games that can be played within it. However, whether an individual user enjoys the situations that come of this potential or is resentful and wary of them, all are aware that exploitation of it is a part of the MUD environment. The flexibility of self-presentation provided by MUDs makes it possible for users to experiment with aspects of behavior and identity in ways not normally possible. The barriers between imagination and manifestation are collapsed within the MUD world. Users are able to create a virtual self outside the normally assumed boundaries of gender, race, class, and age. MUDs challenge and obscure the boundaries between some of our most deeply felt cultural significances and force the creation of new cultural expectations to accommodate this.

The Virtual Stage: Communication and Community

Erik Erikson (1985) writes that "the playing adult steps sideward into another reality" (p. 222), imagination being the central ploy of entertainment. The games that are played on MUD systems involve not just a stepping into but the creation of another reality, the creation of virtually physical contexts. The virtual environments designed on MUDs exist not merely in the databases and computer networks underlying these systems but in the ways in which users can use those technologies to realize what they have imagined and to explore the results of others' imaginings. The program mediates between the users' imaginings and their realization in a form that can be experienced by others. MUDs allow each person to design and interact with computer-generated objects that are imbued with cultural meaning by those who have created them. These objects in MUD universes are treated as if they had the properties of the everyday counterparts—houses are lived in, roses are smelled, and hugs can hold together friendships.

MUD systems promote cultural understandings through the creation of commonly understood ways of symbolizing social and emotional contexts. The medium itself blocks some of the social constraints that users would, under other circumstances, be operating within. Cultural indicators—of social position, of age and authority, of personal appearance—are relatively weak in a computer-mediated context. They might be inferred, but they are not evident. MUD systems leave it open to users to create virtual replacements for these social cues, and interaction on MUDs depends on the creation of replacements and substitutes for physical cues. The textual replacements for context cues used on MUDs are the tools of interpretation that enable players to both overcome the cultural problems created by their environment and create unique environments that house their own specialized cultural understandings. With these tools MUD users form cultural groups—communities —that enable members to form close attachments and to regulate and punish disruptive members. The objects in this virtual environment serve as the stage on which these cultural plays are enacted—houses and toads facilitate the marriages and public trials that are the virtually physical manifestations of users' common cultural understandings.

The degree to which each aspect of the MUD offers information on available options is the degree to which the MUD successfully substitutes text for physical appearances. This virtual scenery provides the dramaturgical cues that tell each person what actions are possible within the MUD world. The MUD program allows what is imagined to be controlled and channeled into meaningful cues upon which other users can base their actions. The imagination of each user creates the context in which all others can act. The more willing each person is to invest his or her imagination in creating objects and descriptions, the richer and more successfully dramaturgical the environment will be. The MUD program serves to actualize what is imagined in ways that can be communicated to or retrieved by other users. The numerous ways in which textual descriptions can be elicited and created allows language to substitute for the nonverbal cues we are used to receiving about our environment and our fellows. The commands provided by the MUD systems enable users to weave a web of communication that ties each person into a sociocultural context. This web of verbal and textual significances that are substitutes for and yet distinct from the networks of meaning of the wider community binds users into a common culture whose specialized meanings allow the sharing of imagined realities.

Notes

1. Although this is true for most MUDs, not all of these commands are available on all MUDs, and different technical implementations of them can demand a slightly different syntax to the one described here. On some systems the emote command is known as pose.
2. Quotations in this format are taken from discussion about MUD use carried out over Usenet, the asynchronous conferencing system available on the Internet.

References

Curtis, P. (1992). Mudding: Social phenomena in text-based virtual realities. *Intertek, 3*(3), 26-34.

Dening, G. (1988). *The* Bounty*: An ethnographic history.* Melbourne: Melbourne University Press.

Erikson, E. H. (1985). *Childhood and society.* New York: Norton.

Kiesler, S., Siegel, S., & McGuire, T. W. (1984). Social psychological aspects of computer-mediated communication. *American Psychologist, 39*(10), 1123-1134.

Kiesler, S. & Sproull, L. (1986). Reducing social context cues: Electronic mail in organizational communication. *Management Science, 32*(11), 1492-1512.

Rice, R. E., & Love, G. (1987). Electronic emotion: Socioemotional content in a computer-mediated communication network. *Communication Research, 14*(1), 85-108.

Rheingold, H. (1991). *Virtual reality.* New York: Touchstone.

Van Maanen, J., & Barley, S. (1985). Cultural organization: Fragments of a theory. In P. J. Frost, L. F. Moore, M. R. Louis, C. C. Lundberg, & J. Martin (Eds.), *Organizational culture* (pp. 31-53). Newbury Park, CA: Sage.

9

THE E-MAIL MURDERS: REFLECTIONS ON "DEAD" LETTERS

Alan Aycock

Norman Buchignani

"Under what circumstances do we think things are real?" William James's famous query (1950, pp. 283-324) raised nearly a century before computers had become ubiquitous in daily life now gains a new dimension of significance: The virtual reality that computer-mediated discourses generate acutely bring to our attention the multiplex ways in which experience may be framed in modern cultures (Goffman, 1974, chap. 1).

In particular, some computer discourses appear to blur the distinction between "being there," "seeming to be there," and "talking about being there" in a fashion that urges us to look at culturally intuited notions of fact and fiction in a new light. This blurring is especially intriguing because in several critical ways computer discourses at least superficially appear to stand outside the conventions of everyday orality and literacy (Crane, 1991, p. 293).[1] Indeed, computer discourses are sufficiently ubiquitous and different that it seems no longer sufficient, necessary, or even possible to fix cultural experience only directly in personal interaction or indirectly through the permanency of the printed text—if ever experience *could* be fixed in such a manner: consider Derrida's (1987, pp. 3-256) remarkable analysis of a series of postcards exchanged with his lover(s). Standard cultural interpretations of the "facts" either based on personal presence or on the stability of a text owned by its author and understood more or less adequately by its readers have been brought into question by computer-mediated discourses. In this sense what is "known" to be true becomes somewhat less certain and what is fantasized perhaps even more so.

The direct application of the naturalist discourse of traditional ethnographic analysis (Geertz, 1988, p. 140) is problematic in the analysis of computer cultures. What is the relationship between realities grounded in the empiricism of directly lived experience and virtual realities generated on-line? Suffering and death, which in nominally "factual" discourses once seemed uniquely referential and embodied, now can be seen in a broader arena to be also, even primordially (*déjà aussi*), the stuff of imagery and representation. As Baudrillard (1983) has suggested, in the cultural constructions of experience the simulation of reality has increasingly supplanted experience itself (p. 2).

A case in point is the remarkable computer-mediated discourse surrounding Valery Fabrikant, who murdered four persons and wounded a fifth at Concordia University in Montreal, Canada in late summer 1992.[2] These violent assaults and the personal circumstances of Valery Fabrikant preceding, (literally) during, and after them became the objects of intense scrutiny on a number of Usenet newsgroups, especially sci.research. careers, sci.research, canada.general, and soc.culture.canada. On several occasions, on-line text and "real" context seemed to intersect and to interpenetrate one another in subtle ways. We examine this discourse, using it in an experimental spirit (Clifford, 1988, pp. 22-23; Marcus & Fisher, 1986, p. 40) to investigate the potential for ethnographic analysis conducted wholly or in part through the new realm of cyberspace (Benedikt, 1991).

To organize our observations, we employ the literary trope of irony, defined simply as the juxtaposition of apparently disparate elements in a manner that highlights and problematizes each of them (Brown, 1977, ch. 5). Irony, of course, provides a convenient and familiar theoretical framework for the interpretation of texts (Muecke, 1970). It also represents an especially powerful juxtapositional strategy (Marcus & Fisher, 1986, pp. 31-40) to interpret this dimension of computer culture, as it helps expose the "seam, fault, or flaw" (Barthes, 1975, pp. 6-7; also Scholes, 1989, p. 8, on centripetal and centrifugal values in narrative) in what otherwise appears to be quite ordinary and "natural" referential (embodied or textual) discourse.

We begin by introducing the institutional context of the Usenet and some of the basic cultural norms that prevail there. We then describe the scope, chronology, and basic thrust of Usenet postings concerning Valery Fabrikant. Thereafter, we employ a trilogy of themes that we take to be ironic in this situation and the data that support our selection: authority, genealogy, and madness. We then show how these three themes bear upon a master irony: the real versus the hyperreal. Finally, we identify a range of issues that the analysis of this discourse has for further anthropological study of computer-mediated discourses.

Usenet Newsgroups

An intentionally reductionist and decentering definition of the Usenet provided by one of its gurus "is the set of machines that exchange articles tagged with one or more universally-recognized labels, called newsgroups" (Kehoe, 1992, p. 29); Usenet postings are received and redirected along a complex web of connections between computers and networks of computers via the Internet. It is, however, much more than this, especially from the point of view of those who make use of it. To them, the technical underbelly of the Usenet is typically invisible, the Usenet groups appearing instead through "software magic" as if they all were sited on a single great machine, whose location is both unknown and irrelevant. Although actually posted asynchronously from many points around the globe to the Usenet at large, groups appear to have a concrete reality and organization. This appearance remains integral despite newsgroups' reduction, for purposes of the ordinary user, to mere labels on files. Individuals may subscribe and unsubscribe to one or more of 1,000 locally, regionally, nationally, or internationally available groups, read anything posted to these groups in the recent past, and post their own contributions. Such postings easily may be sent simultaneously to thousands of people subscribed to many different newsgroups or to a single person. In turn, users may reply only in one such group or in several, or repost original messages generated by others to groups to which they were not originally sent, thus creating new and ever more intricately interwoven connections. Although some newsgroups are nearly moribund, others sustain well over 100 postings a day.

Each newsgroup is loosely organized around a particular theme at the time of its creation. For example, sci.research.careers was nominally created to consider issues relating to access to jobs and advancement in the "hard" sciences. There are, however, not many formal mechanisms to limit postings to the specified theme. The few newsgroups that are moderated are eclipsed in number by the multitude that are not. The latter, having been literally voted into existence by users based on arguments of thematic utility, thereafter provide a venue for almost any kind of postings without editorial control, however peripheral these postings are to the group's central theme.[3]

Published ideal Usenet conventions, or "netiquette" (Templeton, 1991), attempt to restrict postings to themes appropriate to a given newsgroup, and to styles of discourse that mirror those of ordinary polite interaction. However, it is hard to secure the practical observance of these conventions, and in practice the most thematically off-topic and idiosyncratically formed opinions assume equal place with those that are more "mainstream" in content—especially in those groups whose discourse centers on highly topical social issues and social problems.[4] Those who might be more inhibited in direct daily intercourse readily speak out on-line, and the sole recourse of Usenet patrons toward obnoxious, repetitive, vacuous, voluminous, or obscene postings is to protest (usually ineffectually) to "the newsgroup" for sanctions, establish "kill files" to strain out such postings automatically or engage in spiraling "flame wars" that more often heighten discordance than reduce it.

The most central stabilizing factor in all this is a Usenet convention (almost always observed) that a posting should be linked by attribution and subject heading to its predecessor and that, where appropriate, verbatim quotes from previous postings should be included with one's response. This creates immediate relationships between one posting and its successors, the "interlocking" of dialog (Perinbanayagam, 1991, pp. 73-76), called "threads" by reference to the subject heading on the Usenet, even if it does not always constrain a particular newsgroup's or a connected web of newsgroups' range of discussion. The potential for ironically juxtaposed postings in this use of the "indirect speech" of others (Sperber, 1985, p. 19) is consequently immense and frequently realized in practice: Whereas many people keep to the stated subject of threads and follow the rules of polite discourse on the Usenet, many others do not. The result is to set normal expressions of *politesse* alongside commentary that is often blatantly racist, sexist, nationalist, and so forth. The overall effect is inevitably a cacophony of voices struggling to be heard and acknowledged.

Partly as cause and partly as a consequence, one finds a strong, largely subtextual set of values widely dispersed across the Usenet that positively affirm what is perceived to be the extreme leveling and "democratic" tendencies of this comparatively new forum for interpersonal discourse. This ideology is deeply embedded in "computer guru" texts about the Internet—"the possibilities are endless" (Kehoe, 1992, p. 5)—and is, of course, directly tied to the broader popular culture cant regarding the wondrous potential that new technologies supposedly offer for universal human communications and sharing of knowledge (Lyotard, 1984; McLuhan, 1964; Meyrowitz, 1985, chap. 15; Nelson, 1987). The attendant risks to effective communication of a polyphonic, dissonant diversity of interpretive idioms (Clifford, 1988, p. 22) are never mentioned.

At a more general level, the open and unaccountable nature of posting practices does nominally seem to empower a range of persons who might otherwise remain muted and permits their opinions, however deviant or outrageous, to be broadcast internationally. This perception of empowerment is heightened by the marked contrast between the massive but invisible infrastructural arrangements that permit newsgroups to function and the simplistic, almost elementary format in which postings actually appear.

At the same time, actual access to these newsgroups is far from universal. Participation is restricted primarily to individuals who can read and write English (the Usenet *lingua franca*), who know about newsgroups and wish to participate, who have the limited computer literacy required, and, critically, who have computer accounts on networks and mainframes with access to the Internet.[5] In practice, this restricts the core of discussants to a relatively small subset of those who work at First World universities, government institutions, and research corporations willing to pay the hefty annual Internet fee. This in turn must profoundly limit the class, occupational, cultural, national, and gender range of participants in ways not as yet empirically investigated. Indeed, how and to what degree the range of participants, forms of discourse, and patterns of information sharing across these newsgroups actually matches the widely accepted perception of their anarchic and liberating status remains a complex, largely unanswered question, which we address below (albeit in a limited fashion) in our case study of the Fabrikant materials.[6]

Fabricating Fabrikant: A Brief Narrative

On August 20, 1992, Dov Bai of Cornell University forwarded to sci.research.careers and later to sci.research a file that had been sent as e- mail to him as well as to more than 42 others by Valery Fabrikant.[7] The file claimed that as an untenured professor at Concordia University Fabrikant had been forced to extend authorship of his research publications to his administrative superiors who had done little or none of the work, that he had initiated a suit against them, and that for disclosing this miscarriage of natural justice he faced an imminent threat of incarceration for contempt of court.

Bai responded personally to Fabrikant by e-mail requesting further information, which he and many others then received. Of what may have been as many as 500 people who received the material firsthand, Bai alone posted this 25,000-word corpus to the Usenet group sci.research.careers on August 23. These texts were highly dissonant with normal Usenet discourse, especially that on sci.research.careers, which before this was archetypically mundane and, as measured by the daily number and size of postings, rather marginal.[8] The texts were perceived as unusual, we believe, in part because they were symbolically "dirty" in Mary Douglas's (1966) sense of "matter out of place" (p. 48). They comprised highly personal materials normally inaccessible to the public, such as confidential letters assessing Fabrikant's career, "transcripts" of private conversations with his colleagues at Concordia University, confidential reports of university personnel committees considering his further employment and tenure, and the like. The files presented at length the give and take of lengthy disputations between Fabrikant, his colleagues and supervisors, various administrators of Concordia University, his faculty association, and even the campus police.

Throughout, Fabrikant leveled many accusations that are of primordial significance in the scholarly universe of most Usenet participants: charges that he had been denied tenure on purely personal grounds;[9] claims that others in the Department of Mechanical Engineering had forced him to extend coauthorship on papers where he had done most of the research while they had not; the assertion that some of his colleagues were corrupt, siphoning off research funds to private companies entirely owned and controlled by them or their relatives; claims of personal harassment; and assertions that the faculty association was in bed with the administration. Fabrikant's style of portrayal was intensely personal, dramatically vivid, and frequently highly combative.

The remarkable nature of these files generated some initial interest in the hours immediately after their posting, but the next day (August 24) a new, wholly unexpected feature of the controversy began to emerge. Evidently responding to his having seen only the first of Bai's postings, a Concordia doctoral student replied:

> *This trash is unfounded. Fabrikant is one step away from the looney bin. There is an unconfirmed report that he is involved in a hostage taking at Concordia right now (4:40 pm., 24/8).*

This report was quickly "confirmed" not by those at Concordia but by subscribers in distant Oregon and Maryland, who cited international media sources (CNN and NPR) as their authority. This remarkable event, tied as it was to the Usenet, sparked an instant, exponentially increasing interest on sci.research.careers, where the postings increased to 10 times their normal volume. Postings in the next few days were primarily highly conventional expressions of shock and condolence and speculations on the relationship between the Fabrikant texts and the events that had transpired. In particular, subscribers wondered whether the police had been informed about these posted files and whether subscribers could have prevented the shootings by notifying "the authorities" earlier.

Newspaper and television news accounts continued for a while to infiltrate Usenet postings, the former of which sometimes were posted verbatim. It was widely reported that a "computer sleuth" had been employed by the police to investigate Fabrikant's electronically mediated communications. Television news reports (themselves "reported" on the Usenet) subsequently confirmed that Fabrikant's Usenet texts had been downloaded by the police.

Discussion spread quickly as the texts and responses to them were cross-posted to other newsgroups such as sci.research and soc.culture.canada. This in turn increased user subscriptions to sci.research.careers and so presumably the diversity of its discourse. Newsgroup discourses thereafter partitioned themselves in a number of topical threads. Some subscribers attempted to assess the authenticity of these documents and the assertions they contained by questioning Dov Bai, securing and uploading further newspaper reports, researching Fabrikant's credentials on on-line library catalogues, and asking for more information from Fabrikant's Concordia University colleagues.[10] Thereafter, vigorous debates raged on a variety of newsgroups: Subject threads on the Fabrikant matter quickly diffused into arguments about scientific authorship, Fabrikant's state of mind and biography in relation to the potential explanations of his "rampage," to what extent his rage was justified, other instances of campus shootings, the accessibility of firearms in Canada, and so forth.

As the weeks wore on, Usenet postings gradually continued to refocus from specific reference to Fabrikant himself to the more general issues that his "rampage" presumably represented. By the end of September there were only sporadic intrusions by Montreal users reporting on the progress of Fabrikant's incarceration and pretrial legal antics. Even these tangential threads soon were lost and replaced by matters having nothing to do with Fabrikant: As an actor, he disappeared from Usenet newsgroups almost as quickly as he had initially appeared.

Usenet Discourse as Ethnography

We approach this discourse on Fabrikant as an ethnographic text.[11] However, as our preliminary remarks may already have suggested, this narrative poses some unconventional analytical challenges to the traditional means by which ethnographic texts are assessed. Two assumptions in particular are ordinarily made in the "realist" analysis of conventional ethnographies that are problematic here: first, that an ethnographic text refers to an ethnographic reality that is "out there" and therefore that the text is subject to falsification when text and reality are compared; second, that when an ethnographic text is stabilized by publication it ceases to interact with ethnographic reality in any immediate fashion, and thereby ethnographic text and "real" context are enabled to maintain themselves as distinct realms of truth (Clifford, 1986, p. 116; Handler, 1988, chap. 1).

In the discourses on Valery Fabrikant, neither assumption holds true even as a first approximation. Save for a select few linked to Concordia University, Usenet subscribers who participated in this discourse had no access to a reality independent of their postings, other than vicariously through the television and radio news and through their own personal experiences far from the scene. The central comparison between Usenet text and other collectively generated realities involved yet further texts such as newspaper and television reports on the shootings, and even these were largely unavailable to those outside Canada after the day of the first international press announcements of Fabrikant's "rampage."

Further, and even more significant, Usenet postings and the "reality" to which they referred were conflated from the onset. Postings on Fabrikant interacted intensely with the events to which they presumably referred, generating new texts that formed part of the events at hand, the texts themselves produced by readers' diverse perceptions of what was "really" happening. This nearly instantaneous interpenetration of ethnographic text and referential context is a notable feature of computer-mediated communication because it decenters one's normal confidence that text, in some sense, can ever be adequately characterized as representing a reality from which it clearly may be distinguished (Barthes, 1974, pp. 54-55; 1986, p. 145).

Two additional comments seem appropriate at this point. One has to do with the comparison of text and context and the other with their mutual interaction. First, the existence of Valery Fabrikant as a "real" person was never established on the Usenet, except by indirection and intertextual reference; indeed, it is not clear even hypothetically how it could have been—consider Goffman's treatment of the biographical self as a kind of game in which the gap between "virtual" and "actual" identity (1963a, p. 127) can be dealt with as a continuing resource of the play (1974, pp. 287-292). Fabrikant never posted to the Usenet himself, and the relationship of Bai's vicarious postings to the "real" disputes at hand remains equally as obscure as the version of Fabrikant that he himself intended to "fabricate." Although the discourse on Valery Fabrikant appeared to us in retrospect to have maintained a certain overall coherence and "sense" while it unfolded daily, when viewed as a total corpus the documentation on the textual Fabrikant is a choppy, one-sided mèlange of disparate texts whose chronology and credibility is difficult to assess even by careful inspection.[12] This indeterminacy characterizes not only the initial postings of Dov Bai but also later attempts by others to fill in Fabrikant's biography. "What is it that's going on here?" (Goffman, 1974, p. 8) was thus subject to continuous editing and reinterpretation throughout.

Second, in some sense Fabrikant's status has since been elevated from that of mere person to that of a Usenet and Canadian academic culture icon (Browne & Fishwick, 1978). Metaphorical reference to Fabrikant has appeared in Usenet postings wholly unrelated to the original incidents as a stereotype of a particular violation of netiquette: a tendency toward unreasonable aggressiveness and irrational controversy. As an officer of a faculty collective bargaining group, one of us (Aycock) can attest to the influence of Fabrikant's alleged activities on the manner in which "real," unrelated faculty grievances in Canada have been subsequently addressed. That is to say, Fabrikant has perhaps achieved a cautionary status disproportionate to his significance, but it is a status that in "real" terms has become incorporated into everyday conversational and official contexts (Fiske, 1989a, chap. 6). The relationship of text and context in computer-mediated discourses is thus in this case highly reflexive, and this reflexivity is correspondingly difficult to evaluate.

Authorship and Authority

An important theme in the Fabrikant files is the ironization of authorship and authority. These two ideas share underlying cultural notions concerning speaking, power, rights, and the legitimacy of a privileged, fully referential generative presence (whether human or organizational) that monitors and sanctions those who might challenge the authenticity of its pronouncements or even place themselves in a position to do so (Barthes, 1975, p. 27; 1977b, pp. 142-148; Foucault, 1977, pp. 113-138). Authorship and authority are nevertheless often paradoxically opposed to one another in the Fabrikant files.

Fabrikant as Author-Ethnographer

It should be recalled that Fabrikant himself played no active authorial role in on-line discourse after his initial e-mail postings to Dov Bai and others. The representation of Fabrikant was thereafter literally "fabricated" by Usenet writers, who totally and unconsciously appropriated the authority to speak for, against, and about him. This is particularly ironic, as one of Fabrikant's most central claims offered as justification for a variety of his actions was that his authorship had been unfairly appropriated. It was his contention that he had been coerced by promises of tenure into permitting colleagues who had not contributed to his research to share authorship of his scientific papers. This is the introductory theme to all his posted material, appearing in the very first page of his first posting:[13]

Dear Colleague:

The events which I want you to tell about are so outrageous, that one should see it to believe. There will be several mailings with facts and documents. I have little time left because on August 25 I will be in jail for contempt of court, so I need to do the mailing really fast. I have no time for editing so everything will be mailed exactly as it was distributed originally in Montreal.

I raise question of "scientific prostitution." The main difference between scientific prostitution and "honorary authorship" is that in the first case a completely bogus scientist, not capable of doing any research, hires somebody from developing countries or USSR by using governmental grant. This someone does research in which the parasite supervisor is included as co-author. The more publications this parasite accumulates, the greater grant he gets, the more people he can hire, the more publications he gets, etc.

Perhaps the most dramatic presentation of this theme by Fabrikant himself is to be found in the long "transcripts" (Fabrikant's characterization) said to be of conversations among Fabrikant and his colleagues:

Fabrikant: *I mean, if you are called to testify, and I put you a question about the papers I have written: "What was the contribution of* [X]*?"*

Y: *He did not contribute, except for the fact that he paid you. (Laughs)* [end of quote]

Fabrikant: .... *You mentioned several times, "we were doing," "we were investigating," we do this, we do that. I am kind of wondering, how do you feel when you see in print "Method of Fabrikant,"* [A] *and* [B]*? What is your internal feeling?*

[A]: *What do you mean: "What is your internal feeling?"*

Fabrikant: *OK, let us call a spade a spade. What was your contribution to that method?*

[A]: *Which one?*

Fabrikant: *Fabrikant,* [A] *and* [B], *remember, I gave you a copy? (I refer to the paper by Love et.al., entitled "On the method of Fabrikant,"* [A] *and* [B] *. . .") What was your scientific contribution to that method?*

[A]: *I do not know, some of these things we discussed . . .*

Fabrikant: *Discussion is not a contribution. Contribution is contribution, and you know this better than anybody else. Could you name at least one single paper published, I understand that I have given you 16 papers, and you did not overpay me, and at least 18 conference presentations, in the best journals around the world, and, as I mentioned it to you, the papers are bound to become classic, and they are, little by little. I can show you a paper by Rice ([A] tries to interrupt). Would you agree, that actually none of the papers published has any scientific contribution of yours, whatever? Would you agree with that?*

[A]: *Let me tell you. People have short memory. As long as this is fine with them, they do not mind establishing exactly what they have done, and what others have not done . . .*

These transcripts were written out exactly as above, much as dialogue in a play or movie script or, ironically, as are some postmodern "experimental ethnographies" (Crapanzano, 1980; Kracke, 1978; Shostak, 1981; see esp. Dwyer, 1982),[14] with annotations for hesitations, laughs, and grammatically broken sentences. The point has been well made that modern ethnographic writing is intrinsically ironic in that it typically is successful in establishing for its readers a conviction that the ethnographer's subjects are "truly speaking" only when there has, in fact, been massive authorial appropriation by the ethnographer (Geertz, 1968, p. 154; Strathern, 1987, pp. 265-268; Thornton, 1983, p. 516). Fabrikant's "transcripts" and other putatively verbatim texts illustrate the same ironic relationship. It can reasonably be inferred that Fabrikant's intention in presenting these "transcripts" was, as in the selective incorporation of native talk in ethnographic writing, to portray these discussions effectively as "persuasive fictions" (Strathern, 1987), such that a reader was convinced that Fabrikant had, in effect, ceded all meaningful authorship to the "actors" involved. The authorial position suggested by these "transcripts" was that Fabrikant fabricated nothing. Rather, he (like the epistemologically naive modernist ethnographer) was merely a neutral vehicle for the "authentic" transmission of what he and his coactors were doing and saying.

The Fabrikant documents underscored this representational strategy by the presentation of other kinds of material framed in such a way as to substantiate Fabrikant's presentation of evidence supportive to his cause by symbolically minimizing his apparent authorship. Letters and memos to and from Fabrikant reputed to be unaltered are liberally sprinkled throughout, and a massive document is included that is asserted to be an authentic copy of the departmental personnel committee report that recommended he be denied tenure and dismissed. The fact that under the circumstances it is not at all clear how these "transcripts" and other documents were produced (and it occurred to none of the empiricists on sci.research or sci.research.careers to inquire) highlights the interpenetration of text and context here. It also points suggestively to the seductive authority of printed text on the Usenet, ideologies of the "writerly text" notwithstanding (Barthes, 1974, p. 4).

Finally, Fabrikant shared with many traditional ethnographers (Sontag, 1970) one other major trope deployed to raise himself above the status of mere author, to minimize his own role, and to legitimate his claims.[15] He presented himself as a mythic iconoclast struggling against terrible, even cosmic odds:

> *Someone has asked me if I am afraid that the "persons affected" might hire someone to stage my "accidental death" or to frame me in some kind of a crime. Well, I am no longer afraid of anything or anybody. We all have to die one day. Whenever I die, I shall die an honest person. I just wonder, how many administrators can say the same about themselves. Gandhi considered jail as a must*

for an honest person. I am prepared for that too. I just regret that I put up with all this filth for twelve years. Make no mistake, I am dead serious in what I am doing. I can not fight all the crooks in the world, but I shall not rest until the bogus scientists in this university are exposed and the Justice is served.

Usenet as Author-Ethnographer: Authorship

Fabrikant's explicit arguments about authorship became the subject of many postings in which the meaning and political significance of scientific authorship were hotly debated:

co-authorship becomes a form of tribute

**I* have been co-author of a few papers that *I* didn't even know about.*

how would you feel about a supervisor lending his name for co-authorship in order to increase the chances of publication?

It turned out that every paper written by anyone at the Institute he currently directed was required to list him as a co-author.

I believe that there should be absolutely no penalty for a genuine multiple authorship, so that people are not discouraged from working together.

It was pointed out, for instance, that in the area of high-energy physics there might be several hundred "authors" of a research paper, many of whom might even be unaware that their names had been so cited:

The number of authors . . . reflects the reality that nothing can be done in this field by a single individual without help of a team of 50-200 or so people over a period of 10-15 years.

No one questioned Fabrikant's claim to a distinguished research record, especially after several subscribers did on-line literature searches on Fabrikant and then posted summary lists of his books and journal articles. Neither did anyone fail to accept Fabrikant's assertion that he was the primary researcher-writer of the publications in dispute. Rather, postings strongly supported his "right" of authorship —ironically, perhaps, on Usenet groups where at least one of the main ideological architects of the Internet asserts that as the Usenet is perfectly anarchical, users "have no rights" (Kehoe, 1992, pp. 29-30).

Most Usenet posters clearly subscribed to the North American folk notion assumed in Fabrikant's original materials, a notion fostered by a complex mix of culturally emphasized individualism, print technology, and the private ownership of texts, of the "true self" and the individual writer as the main authentic, creative, authorial forces (Barthes, 1982, p. 63; Geertz, 1983, p. 59):

> *'author'—one who writes . . . Period.*
>
> *Only one person, or at most two, can write the paper . . . many can participate in the science.*
>
> *Authorship is reserved for persons who receive primary credit and hold primary responsibility for a published work.*
>
> *Authorship should be limited to those who have made a significant contribution to the concept, design, execution and interpretation of the research study.*

This of course coincides with the netiquette convention (Gier, 1991) that every posting be linked to those before it and that quotes to prior postings (or even newspapers) be fully referenced; more deeply, it subscribes to the supreme folk Usenet value (the pronouncements of Internet gurus such as Kehoe to the contrary) of all subscribers having the "right" to a unique authorial voice of their own making. Various stratagems were even suggested for discerning "true" authorship:

> *I vote that . . . the authors of every paper submitted . . . also submit a one page outline of their contributions to the paper AND ALL the authors sign ALL the outlines!!!*

Others bemoaned the status quo and what researcher-writers had to do to "work the system," inculpating the political, even racial and colonial nature of normal science:

> *a faculty member can require obscene amounts of work from a student or postdoc and threaten withdrawal of support if they don't do it! They all know that if they get rid of this person they can find another from the third world pretty quickly.*

As Fabrikant himself is reputed to have claimed: "A professor at a Canadian university who has a government grant but does not have the brains to do the research can hire talented scientists from the Third World or Russia, they would do the work and he gets all the credit."

The Authorities

Ironically, Usenet attitudes toward "the authorities" were so far from consistent with their generally shared position on "authorship" as to be mutually and severally contradictory. "The authorities" were initially delimited by Fabrikant as his supervisors at Concordia University (Department Chair, Dean, Vice-Rector, and Rector) and their agents, the campus police, who had in his view become instrumental in his tribulations. Fabrikant claimed that these "authorities" had acted inappropriately concerning his research and career. In his own demonology, the widespread dissemination of information concerning his situation was critical, as he already expected to be jailed on August 25 for contempt of court because of his locally distributed electronic expressions of outrage.[16]

Fabrikant's contention that "since Rector Kenniff prefers to cover up fraud at Concordia, I have no choice but to make the relevant information as public as possible" was universally accepted on the Usenet, where there was not the slightest suggestion that it was inappropriate for such materials to be posted, read and discussed.[17] Even after the killings of August 24, many were skeptical of Concordia's official protestations, concentrating particularly on what penalty the interaction of Usenet and everyday reality might bear for the former:

> *The fact that Concordia University is involved may send a chill through every college administrator on this continent, and since administrators are famous for acting out of fear, the implications for free and easy access to CMC* [computer-mediated communication] *and other forms of computer communication may possibly be threatened.*

> *Yes, I'm aware of the laws. And I'm also aware of the law as a tool to suppress undesired speech. While the laws of libel and slander are noble ventures in the battle against hate literature and what not, they are disproportionately implemented by those insecure with the truth.*

> *The letter that Fabrikant mailed* [the texts that were posted] *did not contain any threats against anyone.*

More generally, the authorship of "the authorities" was questioned whenever such pronouncements appeared to contradict the egalitarian premises of the Usenet. As a case in point, official pronouncements from the university were never taken at face value. Fabrikant himself transmitted an electronic message from Dr. Rose Sheinin, Vice-Rector (Academic) of Concordia, who asserted something bound to fall on deaf ears on the Usenet:

> *It is a misuse of University property to communicate in this manner* [campuswide e-mail] *your dispute with the Concordia University Faculty Association.*

Subsequent to the murders, a posting *directly to Usenet* by Dr. Patrick Kenniff, Rector of Concordia, which claimed that

> [Sheinin] . . . *conducted an inquiry into the numerous allegations he raised and reported to the Board of Governors in March 1992 that they were unfounded*

engendered nothing but cynical replies.

By contrast, there was strong Usenet support for Kenniff's further statement that

> *there can be no excuse nor justification for the brutal and senseless actions of 24 August 1992.*[18]

Once Fabrikant had been arrested and accused of murder, certain Usenet discussions of authority became aligned much more conventionally with the interests of the police and of authority in general (Goffman, 1959, p. 220; 1961, p. 128, on the way in which moral agents present themselves *to* themselves and to others as sustaining a coherent moral career). Indeed, many queries were expressions of actively helpful concern for the authorities, especially "the police":

> *Do the police have copies of his recent posts here? I mean, are we sure that they've been handed over?*

> *I believe so; Canadian t.v. news shows Fabrikant's dept head holding fanfolds of offprints from what looks like this newsgroup; certainly the text they've highlighted looks like the stuff he uploaded here.*

> *Should we have done something right away, like notifying some authority, after seeing the parts of the posts where he talks about fearing for his life and being willing to die?*

> *A police investigator might actually USE the net to collect such information (e.g., mailing lists kept by Fabrikant).*

> *I wonder whether there would be anything of interest in his computer directory . . . 'finger ccyfk568vax2.concordia.ca' and check the time of last login"* [a matter conceivably bearing on the legal issues of intent and premeditation][19]

Usenet willingness to cooperate with the police, even to identify themselves with Fabrikant's department head, and (more vaguely) to notify "some authority" suggest the ambivalence expressed by some newsgroup users in relation to the implied antinomies of "freedom to post" and "electronic surveillance" (Foucault, 1979, pp. 195-228; Poster, 1990, chap. 3). These concerns quickly resolved themselves into more self-involved discussions:

> *. . . in posting confidential memos and documentation, did you unknowingly open yourself to a lawsuit yourself?*

> *. . . when the email is forwarded to some 30 or 40 other addresses . . . the recipient may assume this is like a public disclosure.*

"Authority" in this fashion represented for Usenet readers a hierarchy or, more to the point, a leveling of access to interpretations of what was "really" going on: "This anti-hero exists: he is the reader of the text at the moment he takes his pleasure. . . . The text of pleasure is a sanctioned Babel" (Barthes, 1975, pp. 3-4). The comparatively wide access to Usenet postings brought into public view events and texts that would normally have been concealed and exposed to scrutiny the actions of "authorities" in ways to which they are not accustomed.

Indeed, after Fabrikant had been taken into custody his inability to present his own case on the Usenet placed the newsgroups at a distinct disadvantage in interpreting the "facts" of the matter, and reduced their access to repetitive postings taken "without authorization" from media coverage and official statements. This of course, sharply limited the capacity of the Fabrikant case *per se* to be pursued in detail rather than in principle.[20] It also showed complete acquiescence to the iconic textual authority of the "real" news from which subscribers frequently meticulously transcribed verbatim accounts (Fiske, 1989b, chap. 7). The authenticity and authorial voice of the news was, in fact, never questioned, even though Usenet and news discourse were often mutually interdependent.[21]

Authorship/authority was also ironized by bringing into question the very authenticity of the Fabrikant postings while at the same time acknowledging the salaciousness of public access to such private materials:

> [Legal jeopardy] *for what? For posting "electronic" copies of files that I have received, without any real signature on them? The only "signature," (if we may call it so) was the header of Fabrikant's message. Even headers were forged many times on Usenet.*

Does anybody know if it is possible to establish "beyond a reasonable doubt" if Fabrikant sent the e-messages?

. . . what we have here is publicly available copies of notes from a madman before their killing spree. In other situations the individual might write notes that in their distorted view justified what they were about to do, but that would be evidence not readily available to the public.

In short, the circumstances and possibilities of the Usenet opened up contradictory avenues of resistance and compliance in regard to authorship and authority, stances that simultaneously upheld and called into question their conventional meanings in copresent and print-based discourses (Bakhtin, 1984; De Certeau, 1984; Stallybrass & White, 1986). We see the electronically mediated communications of newsgroups as a major contributing factor to this equivocation and ironization of authorship and authority, as the immediacy, reciprocity, and nonreferentiality of newsgroup discourses permitted multiple variations on such themes that otherwise might have been taken for granted or remained largely inaccessible to the general public.

Genealogy

An irony immediately noted by both authors when the postings began involves the name "Fabrikant" itself. As one like-thinking Usenet subscriber remarked, who when first seeing the name thought the postings a possible joke,

Fabrikant means "someone who fabricates" or "someone who creates" in German

Dov Bai also remarked that, on the basis of the name attached to the first e-mail sent him, "I thought the whole thing was a hoax."

This coincidence initiated our consideration of genealogy, defined here as the study of names and their relationships, and in particular the nature of the continuity and discontinuity of related Usenet postings (Foucault, 1977, pp. 139-164; see also Aycock, n.d., chap. 6; Derrida, 1988, pp. 100-104). In this vein, a supreme irony (noted by no one on the Usenet) is the name "Concordia" (harmony) itself in connection with the textual accounts of "threats" and "harassment" on all sides and the denial of tenure to Fabrikant, largely on the grounds of his want of collegiality.[22] More broadly, these ironic connections highlight the larger issue of the genealogy of Usenet postings themselves and the tendency of these postings to exhibit a certain kind of broadly constrained chronological incoherence and to disperse themselves along tangentially related threads of discussion. We look first at the matter of tenure and Fabrikant's Usenet genealogy and subsequently at the notion of genealogy in regard to Usenet postings more generally.

Tenure

In common with many other such Canadian agreements, the collective agreement of Concordia University provides that the "evaluation of full-time faculty shall be based upon the consideration of professional competence and potential for fulfilling academic responsibilities."

Whether balanced or even credible, when read as a sequentially organized whole Fabrikant's posted account of the events leading to his denial of tenure from the beginning deeply ironizes the abyss between the alleged activities of his colleagues in the Department of Mechanical Engineering and the rationale they offered for denying him tenure. It is clear that Fabrikant's "paranoia" evoked in classic style a corresponding "conspiracy" on the part of his colleagues (Lemert, 1962). To take one example, Fabrikant relates a confrontation in the hall of his department during which he was accused of lurking with intent to spy on his colleagues, who were themselves engaged in a secret midnight meeting! On another occasion, Fabrikant claimed that he "was approached [in Fall 1991] by two policemen who said that someone from the University called them and told them that I have a concealed firearm and [am] about to commit a crime." A search of Fabrikant's person produced nothing in the end but an official apology for the incident.

As presented to the Usenet, the mechanical engineering departmental personnel committee (DPC) meetings held to address Fabrikant's contract and career progress show a coherent trajectory that, although clear in retrospect to Usenet posters, may well not have been evident to participating DPC members as they went along. Initial recommendations of his appointment and early evaluations of his performance read as typical bureaucratic code in such matters, generating a highly meritorious if faceless "Fabrikant." A midstream positive recommendation of the DPC began to assign a constellation of less salubrious personal attributes to Fabrikant, requiring "that he show evidence of collegiality" in the future. By their report in November 1991, the DPC emphasized increasingly his alleged belligerence and uncooperative attitude, downplaying both his research and teaching to the point of relative insignificance (cf. Goffman, 1967, pp. 47-95, on the ritual significance of deference and demeanor).

Later DPC discourse sought to establish a connection between the clause of the Concordia agreement quoted above (clearly meant to make academic merit central to the process) and their personal disapproval of Fabrikant. Lack of concord rather than merit is his fatal flaw:

> The success of the Mechanical Engineering Department has traditionally been built around the harmonious relationships between its various members and the Chair; we perceive Dr. Fabrikant's attitude . . . to be detrimental to the . . . spirit of harmonious relationships between department members.

Ultimately, Fabrikant was not recommended for tenure by his DPC, only to have his contract extended a year by the faculty-wide personnel committee.

This feature of his case sparked an intense debate on the Usenet, one that seems largely predetermined by the portrayed chronological development of Concordia reactions to Fabrikant. The issues were these: access to tenure by otherwise meritorious "jerks" (see below) balanced against the rights of the many and the inequities of tenure as an academic caste distinction in a less than ideal world. It is highly relevant to note at this point that while throughout academia the notion of tenure (or at least, one's own tenure) is symbolically prized as a safeguard for academic freedom, both those on the margins of academia and the general public tend to perceive tenure more ambivalently as a way in which established fat-cat professors protect themselves from the otherwise inevitable consequences of their own laziness and incompetence.

Thus the notion of "merit" is itself double-edged and ironic: What might be considered by some as a desirable freedom to speak and work idiosyncratically is taken by others as evidence of unmeritorious performance or even malfeasance. That the DPC wrestled with this ambiguity is clear, if Fabrikant's postings are accurate. That Usenet subscribers were enmeshed in a similar dilemma is even more manifest, and the patterns of their responses are especially ironic, given that most were themselves aspiring or full-fledged academics.

A number of postings dealt with Fabrikant and tenure—or more precisely, they dealt with synchronically constructed images of Fabrikant-as-academic and of Fabrikant-as-killer. That is to say that for the full run of these discourses Fabrikant as idiosyncratic academic persisted, frozen in time in certain Usenet threads, side by side with Fabrikant the murdering madman. Thus Usenet posters could and did discuss whether someone with Fabrikant's "posted personality" should be granted tenure long after it was clear that the real Fabrikant's next tenure would be in jail:

> *Would *YOU* want to work with someone like that on a daily basis? I wouldn't! As far as I'm concerned, if someone is as big a pain as Fabrikant seems to have been, it doesn't matter one whit how good their research was.*

Should they have given him tenure then? To prevent him from going off the deep end?

As far as what the department 'owed' Fabrikant, I don't believe ANY university is obligated to give tenure to such an abusive person.

. . . their response was to deny him tenure. In other words, to deliver a crushing blow to his research career, while simultaneously washing their hands of him.

Jerks

More generally, many Usenet subscribers set Fabrikant in the category of "jerk," a term which itself became the focus of intense debate, even flame wars, as it was tied to the tenure issue and to a leveling, "horizontal" ideal image of collegiality:

Besides, I read the stuff over the weekend, and I did not read into it that he was going to kill those folks. He came out as a jerk, right?

*So, the picture that came through was that of a jerk who had (perhaps he was right about that?) such a high regard of himself as a researcher that he could no longer stand being subordinated to an establishment that was intellectually so *inferior* . . .*

Learn to live with jerks. It's the real world.

to which the response was

Very well. Here is how I have 'learned to live with jerks': I recommend against granting them tenure. Is that real enough for you?

If a school tries to keep jerks out of its tenured faculty, I say 'more power to them'!

Could you please give us a formal and generally acceptable definition of a 'jerk'?

I am afraid that you don't understand what tenure is about. Its purpose is to make sure that you are free to do you own favorite research and voice your favorite opinions without being afraid that one of your bosses may call you a jerk and force you to do something different.

. . . a person given a guaranteed job for life must be able to work with the group of people that are there. If that means they ALL have to be jerks, then so be it!

> *What appear to some faculty as disruptive is actually constructive to teaching + research, and it is often made by innovative individuals, who are disliked by some faculty members.*

One person even proposed a Darwinian version of tenure:

> *. . . jerks just don't last — the requirement for team membership, the collegiality, is an extremely good selector. I am a very strong believer that this is appropriate. Prima donnas and the totally weird have to pay the price for their behavior and sometimes it's a lack of acceptance.*

As measured by frequency of various responses, the posted Usenet consensus seemed to be to deny Fabrikant the right to tenure, this critical dimension of authority and platform for future authorship. Most argued the position, contrary to Usenet ideology, that the good of the many (read: "the department") should be considered before the rights of a dissenting few. Selecting a person with an appropriately collegial attitude took precedence thereby over otherwise meritorious individual "jerks":

> *. . . the department should choose people that can work with the current people in the department, without disrupting the current work. Yes, this will sometimes give you departments that are full of 'jerks', but if that's the way the people at the department and university feel they get the most work done, then let them do it!*

> *. . . if the person is disruptive enough to harm the work of the other people in the department, then they should not granted tenure.*

> *Being disruptive is rarely constructive to teaching + research, except to the person who is being disruptive . . . no single individual should be allowed to harm an entire Department.*

In all of this, it is noteworthy that tenurable merit was perceived on the Usenet much as in the report of Fabrikant's DPC committee—mainly as a capacity to get along with others rather than (as Fabrikant wished to claim) an individual's ability to perform significant research. Remember that these postings, by and large, appeared on sci.*research*.careers, where a central theme in more normal times has been the comparative weakness of meritocratic determinants of access to professional employment (by comparison, say, with the requisites of affirmative action). It was generally held, ironically enough, both by those holding and by those without secure academic positions that collegiality necessitated the expulsion of those who might be noncollegial by temperament or "attitude." One Usenet user summed up the discussion well, if rather understatedly:

> *I conclude from this that personality, attitude, relations to colleagues, etc., are not irrelevant to tenure decisions.*

This stands in marked contrast to the previously remarked Usenet emphasis on the authorship of the individual creator and scientist.

Thus in regard to tenure the genealogical study of postings reveals both topical continuity (an emphasis on collegiality) and discontinuity (the willingness to engage in systematic disfellowship). The name "jerk" juxtaposed to "tenure" (tied subtextually to a contrast between collegiality/equality of authority and hierarchically institutionalized authority) calls to our attention the real disproportion between these two nominations as they were applied to Fabrikant in Usenet postings and in terms of the quite divergent "carceral" implications they posed for subscribers (Foucault, 1979, pp. 293-308).

More generally, however, this instance illustrates how Usenet postings exhibit a tendency to dispute matters of topical continuity and discontinuity while at the same time often fracturing chronological continuity and partitioning discussed reality into contradictory or ironically contrasted images. We believe that from a technical standpoint alone this is a characteristic of computer-mediated communication as a whole, particularly because several dimensions of computer use make inevitable a certain measure of anarchy and disarticulation amid the usually firm orderliness of conversational reciprocity.

In particular, although many messages are genealogically linked in the sense that they cite the text of an immediate antecedent as a warrant for their response, the sequence in which they may actually appear on the Usenet is jumbled both by the multisite conditions under which messages are posted and distributed and by the diverse circumstances of readers, who do not always receive Usenet postings in the same order or choose to read them sequentially or at the same time. This effect is exacerbated by the practice of cross-posting, which allows a message read on one newsgroup to respond to predecessors on another to which the reader may not currently subscribe. Usenet reality is further partitioned by the use of subject descriptors both to establish, become aware of, and read topical threads; once established, threads nominally on "the same" topic, such as Fabrikant, can be genealogically coiled differently and are likely to unwind at differing rates.

This, of course, brings up a critical question: Given these dissonant forces, from where does Usenet order and epistemological certainty arise? The Usenet would be chaotic indeed if no social conventions intervened to reassert the usual style of conversational norms. As we have noted, on a discursive level the genealogical continuity of postings is maintained partially by mutual citation. But it is clear that the sequential unfolding of threads is highly constrained by a widely held stock of conventionally and sequentially acceptable responses to particular thematic bits. In the case of the Fabrikant postings, these surfaced clearly in the highly conventional story lines developing out of the shootings themselves. The initial response, to which all deferred, was muted sorrow ("response cries," Goffman, 1981, chap. 2):

> *. . . cannot express my sorrow at what has happened at my alma mater.*
>
> *. . . sad, distressing and disturbing.*
>
> *My condolences to all involved in the Concordia incident.*
>
> *My sincere sympathy goes out to the families and friends of the victims.*

Some, who evidently found the alleged murders an unexpected twist in the Fabrikant story, expressed disassociative amazement:

> *When I read this newsgroup and see what the local newspapers or TV stations are transmitting, I feel like being a space alien and participating in a debate about something the Earthians are just not aware of.*
>
> *Bizarre. News is an abstract involvement in an untangible world, an almost prosthetic existence with little or no impact on physical reality. To have seen the posts the Fabrikant made before us all, followed by such physical and evil acts, is really disturbing.*
>
> *I think it is obvious how powerless and desperate Fabrikant felt — to laboriously type all of this stuff into a file and transmit it to what is essentially a public BBS* [bulletin-board system]. *He really needed to be heard! Look what is happened now!*
>
> *This raises many interesting questions. It raises the specter of a distraught human being under pressure trying desperately to communicate with the outside world by sitting alone in front of his computer screen and sending out mass mailings of help (the electronic version of the "message in a bottle" or the "prisoner in a Chinese cookie factory").*
>
> *By the way, isn't anybody intrigued by the symbolism hidden in these kinds of cases? "Fabrikant" means "someone who fabricates" or "someone who creates"*

> *in German. Just thought I'd add a little mysticism to this otherwise crazy, surrealistic (I wish) world.*

There are also clearly panoptic forces at work determining what constitutes thematically, contextually, and structurally appropriate postings, as well as providing "net police" in the form of those who will aggressively attack the appropriateness of unconventional discourse (Foucault, 1979, pp. 195-228). To illustrate, a fascinating flame war broke out respecting the posting of Fabrikant's material and the relevance of discussion of his case to sci.research.careers within two days of Bai's first posting. This initially was ironically interspersed with disconnected postings reporting Fabrikant's alleged mayhem on August 24 and was finally quenched by the realization across the relevant groups of what had just happened at Concordia. Some thought that the postings were appropriately sited; others did not:

> *1). Brevity in writing style is desirable 2). Care should be taken in selecting a forum for your views 3). Discuss only issues appropriate to the selected forum . . .*
>
> *If you can't find some redeeming qualities in the topic at hand, please take the discussion off line.*

> *Get this Fabrikant crapola out of this group and into its own forum. Perhaps alt.justifiable.homocide or rec.murder.for.promotion.*

> *STOP! Take a moment, edit your Subject-lines, your Newsgroups: fields, and Follow-up lines. If you want to ask for expertise about Fabrikant's sanity, please ask in psy.psychology . . . The legal questions can be taken to misc.legal . . . This way the readers of this group don't need to concern themselves with murder events, and can concentrate on career issues . . . Academic? Make sense? Got that? Great?*

> *Just because you use the group to get career information doesn't justify your request to censor this thread . . . There may even be some useful career lessons there if you take the time to look.*

> *Lighten up, oh diplomatic one. This is the Internet. Use your kill key.*

> *Who died and made you Elvis?*

These flames point to a contradiction that may be inherent in the culture of scientific research: On the one hand, it is often maintained that through science there develops social progress and, on the other, that science itself is and should be objective, dispassionate, and distinct from social issues (Kuhn,

1970). Again, there arises through observation of the genealogy of Usenet postings an awareness of the fragility of science as ideology:

> *I can't believe what I'm reading here, day after day. A man murders three people . . . and he develops a fan club in sci.research.careers!*
>
> *In a research career newsgroup a professional compatriot has posted a succession of charges which were very much an appropriate contribution to the theme of the group. He then (allegedly) commits mass murder in a shooting spree, apparently in response to unbearable pressures, again which are very topical to careers in research and academia. And YOU don't think this warrants further discussion in this newsgroup?*
>
> *I think that this news group is the ideal place for a discussion of the issues of co-authorship and 'politics' in the academic environment.*

In this context, therefore, the trope of irony and the genealogical method converge. This convergence becomes pointed when Usenet threads disperse themselves among apparently peripheral topics, as the choice of such topics exposes yet further mythologies, discrepancies ("de-fabricating" the discourse in several senses), and discontinuities in the culture that is constructed by and in its turn, constructs the Usenet and its subscribers themselves: "Discourses are . . . practices that systematically form the objects of which they speak" (Sarup, 1989, p. 70). We consider two such here: guns and the use of the English language. These initially attracted our attention because they seemed so tangential to the more obvious issues at hand and then later because they seem to illustrate so neatly the double-edged meaning of genealogy in this context.

Guns

Fabrikant's access to guns apparently became a "real world" issue long before the actual shootings, as evidenced by the police search mentioned above. It also appears that when Fabrikant applied for a permit to carry a gun between his home and gun club, the required five letters of recommendation (including one from his employer) became a serious issue in his continuing disputes at Concordia, as "the permit department got a call from Concordia warning that Fabrikant had threatened people." One poster remarked that

> *Dr. Fabrikant made it a point to go round and ask for signatures from anybody he had difficulties with including . . . secretaries, support staff, and administrators.*

Another poster burlesqued his quest for a letter of recommendation:

> *Fabrikant, unshaven and disheveled, enters your office without knocking. He creeps up to your desk, silently. 'What?!?!?! Oh, it's you, Fabrikant! Wh-wh-what do you want?' 'Oh, nothing really. (circling behind you) I just wanted (pant, pant) you to sign (drooling) my GUN PERMIT!!!!!! BHA HA HA HA HA HA HA HA HA!!!!!!!!!!!!!!'*

Charles Bertrand, Vice-President of Administrative Services at Concordia, eventually stated that "the university has strong reason for concern about the issuing of a gun permit to Dr. Fabrikant." Two of the guns allegedly used by Fabrikant belonged to his wife, Maya Tyker.[23] Ms. Tyker belonged to a gun club and claimed to have given her husband the guns "for safekeeping." The fact that five persons at Concordia had been assaulted with guns, four of them (eventually) fatally, seems to have evoked a distinct thread of discourse on the Usenet focused on gun control. The entire conventional panoply of pro- and anti-gun debates was exhausted through many postings (particularly in canada.general and soc.culture.canada), including the following:

> *Can anybody out there really justify the sale of fire arms in this society?*

> *It ensures that the population is not totally helpless in the event that civic order collapses.*

> *I could use a tank!! Think how safe I would be then . . .*

> *The number of crimes committed each year with properly registered handguns in canada, is very low. much lower than deaths attributed to knifings.*

> *If you want to reduce violent crimes, you'd do better by looking at a society that glorifies all kinds of violent acts . . . Picking on any particular tool is a waste of time.*

And, of course,

> *Guns don't kill people, criminals kill people.*

The central genealogical point to be made concerns the discourse's automatic "natural" association of violence and guns. Although Fabrikant could have dispatched his enemies in any number of ways (and did attempt to do so through memo wars and legal maneuvers), the fact that he chose a hand gun was deemed highly symbolic by Usenet posters. In some ways, it seemed to confirm their image of him as a scientific rebel and prefigured their judgment of him as "insane" or "mad" (see below). It also powerfully associated him with "crime" and "criminality"—both predominant themes lending further credence to "the authorities."[24]

It is perhaps too much to argue that Fabrikant became the prototypic mad scientist for Usenet subscribers. It is not at all remarkable to point to this thread of debate as genealogically continuous *and* discontinuous with his fight for authorship and tenure and his alleged activities against the Concordia "parasites"—continuous, because Fabrikant throughout was seen to speak in a violent idiom whose mood was captured in the gun control debate, and discontinuous, because it forcibly associated Fabrikant, in other contexts portrayed as an elite academic who had claimed scientific sanctity, with the secular, decidedly unscientific and déclassé matter of "vulgar" violence (cf. Bourdieu, 1984, pp. 215-218, on the class implications of violence in sport, a homologous cultural "game").

Language

Another thread of debate that attracted Usenet postings concerned the language used by Fabrikant:

> *What struck me is his poor command of English after having lived in Canada for a dozen years or so. Perhaps the delay in granting of tenure is related to this. I mean, no matter how brilliant his research papers may be, if they must be edited by a grammarian every time, it would be a bit embarrassing for Concordia, don't you think?*

As noted, the Usenet has adopted English as its *lingua franca.* For this reason alone, facility in English could be anticipated as an issue that would draw attention. However, the status of English as an international language, and particularly as a language of science and applied science, also highlighted Fabrikant's image as an outsider, inviting aspersions on his general competence and credibility:

> *If you read through his other letters, you'll notice he doesn't have a complete mastery of our language.*

This immediately became caught up in a debate about bilingualism in Canada, also an issue of nationalist and even grammarian passions:

> *I assume you mean English by 'our language' though in Quebec that may not be the case of course.*

> *. . . if this was in a French-speaking university,* [as it is not] *I don't see the relation between someone's English being worse and impeachment of tenure.*

> *Having spent 4 years at Concordia (84-88), I honestly don't think that mastery of the English language is a criterion for granting tenure. There were a few professors in engineering that could barely speak English, yet they did get tenure.*

> *I find that Canadians, in general, seem to be very lax when it comes to writing standards.*

There were dissidents who claimed

> *His English isn't bad . . . I doubt that this has had any bearing on the case at all.*

But the tenor of this discussion nevertheless worked to undermine his represented position: In the original Fabrikant postings, there was a noticeable discrepancy between the rather passionate yet stilted "transcripts" of his conversations with his antagonists and the cold textual fluency of the latters' memoranda. In short, if Valery Fabrikant dropped his prepositions and articles, he might be suspect in other ways as well (Barthes, 1986, pp. 106-110, on the "encratic" nature of language). This remained a commonly expressed view despite, as one poster noted, Fabrikant's main opponents being of "South Asian" ancestry (which, in the worst-case scenario, might have led to a "plague on both your houses" response, although it did not).

To summarize, the method of genealogy draws our attention both to continuities and discontinuities in names and their relationships. These elisions and breaches, in their turn, deconstruct for us the significant mythologies that attend science, research, tenure, violence, language, and several other themes. Ironies reside aplenty in these themes, particularly those that problematize the relationship between the individual and the collegial, between science as an eremitic enterprise and science as a project of association. Yet to be explored are the passions attending such relationships and how they are understood.

Madness

> *He was ranting like a lunatic. Much of what he said may have been the exaggerations of a paranoid.*

> *I find it very interesting what motivated a man of rather high intellect to stoop to such an extreme course of action.*

Back in my country there is a proverb 'You can chase a cat up to a corner, and then it is going to pounce back at you.'

It's too easy to dismiss his 'rantings.'

Mr. Fabrikant, you are not the Robin Hood of academia.

Truth can motivate evil acts, and falsehood good acts.

Now you are calling me a crazy murderer. I want to ask you, who is crazy now?

The irony that overflows these citations is that of contested images of Valery Fabrikant as an agent of misfortune, "bad, sad or mad." Whether the Fabrikant of "everyday reality" was mad or angry is itself, of course, at least partly a cultural construction (Szasz, 1974); however, the various Fabrikants on the Usenet were almost entirely so inscribed. On-line discourses offered opportunities for many constructions that became juxtaposed ironically to one another, all of them relatively unfettered by personal experience of the man himself or of his sociocultural context.

Usenet subscribers resorted to a variety of stratagems to interpret or "account for" Fabrikant's activities and thereby to constitute him as a conventionally understandable "agency" of a recognized sort, functioning within a specific "game" whose stakes, among others, included scientific reputation and assassination (Bourdieu, 1984, p. 12; 1990, p. 103). For our purposes, these strategies may be gathered into three general categories: biographical construction (and its discreditation), contextualization with regard to other incidents, fictional or real, and the attempts of scholars to segregate persons from issues. We address each in turn and point to the conflicts and accommodations they represent in regard to Valery Fabrikant, Usenet prototype of the "mad scientist."

Biographical Containment

Goffman (1963) has shown in detail how stigmatization and consequent marginalization stimulates and then interrupts the arrangement of a coherent and credible biography (chap. 2; see Aycock, n.d., chap. 7, for an analysis of Goffman's strategies in this regard). Fabrikant himself singled out stigmatization as a muting tactic used against him by his enemies:

They had to invent something, and they did. They know how everyone hates violence, so they have decided to use this, but they needed facts that I am violent

> *or potentially violent . . . they figured that the more lawless the action, the greater is the probability that I loose [sic] my temper and do something outrageous . . . they try to destabilize me psychologically and to damage my reputation, so that nobody would pay much attention to my accusations.*

Indeed, Fabrikant's antagonists, taking this cue, referred again and again to his violent and contentious nature:

> [Fabrikant] *seems determined to see the inside of a courtroom*

> *Many respected and important people from outside the University have also been disturbed by Dr. Fabrikant's behavior*

> *Fabrikant involved in a host of legal actions [Usenet citation of a newspaper report, detailing his disputes with Tilden Rent-a-Car, Royal Trust, Prudential Insurance, and Royal Air Maroc]*

> *2 ½ hours of demands and complaints by Fabrikant at the opening of his preliminary hearing* [Usenet citation of a newspaper account of Fabrikant's arraignment]

Usenet postings conventionalized his "rampage" by strongly subscribing to the implication that if Fabrikant had committed a murderous atrocity it was because he was already primed by his idiosyncratic nature to do so (cf. Goffman, 1961, p. 145, on the retroactive nature of "moral careers"). His actions on August 24 were perceived as an inevitable outgrowth of his "abusive" and "arrogant" personality (two adjectives prominent in Usenet accounts). First, Fabrikant's colleagues and supervisors and then his media biographers construed his actions as "irrational" violence from their perspective, conveniently without either external justification or accounting. This "genetic" demonstration, ironically, situated Fabrikant in a discredited biography that might well have been related quite otherwise had he remained in the former Soviet Union: "Sure enough, it was like Soviet Russia: people are raised in a very oppressive, authoritarian environment; then they get out, and they take literally the promises of justice . . . and the judicial system finds them 'arrogant'."

Some attempted to gloss Fabrikant's stigma:

> *. . . these postings, while most likely biased, do contain elements of verifiable fact . . . Fabrikant's publication list, the publication list of the head of his department, the personnel department recommendations, contract awards . . .*

. . . I begin to wonder whether if some of us are acting in a haste in dismissing him as a mad man . . .

I've used the Melvyl system of the Univ. of California to look for the books and articles of Dr. Fabrikant in the period 7/89-7/92. As it can be seen below, the list is pretty impressive . . .

Others universalized his biography in characteristically discrediting terms of dismissal or caveat:

. . . the man was abusive, arrogant, and more than a little unstable.

. . . he had said on more than one occasion that he would settle his disputes 'the American way', with an accompanying pistol-like hand gesture.

. . . Fabrikant appears to be using the same bullying tactics in court of warnings of dire consequences if he doesn't get his way as he is seen doing over the years . . .

The DPC's observation of the pattern of behavior of Dr. Fabrikant . . . was confirmed by a part of the motions passed in the meeting of the senior faculty members of the department on October 25, 1991 . . .

In the case of murder _every_ human collective places a high value on human life and recognizes its fragility. Therefore murder is an egregious crime everywhere which demands that decisive and effective steps be taken to limit such behavior.

Even Fabrikant himself, ironically, seemed to acquiesce at some points in this biographical reconstruction through his own statements:

. . . I am no longer afraid of anything or anybody. We all have to die one day . . .

This particular act of violence was carefully planned and nurtured and I have documents for that . . .

I am a great danger to such people . . .

Thus the virtual biography of Valery Fabrikant is extremely flexible, susceptible both to justification and vilification by reference to divergent interpretations placed upon the "facts" of his personal history and to those that seemingly discredit his actions. Goffman sees the construction and presentation of self as "inherently political" (1963a, pp. 123-125) and the self as essentially "recalcitrant" (1961a, p. 319). There can be no greater ironization, perhaps, than that of a biography turned against itself to highlight its own contradictions (cf. Barthes, 1977a).

Containing Difference

A second strategy employed by the Usenet subscribers was to account for Fabrikant's actions by contextualizing them in relation to other, putatively similar "mad" or "crazy" deeds. Notably in terms of the previously remarked blurring of text and context in computer-mediated discourse, some of these were apparently "real" while others were "fictional." The fact that no one seemed concerned about this distinction (in a company, remember, mainly of empiricists) is in itself highly ironic and a tendency that we surmise is intensified by the textually concrete yet virtual nature of on-line discourse.

It was inevitable that the most popular comparison was between Fabrikant's actions and those of Marc Lepine:

> *The attack recalled a December, 1989, massacre when gunman Marc Lepine shot and killed 14 women* [engineering students at the École Polytechnique] *at the University of Montreal.*

Some accepted the comparison:

> *They both concerned a frustrated man with a gun.*

Others rejected it:

> *The situation at Concordia was quite different from the incident at la Polytechnique.*

Yet the standard of contextualization itself—madness, and the consequent conceptual merging of Fabrikant's actions with those of others who were deemed "crazy"—was rarely questioned.

Again, some such associations were made with "real" events:

> *. . . an article in the Philadelphia Inquirer told of a break-in at the residence of . . . Chancellor, Berkeley. If I remember correctly, the intruder was characterized as a female *radical*, was carrying a hunting knife and machete, and was mortally wounded by the police.*
>
> *1) In the late seventies a math professor at Stanford was killed by a graduate student with a hammer . . .*

2) Last fall 3 professors at the University of Iowa were shot to death by a former graduate student . . .
3) At Utah State a professor I knew was denied tenure . . . he made a death threat against another professor . . . he died (of natural causes) on the day he was to vacate his office.

Dan White, who murdered Mayor Moscone of San Francisco 12 years ago, successfully argued a multi-day rage in reducing his conviction . . .

Others were entirely textual:

In the [Goldbug Variations] *the protagonist shares a number of similar characteristics with Fabrikant . . .*

I recommend reading an excellent novel about honesty and integrity in scientific research: _Cantor's Dilemma_ . . .

I find the Fabrikant affair very intriguing; it's almost like real-life Dostoyevsky.[25]

The urge to contextualize in conventional terms as a means to comprehend and situate discourse seems to be quite powerful in this electronic environment despite its ideology of resistance to contextualization. We note that it appears to return textual authority to that of the body and of personal presence, both popularly thought to be certain precursors of authenticity (e.g., Derrida, 1982, pp. 15-16; see also Aycock, n.d., chap. 6, for an extended discussion of Derrida's position).

A number of Usenet subscribers took this opportunity to recount other, allegedly similar incidents of academic "fraud and extortion" from the perspective of a construed victimology and human ecology of madness:

I've seen similar things happen to people who seem entirely reasonable people.

This is not an isolated matter. Things like this are occurring all over the continent.

Here is a story told to me by a mathematician . . .

I posted also a copy of a 'plea for help' from a tenured professor . . . regarding what he thought was an unjust denial of tenure to a couple of young faculty at that university . . .

. . . I know from personal experience that such type of events are becoming all to [sic] *common in academia . . .*

These efforts to fix Fabrikant's textually ascribed actions in more familiar, and thereby more persuasive, contextual events here owns close, ironic parallels with the ethnographic enterprise: Both attempt to make the foreign understandable through reference to the conventional while preserving the flavor of the exotic and different through a highly selective symbolism of *différance* (Clifford, 1986, p. 101; Crapanzano, 1986, p. 52; Derrida, 1982, pp. 1-27).[26]

As against the first strategy of enclosing "Fabrikant" in a suitable biographical schemata, this second strategy disperses his actions toward supposedly comparable deeds, catching up and displaying him within a cultural recognizable typology of violent acts, rendering them meaningful and significant as "different but understandable"; thus the association of Fabrikant the iconoclast with other real and imagined iconoclasts of "the same class" rendered him strangely normative in the frameworks of both strategies.

Institutionalizing Madness

The third strategy that constituted Fabrikant for the Usenet, however, is the most elaborate and telling of all. Should the disputes that he described and their horrific aftermath be interpreted as anger or madness? The first two strategies chiefly address this issue by circumscribing it: the third strategy is one of direct engagement. Foucault's (1975) collection of essays surrounding the case of Pierre Riviere, the man who "slaughtered" his family, offers a template for our discussion.[27] Riviere's imprisonment, trial, and execution were permeated with the contentions of those who wished to stabilize his actions in their own official discourse of madness, legal responsibility, and the like and by so doing to establish their discourses as dominant and authoritative (Riot, 1975). The motivating emotions underlying Fabrikant's actions were no less hotly contested, and as set in a "regime of truth" (Foucault, 1980, p. 133) in no lesser way verified the sciences that claimed him for their attention and remediation. The irony here is immediate: Those who believed their own accountings (both on-line and professional) to be factual, indisputable relations of truths susceptible of independent substantiation according to the strictures of reason and empiricism did not perceive the extent to which reason and truth problematize one another in the realm of on-line discourses (Foucault, 1973, p. 107; 1980, pp. 131-132).

An initial impulse of Usenet subscribers was to struggle among themselves between common, garden-variety expressions of folk wisdom or sympathy and a desire to discern what "really" happened at Concordia:

Nobody's justifying what Fabrikant did.

Even if everything was true, it doesn't justify cold blooded murder.

Before I read the article, I thought Fabricant was a victim in this whole tragedy (although not as much as the three people he killed). Now, I'm not sure.

What Fabrikant did was senseless and abhorable [sic] yet the points he raised before, are quite valid.

**I* believe his evidence too, but his evidence doesn't bear out the charges he made.*

When Fabrikant was a disgruntled academic, I thought his claims should be examined. Now that he's a murderer, I think his claims should be tossed immediately into the nearest garbage can . . .

Fabrikant's actions do not 'validate' his claims. Fabrikant's actions do not 'invalidate' them either!

Although I don't agree with, or even understand, the impulse to commit homicide, I can understand the frustration that led to it.

Although there may be some small degree of truth to what Fabrikant claimed, I highly suspect that any person for whom these things could and does drive them to commit a killing spree would be greatly distorting the truth for themselves, and in this case for us as well.

I sided with him, totally, I believed his evidence. Now that I hear what he's done . . .

At this juncture, opinions diverged sharply. Overall, there was a generally expressed wish that the issues Fabrikant raised nevertheless be investigated without "passion," irrespective of Fabrikant's impassioned actions:

Dr. Fabricant's [sic] *accusations of unethical conduct . . . will be thoroughly investigated despite his violent acts.*

His accusations clearly indicate that he went over the edge, but that doesn't necessarily mean his accusations were false . . .

. . . the academic community should take the opportunity to examine its practices.

All of us would like to know the true story . . .

Hopefully, someone will take the time to investigate this situation and try to come to some understanding of what happened.

> *The underside of the rock he has turned over should be looked at objectively and dispassionately.*
>
> *. . . it sure sounded to me as if Dr. Fabrikant may have had some valid serious complaints.*
>
> *There was clearly something going on inside the ME department at Concordia.*
>
> *The veracity of his claims is a question independent of his subsequent actions, regardless how vile or attractive those actions might be.*

These attempts to segregate the structural determinants of Fabrikant's actions from approval of the man himself constitute a kind of discursive purification that sought to separate science, in its most ideologically exalted form, from raw history and individual experience as a kind of protective mantle for its faithful practitioners:

> *Science is no longer blessed by the historical peace and cooperative spirit that gave it its noble reputation.*

From a rearguard position, therefore, came the plea to:

> *please keep the two issues apart!*

Indeed, the traditional scientistic ideology that "facts" may usefully be known apart from lived personal experience and sociocultural context is central to the narratives surrounding Fabrikant and, possibly, to computer-mediated discourses in general. Bai's query to Fabrikant after receipt of his first e-mail characterizes this search for truth, independent of the "bias" of concrete events:

> *There are not enough facts in your message. . . . People cannt* [sic] *just speak up for something they dont know these facts about. . . . It will make your case stronger and easier for other people to help you if you let more facts be known.*

From this point, two positions may be loosely distinguished between those that were commonsensical (Geertz, 1983, chap. 4) and those that were psychoanalytic in nature. These two positions, although starting from a shared assumption of factuality, realign Fabrikant's situation in distinct, though overlapping ways. Ironically, it is as if those who subscribe to the Usenet, most of them nominally scientists, could not themselves distinguish readily between the folk wisdom of North American proscriptions against violence of a certain kind and that of certified scientific interpretations of that wisdom (Sedgwick, 1982).

The commonsensical position was reflected in this reference to the Mosaic decalogue:

> *Thou shalt (6) not murder; (8) not steal; (9) not give false evidence; (10) not covet . . . violations of (10) are . . . daily occurrences in academic life . . . violations of (8) and (9) are uncommon, but intellectual stealing and intellectual giving-of-false-evidence are often as much part of the infrastructure of our post-secondary institutions as are the campus sewerage and garbage collection systems.*
>
> *It doesn't take much to imagine a distressed alienated mind, hyper-sensitive to perceived massive violations of (8) (9) and (10), to fail (6).*

One suggested remedy:

> *I find the InterVarsity Graduate Christian Fellowship at my school to be an excellent source of support.*

Other commensensical approaches refer to Fabrikant's loss of "perspective," "desperately seeking help," or "activist's syndrome":

> *Somebody starts with a completely reasonable cause, but they run against a bureaucracy . . . who refuses to let them have their way. Such people can lose their perspective . . .*

As noted before, some simply saw him as a

> *jerk who had . . . such a high regard of himself as a researcher that he could no longer stand being subordinated to an establishment that was intellectually so *inferior* . . .*
>
> *These lawsuit actions by Fabrikant against the world speak much about his character.*

Proposed remedies included the suggestion to consult "books available on how to protect yourself from backstabbing and unethical power trips in an organizational setting," "not becoming isolated," "wise counsel," "some intervention," or forcible "counseling":

> *when someone is going off the deep end, and it's visible to everyone around him, then everyone around him shares the responsibility for getting him help, IMHO* [in my humble opinion]

A unique suggestion was "working off stress with athletics."[28]

These commonsensical approaches faded imperceptibly into more formal, psychoanalytic arguments that carried with them their own impedimenta of explanations for action, basis for labeling, and prescribed response.

Generalizations about Fabrikant's "instability," for example, led to heated discussions about whether he was "really" a "paranoid schizophrenic." Such labeling permitted users to ground Fabrikant's seemingly irrational behavior in the relative certainty of psychology and biochemistry:

> *My understanding is that paranoid schizophrenics can create quite detailed and often internally self-consistent delusions.*
>
> *I find it hard to believe that any biochemical imbalance in the brain (I'm sure you would agree that schizophrenia and like neuroses can be linked to biochemistry) would allow a man to function at the top of his intellectual ability.*
>
> *Sudden degradations in work relationships are a classic sign of paranoid schizophrenia.*
>
> *Dr. Fabrikant's actions . . . are those of a very, very sick mind.*
>
> *He had reached an unstable frame of mind. Maybe persecution complex and extreme paranoia.*
>
> *. . . those postings, plus his actions, should be quite enough to convince a jury that he belongs in an institution . . .*
>
> *. . . when he started threatening people and acting violent, they should have said, 'OK, well now we know why he has been so abusive and difficult; it's not that he just has a personality problem, it's that he is mentally unstable.'*

It is quite interesting that such well-established "scientific" definitions of Fabrikant encountered resistance on the Usenet. It is difficult, however, to discern the degree to which this resistance was inspired by scientific skepticism, as opposed to characteristic Usenet anti-authoritarian sympathies. For instance,

> *Very little is known about the human mind. Using the term 'madman' is about as appropriate as labeling people with disabilities as 'retards or imbiciles'* [sic]
>
> *If by 'mad' you mean frustrated/angry/desperate to the point of considering violence, then that's tautologically redundant, since it is clear that his actions*

> *were preceded by such consideration . . . However, if you mean 'mad' in the modern forensic-psychiatric sense, you appear to have no grounds for such a judgment.*

> *I think it's unfair to simply dismiss Fabrikant as a madman . . . in general there are people who provoke others in order to make the other guy come out looking like the bad guy.*

> *We do *ourselves* a great disservice by automatically labeling those who commit these types of crimes as madmen.*

> *Dr. F. didn't sound that unstable to me. Many of his letters seem very sober and articulate. He just sounded VERY angry at the injustice.*

And perhaps most telling,

> *Often, those that are seen to be threatening to an establishment, are branded by that establishment as being 'unstable, schizophrenic, dans-la-lune, etc.'*

Some even responded to the claim that Fabrikant could not have retained his scientific productivity if he were mad by a truncated class analysis:

> *How would *YOU* feel if your bosses are treating you like he was treated?*

> *He* [Fabrikant] *had very high expectations and couldn't tolerate . . . the conflict between his idealism and the reality of the corruption that is probably standard in all universities.*

> *I am willing to believe on the face of things that his department was very political and very vicious.*

There was, of course, no resolution to these debates about Fabrikant's biography, the contexts of violence in North America, or attempts to discern whether Fabrikant was after all "bad" or "mad." And how could there be? It is surely typical of computer-mediated discourses that such debates may be juxtaposed, interpenetrate and contradict one another, and then drift off almost idly into irresolution.

All the more so, it is ironic that such debates mirrored those that might have transpired among ordinary persons with no pretension to scientific accomplishment. It is also ironic that subscribers to the Usenet, many of whom *did* claim scientific accomplishment, could not agree fully among themselves on the overall framework required to comprehend Fabrikant, the most likely interpretation of his actions, or the general import of his claims and deeds for the scientific enterprise as a whole. This posits, although it does not satisfy, an argument that subscribers to the Usenet, those who are also mainly subscribers to an overarching ideology of science, are not, despite themselves, "playing in the same ballpark."

Thus even as Usenet subscribers sought to distinguish themselves from the flux of history, they were embroiled in it; even as they sought to except themselves from unscientific interests and explanations, they were enmeshed in them; even as they sought to disclaim Fabrikant as a legitimate agent of the "game" of science, they acknowledged him as such.

As Fabrikant "stared out at the packed courtroom," he asked the most incisive, and ironic question of all: "Is anyone here really afraid of me?"

Conclusion: The Ironic Cage of Hyperreality

> *Incidently, anyone want to guess how many slimeballs analysed the situation and decided that what all of this means is that Concordia now has several open billets for tenure track faculty?*
>
> *Then, of course, there are those of us non-tenurable scum who get only a fraction of a faculty position, spend most of our time teaching, serving on commitees* [sic], *writing proposals, reviewing papers and proposals, going to meetings, and directing the research of others, but have zero job security and have to scrape for soft-money salary justified only by that 30% of time available to do research.*

When we "think that things are real" we achieve something that is not only epistemological or ontological but experiential as well. Such insights arise from the daily discourses that produce and constitute our experiences, and in their turn, our experiences affirm those discourses as "real" (Foucault, 1980, p. 39). Yet not all discourses produce experience in the same way, nor do all discourses share the same sense of what is "real." We shall contrast three kinds of discourses here: interpersonal, print-based, and computer-mediated.

Interpersonal discourses confer upon the individuals who engage in them an immediate sense of authorship and authority. These discourses are reciprocal and renegotiable (no matter how unequally such negotiation proceeds) and have direct, embodied consequences. Interpersonal discourses lack permanency. As Ong (1982) has put it, they depend chiefly upon the production of vocal sounds generated precisely at the moment they are going out of existence (p. 32). Instead, they rely on embodied recall and ongoing social relationships to construct and stabilize their reality.

Print-based discourses (PBDs) delimit texts that are forever fixed in place and identified with a specified author or authors. Ong points out that unlike interpersonal discourses, PBDs have an objective, highly visual quality about them that permits them to be owned, acquiring in the process the factuality of private property (see his chap. 5; also Barthes, 1981, p. 91, on the "violence" of images reproduced visually). PBDs direct themselves toward a relatively passive, distanced readership that responds mainly through rereading and interpretation, occasionally through further print-based discourses. Although PBDs lack the immediacy of interpersonal contact, they have a capacity to mobilize powerful institutions that sustain themselves across great distances of time and space (Goody, 1986).

Computer-mediated discourses (CMDs) partake of some of the characteristics of interpersonal and print-based discourses, but extend them in particular ways. CMDs are potentially reciprocal and even in some instances almost immediate, but they are also disembodied, typically having no greater personal consequences than reading a book. While CMDs are at least hypothetically permanent, their main significance is often measured in days. Although CMDs are always authored, their authorship is always dubious. They appear to lack the authority of printed text to which they frequently overtly defer. CMDs possess an unambiguously textual format, yet one that is nevertheless interactive. The visual quality of CMDs lends itself to a sort of ownership and transferability ("my" files; sent me from "her"), yet the ultimate ownership of CMD is always open to question. Finally, CMDs may create and underwrite institutions capable of persisting across time and space (such as the Cleveland Free-Net, the Gutenberg project, or the Usenet University), but these institutions are usually imbued with relatively egalitarian ethos rather than a hierarchical one.

Like interpersonal and print-based discourses, some of the qualities of CMDs are simply functions of the technology employed, and indeed the frequent celebration by high-tech gurus of CMDs is sometimes predicated upon a naive technological determinism of its "liberating" potential along with that of other forms of computer-mediated information dissemination (Crane, 1991, p. 297; Nelson, 1992, p. 44). Yet we have also found in our analysis of the Fabrikant materials that, when considered in isolation from social convention or custom, the technological circumstances of CMDs predict little about the discourse's shape and substance. A reprise of our main points illumines this crucial ambiguity respecting CMDs.

On the one hand, the Fabrikant files first assert and then belie the role of authority and authorship. Far removed from the actual scene of events, we have no direct evidence that a short, middle-aged, bespectacled engineer now languishes in prison. Even so, we cannot disbelieve his iconography on the

Usenet, nor the manner in which his tale inscribed there cast a fleeting shadow over the verities of scientific achievement, scholarly integrity, and academic promise. By the same token, genealogy continued its narratives of scandal and trial, yet breached by so doing the *grand rècits* of scientific progress and methodological purity: Did Fabrikant stand for the former or the latter, scandal or purity? Such matters are undecidable (*en abyme*) in the Usenet texts that as often denied them as it asseverated their universality. Finally, the line between anger and madness wavers and then blurs in attempts to account for Fabrikant's situation. Causality itself, so highly acclaimed in traditional scientific discourses, becomes implicated, even dissolved in the mélange of the Fabrikant files. In all these ways CMDs seem to uphold the most broadly sketched claims of the role of the hyperreal in modernity: The simulation of reality displaces direct experience, and comes to reside in its stead (Baudrillard, 1983, p. 2). Text and context miscegenate promiscuously, destabilized by the circumstances of their production and reproduction on-line.

Yet, on the other hand, we have found good reason not to affirm uncritically the often asserted liberating and globalizing qualities of CMDs. There is a sobering lesson here that undermines Lyotard's (1984) incantation to throw open the databases, his injuncture to enliven experience with information freely served (p. 67). Hence the "cage" of CMDs: To what degree is our experience enlarged, or our cage of conventionality burst asunder, by the Fabrikant files? Those who questioned authority usually did so in a highly conventional fashion; frequently, they truckled to its demands for surveillance and containment. Often those who, in the best "pomo" fashion, should have relinquished claims of authorship instead vigorously defended it. The genealogy of on-line discourses was attested, not diminished, by the flame wars surrounding the ownership of guns, the purity of the English language, and, most important, the segregation of science from its social environs and consequences. Never was the continuity of science as a valued cultural project brought even remotely into question; the most superficially radical postings often were in a deep sense reactionary, hearkening to the nostalgic days of science's "nobility" and its latter-day "corruption." Finally, the passions that overflow every sentence of Fabrikant's own pleas for support were repeatedly discounted by those who wished to contain them by bromidic expressions of "sorrow," by labels of "paranoid schizophrenia," or by calling for "objective and dispassionate" investigation of the whole affair.

Thus the decentering that is often claimed as the primal feature of CMDs was only sporadically evidenced by the discourse we examined. While we partially agree with Barthes (1977b, pp. 146-148) that much of "a text's unity lies not in its origin but its destination"—in the diverse interpretive strategies of readers—we see little of this diversity reflected in the texts themselves.

By contrast, CMDs appear to have been overwhelmed again and again by the normative, conventional, and even reactionary intimations of those who posted to the Usenet. Here, "the foreign" typically was made *so* familiar as to be banal. Even our brief foray into these files strongly suggests the potential for the foreclosure of CMD along long familiar culturally prescribed lines: "Situational proprieties . . . transform the gathering [into] a social reality" (Goffman 1963b, p. 196). Although in some measure the sinews and integuments of the "cage" of the real are relaxed in CMDs, in other respects they remain taut and secure against the seductiveness of the hyperreal.

In conclusion, we suggest several avenues for further investigation of CMDs. First, in pursuit of the "end of history" proclaimed by postmodern thought (Featherstone, 1991, p. 33), may we indeed disaggregate text from context? Or must we instead renegotiate the interface of the two in a fashion that recognizes the sociocultural dispositions of those who produce them on the Internet? Second, do the conventions of Usenet newsgroups erode copresent or textual reality in favor of the hyperreal (Baudrillard, 1983, p. 3), or do they resituate these more traditional intimations of the real in new, even more carceral and deeply felt experiences? Third, shall we work uncritically toward an eschatology of liberation formed by CMDs ("THE PURPOSE OF COMPUTERS IS HUMAN FREEDOM," Nelson, 1992, p. 44, capitals in the original), or must we interrupt our progress toward an ethical millennium by discerning ever more carefully its attendant responsibilities, its hesitations, flaws, and even retrograde directions? Finally, the conflation of is/ought/seems that has been proclaimed by the "masters of suspicion" (Nietzsche, Marx, and Freud) leads, in virtual discourses, not to their resolution but to indeterminacy at a greater and perhaps more sophisticated level of inquiry (Hayles, 1990). Fabrikant closes this investigation with a rhetorical flourish that has resonated throughout this chapter, but in so doing he opens another interrogation that, we surmise, exposes indisputably the contentions that we have sketched between the real and the hyperreal:

> *I am no longer afraid of anything or anybody. We all have to die one day. Whenever I die, I shall die an honest person . . . Gandhi considered jail as a must for an honest person. I am prepared for that too.*

Notes

1. Crane (1991) suggests that computer discourses are "at least as different from print as film is from stage and perhaps as different as written literature is from poetry" (p. 293).

2. Fabrikant was found guilty of these offenses and sentenced to life in prison in August 1993 after a more than 3-month-long trial during which Fabrikant dismissed a string of court-appointed lawyers and eventually defended himself.

3. Indeed, newsgroups are sometimes completely disrupted by a single monomaniacal poster, as soc.history has been for a year.

4. In this regard, there is a rather clear difference in everyday netiquette between highly technical groups, such as comp.sys.ibm.pc.hardware, and social issue groups, such as alt.discrimination. The former tend to be grounded on a call and response of technical questions and afford polite, usually helpful responses (many of which involve considerable effort to generate); the latter frequently devolve into two or three ongoing flame wars, where defense of one's position against all comers seems to be the primary objective.

5. While Usenet access is potentially available to otherwise unaffiliated individual personal computer owners who enter Usenet gateways through public access numbers, personal bulletin boards, virtual communities such as the Cleveland Freenet, or private multiuse companies such as CompuServe® (and in the near future, Prodigy®), each of these options entails personal financial costs to users that has so far restricted their participation.

6. The methodology of this study of computer-mediated discourses is quite informal. We downloaded from Usenet newsgroups a full set of relevant postings from sci.research.careers, sci.research, canada.general, and soc.culture.canada amounting to thousands of pages of hard copy. We briefly considered and then discarded the prospects of a quantitative content analysis, deciding instead to rely on our intuitions of what might be ethnographically relevant. One of us (N.B.) corresponded with Dov Bai but obtained little information that was not available elsewhere; the initial Fabrikant postings were eventually placed on a public FTP site, where they are still available: davros.acs.ohio- state.edu in pub/. We have selected only those elements of the Fabrikant data for presentation that are appropriate to our purpose here, just a small proportion of the materials known to us. Our claims are thus mainly tentative and exploratory, serving chiefly to illustrate our preliminary understanding of some of the characteristics of this form of computer-mediated discourse.

7. Our investigations show unambiguously that people other than the 43 individuals listed on the header of the e-mails to Bai received this material directly from Fabrikant.

8. An average day's postings to sci.research.careers would be three or four one-page messages.

9. This is apparently confirmed by what Fabrikant implied was a literal transcription of a departmental personnel committee report recommending his termination and by another document purporting to be a rejection of that report by a faculty-wide personnel committee.

10. To the best of our knowledge, no poster save perhaps the Rector of Concordia University appeared to have known Fabrikant personally. Certainly, no poster made this claim.

11. We are suggesting a parallel here that is more than metaphorical, but space constraints make it impossible to support this contention here. On the analysis of ethnography as text, see Marcus and Cushman (1982) and Marcus and Fisher (1986).

12. The nature of the Usenet is such that specific postings reach users at widely varying times. This makes a fully chronological discussion by more than two people of any issue on a high volume group impossible to sustain.

13. Quotes have been made anonymous and, although in some cases their margins have been altered, are verbatim.

14. For a review of contemporary experimental ethnography, see Marcus and Cushman (1982).

15. From Malinoski (1922) on, a seductive introductory convention of many ethnographies has been to portray the ethnographer's initial struggles with adversity: unfriendly (Evans-

Pritchard, 1940) or warlike (Chagnon, 1968) "natives," strongly felt marginality (Lévi-Strauss, 1961; Rabinow, 1977), and so forth.

16. None of these locally posted e-mail messages ever appeared on the Usenet, unless of course they were identical to those posted by Dov Bai.

17. There was some initial objection to the length of the Bai postings and to the discussion being appropriate topically for sci.research.careers. This evaporated soon after the murders were reported.

18. Indeed, Usenet discourse was profoundly seduced by the symbolism of disorder connected to these killings. This symbolism can be seen clearly here. The "senseless" nature of Fabrikant's actions is, of course, interpretable as a standard attribution of irrationality, violence done *without just cause*, to those who proclaim themselves in opposition to the authorities. The claim of "misuse of University property" appeals in a similar vein to the most basic tenets of bourgeois society: To misuse property is de facto to discredit one's case.

19. "Finger" was in fact used to find the last time someone with Fabrikant's password was logged on to his university computer: "Monday, August 24, 1:23 pm EDT."

20. In this respect, subsequent discourse was analogous to what Rosaldo (1987) has termed dead, "dehumanizing" rather than "transformative" ethnographic discourse (p. 105).

21. Examples of massive interpenetration are easy to spot, as when users posted verbatim accounts from newspapers, which in turn were based on quotes taken from the Usenet.

22. Indeed, it is doubly ironic, in that "harmony" was a consistently used phrase in the Fabrikant material both to characterize Fabrikant's lack of it (see below) and some of Fabrikant's complaints: "Our [faculty] negotiating team is quite harmonious with the administration, except for the case when the administration tried to limit huge increases to even more huge salaries of some of the members."

23. "Maya," yet another name to be played with, signifies "illusion" in Hindi and Sanskrit (Laing & Esterson, 1970, chap. 1).

24. We will not pursue here this nationalistic theme that while violence might be, as claimed by Fabrikant, "the American way," it was definitely not that of Canada, where violence with guns is a factor of 10 less common than in the United States.

25. It is irresistible to speculate: Did the poster have in mind *Crime and Punishment* or a lesser known but perhaps equally pertinent novel by Dostoyevsky, *The Idiot*?

26. "If the alterity of the other is posed, that is only posed, does it not amount to the same, for example in the form of the 'constituted object' or of the 'informed product' invested with meaning, etc? From this point of view, I would even say that the alterity of the other inscribes in this relationship that which in no case can be 'posed.' Inscription, as I would define it in this respect, is not a simple position: it is rather that by means of which every position is of itself confounded . . différance" (Derrida, 1981, pp. 95-96).

27. The parallel is quite remarkable. Riviere, imprisoned for murder, wrote a memoir narrating his circumstances in much the same fashion as Fabrikant. Foucault (1975) points out, "In all these transformations the text and murder kept changing places, or, to put it more precisely, moved one another around . . . the successive placing of the text and the deed are simply stages in the operation and production of a mechanism: the murder/narrative" (p. 202). Foucault observes, in a phrase that is nicely ironic here, "The memoir had been so to speak *fabricated* along with the crime" (p. 200, emphasis added).

28. Ironically, Usenet news "reports" suggested that Fabrikant had suffered a mild heart seizure during his "rampage."

References

Aycock, A. (n.d.). *Chess/pieces: Play in the postmodern.* Unpublished manuscript.
Bakhtin, M. (1984). *Rabelais and his world.* Bloomington: Indiana University Press.
Barthes, R. (1974). *S/Z.* New York: Noonday Press.
Barthes, R. (1975). *The pleasure of the text.* New York: Noonday Press.
Barthes, R. (1977a). *Roland Barthes by Roland Barthes.* New York: Hill & Wang.
Barthes, R. (1977b). *Image/music/text.* New York: Noonday Press.
Barthes, R. (1981). *Camera lucida.* New York: Hill & Wang.
Barthes, R. (1982). *The empire of signs.* New York: Noonday Press.
Barthes, R. (1986). *The rustle of language.* New York: Hill & Wang.
Baudrillard, J. (1983). *Simulations.* New York: Sémiotext(e).
Benedikt, M. (1991). *Cyberspace: First steps.* Cambridge: MIT Press.
Bourdieu, P. (1984). *Distinction: A social critique of the judgement of taste.* Cambridge, MA: Harvard University Press.
Bourdieu, P. (1990). *In other words: Essays towards a reflexive sociology.* Stanford, CA: Stanford University Press.
Brown, R. (1977). *A poetic for sociology.* Cambridge: Cambridge University Press.
Browne, R., & Fishwick, M. (Eds.). (1978). *Icons of America.* Bowling Green, OH: Popular Press.
Chagnon, N. (1968). *The Yanamamo, the fierce people.* New York: Holt, Rinehart & Winston.
Clifford, J. (1986). On ethnographic allegory. In J. Clifford & G. Marcus (Eds.), *Writing culture: The poetics and politics of ethnography* (pp. 98-121). Berkeley: University of California Press.
Clifford, J. (1988). *The predicament of culture: Twentieth-century ethnography, literature, and art.* Cambridge, MA: Harvard University Press.
Crane, G. (1991). Composing culture: The authority of an electronic text. *Current Anthropology, 32*(3), 293-302.
Crapanzano, V. (1980). *Tuhami: Portrait of a Moroccan.* Chicago: Chicago University Press.
Crapanzano, V. (1986). Hermes' dilemma: The masking of subversion in ethnographic description. In J. Clifford & G. Marcus (Eds.), *Writing culture: The poetics and politics of ethnography* (pp. 51-76). Berkeley: University of California Press.
De Certeau, M. (1984). *The practice of everyday life.* Berkeley: University of California Press.
Derrida, J. (1981). *Positions.* Chicago: University of Chicago Press.
Derrida, J. (1982). *Margins of philosophy.* Chicago: University of Chicago Press.
Derrida, J. (1987). *The post card: From Socrates to Freud and beyond.* Chicago: University of Chicago Press.
Derrida, J. (1988). *The ear of the other: Otobiography, transference, translation.* Lincoln: University of Nebraska Press.
Douglas, M. (1966). *Purity and danger: An analysis of concepts of pollution and taboo.* Harmondsworth: Penguin.
Dwyer, K. (1982). *Moroccan dialogues: Anthropology in question.* Baltimore, MD: Johns Hopkins University Press.
Evans-Prichard, E. E. (1940). *The Nuer.* Oxford: Clarendon.
Featherstone, M. (1991). *Consumer culture and postmodernism.* London: Sage.
Fiske, J. (1989a). *Understanding popular culture.* Boston: Unwin Hyman.
Fiske, J. (1989b). *Reading the popular.* Boston: Unwin Hyman.
Foucault, M. (1973). *Madness and civilization: A history of insanity in the age of reason.* New York: Vintage.

Foucault, M. (Ed.). (1975). *I, Pierre Riviere, having slaughtered my mother, my sister, and my brother . . .: A case of parricide in the 19th century.* Lincoln: University of Nebraska Press.
Foucault, M. (1977). *M. Foucault: Language, counter-memory, practice. Selected essays and interviews.* Ithaca, NY: Cornell University Press.
Foucault, M. (1979). *Discipline and punish: The birth of the prison.* New York: Vintage.
Foucault, M. (1980). *Power/knowledge: Selected interviews and other writings, 1972-1977.* New York: Pantheon.
Geertz, C. (1968). Thinking as a moral act: Ethical dimensions of anthropological fieldwork in the new states. *Antioch Review, 28,* 139-158.
Geertz, C. (1983). *Local knowledge.* New York: Basic Books.
Geertz, C. (1988). *Works and lives: The anthropologist as author.* Stanford, CA: Stanford University Press.
Gier, S. (1991). *Communicate for success: How to use electronic mail and bulletin boards successfully.* Harrisonburg, VA: James Madison University, Office of Information Technology.
Goffman, E. (1959). *The presentation of self in everyday life.* Garden City, NY: Anchor.
Goffman, E. (1961). *Asylums.* Garden City, NY: Anchor.
Goffman, E. (1963a). *Stigma: Notes on the management of spoiled identities.* Englewood Cliffs, NJ: Prentice Hall.
Goffman, E. (1963b). *Behavior in public places: Notes on the social organization of gatherings.* New York: Free Press.
Goffman, E. (1967). *Interaction ritual: Essays on face-to-face behavior.* Garden City, NY: Doubleday.
Goffman, E. (1974). *Frame analysis.* Cambridge, MA: Harvard University Press.
Goffman, E. (1981). *Forms of talk.* Philadelphia: University of Pennsylvania Press.
Goody, J. (1986). *The logic of writing and the organization of society.* Cambridge: Cambridge University Press.
Handler, R. (1988). *Nationalism and the politics of culture in Quebec.* Madison: University of Wisconsin Press.
Hayles, K. (1990). *Chaos bound: Orderly disorder in contemporary literature and science.* Ithaca, NY: Cornell University Press.
James, W. (1950). *Principles of psychology* (Vol. 2). New York: Dover.
Kehoe, B. (1992). *Zen and the art of the Internet.* Downloaded from the Internet.
Kracke, W. (1978). *Force and persuasion: Leadership in an Amazonian society.* Chicago: University of Chicago Press.
Kuhn, T. (1970). *The structure of scientific revolutions* (2nd ed.). Chicago: University of Chicago Press.
Laing, R., & Esterson, A. (1970). *Sanity, madness, and the family.* Harmondsworth: Penguin.
Lemert, E. (1962). Paranoia and the dynamics of exclusion. *Sociometry, 25,* 2-20.
Lévi-Strauss, C. (1961). *Tristes tropiques.* New York: Criterion Books.
Lyotard, J.-F. (1984). *The postmodern condition.* Minneapolis: University of Minnesota Press.
Malinowski, B. (1922). *Argonauts of the Western Pacific.* New York: Dutton.
Marcus, G., & Cushman, D. (1982). Ethnographies as texts. *Annual Review of Anthropology, 11,* 25-69.
Marcus, G., & Fisher, M. (1986). *Anthropology as cultural critique: An experimental moment in the human sciences.* Chicago: University of Chicago Press.
McLuhan, M. (1964). *Understanding media: The extensions of man.* New York: McGraw-Hill.
Meyrowitz, J. (1985). *No sense of place: The impact of electronic media on social behavior.* Oxford: Oxford University Press.
Muecke, D. (1970). *Irony.* London: Methuen.

Nelson, T. (1987). *Computer lib/dream machines* (rev. ed.). Redmond, WA: Tempus Books of Microsoft Press.

Nelson, T. (1992). Opening hypertext: A memoir. In M. Tuman (Ed.), *Literacy online: The promise (and peril) of reading and writing with computers* (pp. 43-57). Pittsburgh, PA: University of Pittsburgh Press.

Ong, W. (1982). *Orality and literacy: The technologizing of the word.* London: Methuen.

Perinbanayagam, R. S. (1991). *Discursive acts.* New York: Aldine de Gruyter.

Poster, M. (1990). *The mode of information: Poststructuralism and social context.* Cambridge: Polity Press.

Rabinow, P. (1977). *Reflections on fieldwork in Morocco.* Berkeley: University of California Press.

Riot, P. (1975). The parallel lives of Pierre Riviere. In M. Foucault (Ed.), *I, Pierre Riviere, having slaughtered my mother, my sister, and my brother . . .: A case of parricide in the 19th century* (pp. 229-250). Lincoln: University of Nebraska Press.

Rosaldo, R. (1987). Where objectivity lies: The rhetoric of anthropology. In A. Megill & D. McCloskey (Eds.), *The rhetoric of the human sciences* (pp. 87-110). Madison: University of Wisconsin Press.

Sarup, M. (1989). *An introductory guide to post-structuralism and postmodernism.* Athens: University of Georgia Press.

Scholes, R. (1989). *Protocols of reading.* New Haven, CT: Yale University Press.

Sedgwick, P. (1982). *Psycho politics: Laing, Foucault, Goffman, and Szasz and the future of mass psychiatry.* New York: Harper & Row.

Shostak, M. (1981). *Nisa: The life and words of a !Kung woman.* Cambridge, MA: Harvard University Press.

Sontag, S. (1970). The anthropologist as hero. In E. N. Hayes & T. Hayes (Eds.), *Claude Lévi-Strauss: The anthropologist as hero* (pp. 184-196). Cambridge: MIT Press.

Sperber, D. (1985). *On anthropological knowledge.* Cambridge: Cambridge University Press.

Stallybrass, P., & White, A. (1986). *The politics and poetics of transgression.* Ithaca, NY: Cornell University Press.

Strathern, M. (1987). Out of context: The persuasive fictions of anthropology. *Current Anthropology, 28*(3), 251-270.

Szasz, T. (1974). *The myth of mental illness: Foundations of a theory of personal conduct* (rev. ed.). New York: Harper & Row.

Templeton, B. (1991). *Emily Postnews answers your questions on netiquette.* Downloaded from mail-server@pit-manager.mit.edu.

Thornton, R. J. (1983). Narrative ethnography in Africa, 1850-1920: The creation and capture of an appropriate domain for anthropology. *Man, 18,* 502-520.

INDEX

ABOUT THE CONTRIBUTORS

Alan Aycock (aycock@hg.uleth.ca) is a professor of anthropology at the University of Lethbridge in Lethbridge, Alberta, Canada. He has published widely in structural and poststructural/postmodernist thought, including several articles in virtual journals. His interest in the Internet stems in large part from efforts to teach undergraduates the fundamentals of virtual discourses.

Nancy K. Baym is an assistant professor of communication at Wayne State University. She received her Ph.D. in speech communication from the University of Illinois at Urbana-Champaign. Her work on computer-mediated community in rec.arts.tv.soaps can also be found in the *Journal of Folklore Research* and *Cultures of Computing*.

Norman Buchignani (buchignani@hg.uleth.ca) is a professor in and currently chair of the Department of Anthropology at the University of Lethbridge in Lethbridge, Alberta, Canada. He has been involved in studies of ethnic diversity and community-based systems of meaning in Canada and elsewhere for two decades. He is author of *Fijian Indians in Canada: The Structural Determinants of a New Community* (AMS Press, 1993) and coauthor of *Continuous Journey: A Social History of South Asians in Canada* (McClelland & Stewart, 1985).

Ted Friedman (tfriedma@acpub.duke.edu) is a doctoral student in the program in literature and literary theory at Duke University and a contributing writer for *Details* and *Vibe* magazines. He also used to work as Deputy Commissioner for Prodigy®'s Baseball Manager game.

Mary Fuller (mcfuller@mit.edu.) is an associate professor of literature at Massachusetts Institute of Technology. Her major interest is the English Rennaissance and she is the author of *Voyages in Print: English Travel to America 1576-1624* (forthcoming).

Henry Jenkins (henry3@mit.edu) is the director of film and media studies at Massachusetts Institute of Technology. He is author of several books on popular culture, including *Textual Poachers: Televison Fans and Participatory Culture.* His current research is on children and popular culture in postwar America.

Steven G. Jones (comm_sj@vax1.utulsa.edu) is associate professor and chair of the faculty of communication at the University of Tulsa. He is author of *Rock Formation: Music, Technology and Mass Communication* and an active scholar in the field of popular music studies. His recent research includes work on virtual audio and cybersociology.

Cheris C. Kramarae (cheris@ux1.cso.uiuc.edu) is a professor of speech communication and the director of women's studies at the University of Illinois at Urbana-Champaign. She has authored, edited, or coedited 11 books, including *Technology and Women's Voices* and *Women, Information Technology, and Scholarship* (WITS). She is coediting, with Dale Spender, *The Women's International Studies Encyclopedia,* which will be available in print and electronically.

Richard C. MacKinnon (spartan@cup.portal.com) is currently pursuing a doctorate in government at the University of Texas at Austin. He originally produced his work on computer-mediated communication and Leviathan as a master's thesis in political science at San Jose State University. His research interests are political theory, computer-mediated communication, and governance within virtual systems.

Margaret L. McLaughlin (mmclaugh@almaak.usc.edu) is a professor in the Department of Communication, Annenberg School for Communication, University of Southern California, Los Angeles. She received her Ph.D. from the University of Illinois at Urbana-Champaign. She has authored, edited, or coedited several books, including *Conversation: How Talk Is Organized, The Psychology of Tactical Communication, Explaining One's Self to Others: Reason-Giving in a Social Context,* and two forthcoming volumes, *Intimate Decisions: Accounting for Risk-Taking in Sexual Behavior and Courtship* and *Network and Net-Play: The Virtual Group on the Internet.* She has served as editor of *Communicaton Monographs* and *Communication Yearbook* and is a past president of the International Communication Association.

Kerry K. Osborne (osborne@almaak.usc.edu) is a doctoral candidate in the Department of Communication, Annenberg School for Communication, University of Southern California, Los Angeles, where she serves as system manager for the CAAS computer laboratory. Her interests include gender studies and computer-mediated communication. She received her M.A. from California State University, Northridge.

Elizabeth Reid (emr@rmit.edu.au.) is a doctoral student in the Department of Communication Studies at the Royal Melbourne Institute of Technology, Australia. She is currently writing a history of the Internet, with particular emphasis on tracing the evolution of its fractionated social structure and attendant lack of centralized and hierarchized control.

Christine B. Smith (cbsmith@almaak.usc.edu) is a doctoral candidate in the Department of Communication, Annenberg School for Communication, University of Southern California, Los Angeles. Her interests include interpersonal communication and computer networking. She received her M.A. from the University of West Florida.